Luminos is the Open Access monograph publishing program from UC Press. Luminos provides a framework for preserving and reinvigorating monograph publishing for the future and increases the reach and visibility of important scholarly work. Titles published in the UC Press Luminos model are published with the same high standards for selection, peer review, production, and marketing as those in our traditional program. www.luminosoa.org

NEW INTERVENTIONS IN JAPANESE STUDIES

1. *Language, Nation, Race: Linguistic Reform in Meiji Japan (1868–1912)*, by Atsuko Ueda
2. *A Proximate Remove: Queering Intimacy and Loss in the Tale of Genji*, by Reginald Jackson

Language, Nation, Race

Language, Nation, Race

Linguistic Reform in Meiji Japan (1868–1912)

Atsuko Ueda

UNIVERSITY OF CALIFORNIA PRESS

University of California Press
Oakland, California

Suggested citation: Ueda, A. *Language, Nation, Race: Linguistic Reform in Meiji Japan (1868–1912)*. Oakland: University of California Press, 2021.
DOI: https://doi.org/10.1525/luminos.103

Library of Congress Cataloging-in-Publication Data
Names: Ueda, Atsuko, author.
Title: Language, nation, race : linguistic reform in Meiji Japan (1868–1912) / Atsuko Ueda.
Description: Oakland, California : University of California Press, [2021] | Includes bibliographical references and index.
Identifiers: LCCN 2020046901 (print) | LCCN 2020046902 (ebook) | ISBN 9780520381711 (paperback) | ISBN 9780520381728 (ebook)
Subjects: LCSH: Japanese language—Reform—Meiji period, 1868–1912. | Language policy—Japan—Meiji period, 1868–1912. | Nationalism—Japan—Meiji period, 1868–1912. | Japan—Race relations—Meiji period, 1868–1912.
Classification: LCC PL525.6.U34 2021 (print) | LCC PL525.6 (ebook) | DDC 306.44/952—dc23
LC record available at https://lccn.loc.gov/2020046901
LC ebook record available at https://lccn.loc.gov/2020046902

28 27 26 25 24 23 22 21
10 9 8 7 6 5 4 3 2 1

For Naoharu and Yasuko Ueda

CONTENTS

ACKNOWLEDGMENTS

I finally get to thank the many people who have supported me in various ways throughout this project. Among my colleagues at Princeton, present and past, who have given me not only a great intellectual community but also pleasurable company throughout the years, I thank Eduardo Cadava, Ksenia Chizhova, Steve Chung, Ben Elman, David Howell, Erin Huang, Paize Keulemans, David Leheny, Federico Marcon, Susan Naquin, Willard Peterson, Franz Prichard, Anna Shields, and Brian Steinenger. I'm particularly grateful to Joowon Suh for her continued friendship and support over many years. I thank Setsuko Noguchi, a friend and librarian without whom this work could not have been completed. Many of my former and current students engaged with my ideas on which this book is based: David Boyd, Will Bridges, Junnan Chen, Miyabi Goto, Claire Kaup, Jessica LeGare, Qinyuan Lei, Bernard Shee, Tomoko Slutsky, Ajjana Thairungroj, and Ron Wilson. I also thank Joseph Henares for his help in compiling the bibliography.

My mentors—Brett de Bary, Ken Ito, and Mizumura Minae—have supported me for many years. Formal and informal conversations with many colleagues were essential in bringing this project to fruition. I especially thank the many close friends in my field who have brought intellectual inspiration along with their capacity to drink pleasurably: Michael Bourdaghs, Rich Calichman, Jim Dorsey, Mayumo Inoue, Thomas LaMarre, Michele Mason, Simone Müller, Doug Slaymaker, Toba Koji, and Toeda Hirokazu. In addition to being great company, I also thank Pedro Erber for his incisive comments on my manuscript. I am also grateful to Richi Sakakibara not only for being a long-term friend but also for sharing with me the desire to continually think about what constitutes "Japan" and the "Japanese" language. I thank Jim Reichert for his professional support and for visiting New York when possible to continue our Michigan reunion.

An earlier version of chapter 1 appeared in *Rethinking Asian Languages*, edited by Benjamin Elman (Leiden: Brill, 2014), while a version of chapter 2 has appeared in *Translation in Modern Japan*, edited by Indra Levy (New York: Routledge, 2010). A small portion of chapter 5 has also appeared as "*Bungakuron* and 'Literature' in the Making," *Japan Forum* 20, no. 1 (March, 2008).

I am grateful to Reed Malcolm at the University of California Press for his enthusiasm and encouragement. I also thank Archna Patel and Enrique Ochoa-Kaup for shepherding this manuscript through. Additionally, I thank one anonymous reviewer, whose comments were extremely helpful in revising the manuscript.

Oddly enough, I feel that there is a strong affinity between this project and my family. In many ways, it is precisely how my parents raised me that shaped my interest in "Japanese" language, national community, and race. As difficult as it was growing up in different countries and being educated in multiple languages, that experience was essential for me to critically engage with "Japan," nationalism, and linguistic modernity. I thank my sister, Tomoko, for sharing the experience with me, and for all the emotional and material support she has given me throughout the years. And I am immensely grateful to my parents, Naoharu and Yasuko Ueda, for raising me the way they did and for all the support they have continued to give me. This book is dedicated to them.

Introduction

This book is about a variety of language reforms that occured in Meiji Japan (1868–1912). It is certainly not at all comprehensive, but is rather an attempt to intervene in the vast scholarship of language reform that has defined the past two decades. In thinking about linguistic reforms, it is of course vital that we consider issues of nation formation, as many scholars have done in the past. Lee Yeounsuk, Komori Yōichi, Yasuda Toshiaki, and Osa Shizue all published works in the 1990s and beyond, and to this day their works define the field of language reform.[1] It is not a coincidence that with the proliferation of postcolonial and nationalization theories in the 1990s, scholarship began to adopt a new focus with regard to the production of national language and its ideological implications. Many works, engaging with Michel Foucault's theory of systems of power and governmentality, began to focus on the structure of violence constitutive of any nation within which the construction of language, especially national language, played an integral role.[2] These texts have produced fruitful analyses that rewrite the somewhat facile teleological narrative of modernization and vernacularization that shaped previous scholarship, as represented by the monumental works of Yamamoto Masahide from the 1960s.[3]

The trend of postcolonial and cultural studies, accompanied by various studies of imperialism and nationalism, is worthy of reflection, as it extends far beyond the scholarship of Meiji language reform. As early as 2000, scholars such as Harry Harootunian issued an apt warning regarding the link between postcolonialism and area studies. In his *History's Disquiet*, Harootunian discusses the trap of postcolonial theory as follows:

> Postcolonial theory's promise to supply a critique of Eurocentric conceptions of knowledge and provide a forum for the hitherto excluded to speak in their own voice from the margins where domination and power had held them silent since the beginning of modernity—now reread as colonialism—stands as the true successor of area studies, which can be seen as their prehistory. Yet the search for the excluded

> voice often leads to the futile pursuit of authenticity and restores the Eurocentric claims of the sovereign subject it wishes to eliminate.[4]

Elsewhere, he also states:

> Rather this obsessive Foucauldianism has often found power everywhere, as well as an opportunity for resistance everywhere. Too often this has resulted in lavish declarations of resistance by the powerless and weak. . . . Sometimes, the mere enunciation of cultural difference and thus the claim of identity is made to appear as an important political act when it usually signals the disappearance of politics. The politics of identity based on the enunciation of cultural difference is not the same as political identity whose formation depends less on declarations of differences than on some recognition of equivalencies.[5]

What Harootunian incisively demonstrates here is that what began as a critical examination of the ideological nature of knowledge produced in area studies turned into something slightly but crucially different. Postcolonialism and cultural studies instead discovered a new space that worked to relieve the frustrations that many felt about the Eurocentric tendency of theoretical discourse. As a result, focus shifted to the recovery of the voices of those unjustly oppressed. This resulted in a scholarly surge toward identity politics, which, despite its historical importance, contains an intrinsic trap. The discourse of identity inherits the culturalism inscribed in area studies—one that postcolonial studies and cultural studies set out to criticize in the first place. In other words, scholars tend to seek out unique voices of the oppressed, and as such end up essentializing identity—whether this be the identity of the subaltern or the oppressed non-West. Furthermore, what is symptomatic of such trends is a naive opposition posed between the oppressor and the oppressed. The desire to give voice to the oppressed, however just and moral it may sound, tends to demonize the oppressors operating within the system of authority. I of course understand this sentiment, but demonizing these figures ultimately attributes an excess of power to them, reifying the very thing that it seeks to undermine. I am entirely sympathetic with such desires, but I also want to be vigilant against inadvertently strengthening the systems that we attempt to criticize.

I raise this issue in order to reflect on the ways in which the "nation," a structure of modernity within which we live, has been approached by scholarship in the past two decades. It is not a coincidence that the nationalism studies that have shaped our scholarship since the 1990s grew alongside postcolonial and cultural studies that focused—rightly or wrongly—on systems of power, as embodied by the "nation." A tremendous amount of work has been produced engaging with Benedict Anderson's *Imagined Communities*, coupled with Foucault's many theorizations of systems of power as inscribed in the institutions of the modern nation.[6] I of course believe that a nation is a system of violence, and it is imperative that we explore the ways in which such violence is implemented. We must, however, be mindful of the implications of this scholarly trend. The inextricable relationship between such works and the rise of postcolonialsm and cultural studies in our field is one that requires attention, for here too we find signs of Harootunian's warning. The systems of power that Foucault delineates are structural, and by no means offer a space outside of which subjects can exist. But here again the desire to give voice to the oppressed, in this case minorities who are excluded from the so-called "authentic citizens" of the nation—oppressed by such factors as class, ethnicity, and gender—leads to the excessive attribution of power to the very thing that it seeks to undermine. It is one thing to expose the ideological structure by which the nation sustains itself. But it is quite another to suggest that such awareness can open up a space in which oppressed voices can be redeemed and given their rightful, "equal" status.

National language scholarship of the 1990s was not free of this trap. This is apparent in the focus on Ueda Kazutoshi, the "founder" of *kokugo* (national language) and father of Japanese linguistics, who trained many of the scholars who went on to institute language reforms in Japan's colonies. Here Ueda is situated as an evil nationalist/imperialist whose project entailed the oppression of local dialects and colonized subjects—as for example Okinawans, Ainu, Koreans, and Taiwanese.[7]

I do not doubt that these minorities and their languages were oppressed in light of Ueda's *kokugo* reform, which sought to produce a standardized language shared by the occupants of "Japan" and its empire. And it is certainly important to study these "minority" languages that are too often disregarded. But what we must pay attention to is precisely what the scholarship that demonizes Ueda takes for granted, which ultimately contributes to the oppression of these minority voices. For example, binary thinking of oppressor and oppressed makes us lose sight of the fact that a nation, in order to sustain itself, *needs* minorities. That is to say, no one is inherently an "authentic citizen." Such a fictive group—in Japan's case, *yamato minzoku*—needs to be constantly fabricated, marking and remarking boundaries between self and other. *Yamato minzoku* does not exist. It is only through the constant reproduction of minorities that such "authentic citizens" can be sustained. Authentic citizens, in other words, can only be defined by the various minorities that make them "authentic." Structurally speaking, anyone can be designated a minority, as anyone is prone to markers of difference. Just as no one is inherently an "authentic citizen," no one is inherently a minority. In effect, the facile binary of oppressor and oppressed cannot sustain itself, as one is invariably defined and contaminated by the other. And to valorize minority identities without critically understanding this system can only reinforce the system that is the nation.

What I want to call attention to is that studies of identity politics, in having recourse to so-called "exteriorities" of Japan (Korea, Taiwan, Okinawa, etc.), perhaps too hastily conceive of the notion of Japanese exteriority. Such research is absolutely crucial in relativizing Japan's claims of national sovereignty, and must be supported. At the same time, however, without first reflecting on what it means to be "outside" Japan, one runs the risk of repeating the traditional conception of what belongs within and without the nation. This tendency, I believe, is of a piece with those traditional notions of nationalism that privilege national "interiority"—that is, *yamato minzoku*. In other words, unless one reflects on what it means to be outside Japan, one risks reifying the notion of Japanese interiority. In this sense, ironically, certain forms of identity politics may ultimately be seen as complicit with a very traditional notion of nationalism. I would like to problematize the very notion of national interiority and exteriority. In my view, a certain exteriority of Japan can be seen within "Japan" itself. This integral relationship between the majority and minority is a crucial one that I will develop further in the discussion of race later in this introduction.

In this book, I make interventions in these scholarly trends from two different angles, coinciding with the two parts of this volume. The first part, entitled "Pre-Nation: Linguistic Chaos," examines the first two decades of the Meiji period prior to the emergence of Ueda Kazutoshi, with a specific focus on the chaotic nature of language reforms. What is symptomatic of the scholarship that focuses on Ueda is that the "nation" appears to preexist the nation. In the effort to condemn the nation and its creators, the nation is posited as a preexisting telos to which the leaders aspired, as it focuses on the production of an ideologically-charged "national language" (*kokugo*), which forcefully excludes or assimilates otherwise heterogeneous languages. The following passage by Yasuda Toshiaki captures the trend most clearly:

> The construction of 'language' in the modern sense is a political process. When the nation-state is established and 'linguistic modernity' emerges together with the awareness of the role language plays within it, the vernacular language is molded as '*kokugo*,' which is a process that is often considered a national development toward progress. '*Kokugo*' is then deemed homogeneous; it begins to embody the institutions (such as law, education, military and media) that consolidate the *kokumin* (there are many efforts to organize such consolidation), exerting its power on 'dialects' and other non-national languages that were unable to attain the status of *kokugo*. It is possible to say that such a scheme appears in any nation when the modern nation-state is formed. (I have inserted scare quotes around concepts that are constructed).[8]

Yasuda appears conscientious when making his parenthetical remarks about key concepts such as "*kokugo*" and "dialects" being constructs. But in his and similar accounts, the process of said construction is predetermined by that of nationalization, which "appears in any nation when the modern nation-state is formed": the "vernacular" becomes "*kokugo*," consolidating the national community, which then begins to exert power on "dialects and other non-national languages." In effect, he logically posits the nation as a preexisting entity. In large part, the scholarly trend of which Yasuda is an example reflects the notion of "imagined communities" put forth by Benedict Anderson, who theorized the ideological formation of the nation-state in which the production of "national language" played a significant part. 1990s Japanese scholarship appropriated this theory, producing a teleological narrative that posits the "national language" of the imagined nation as the putative telos, often producing an inverted narrative that figures the nation as the entity that inspired the movement that created it. Of course, scholars are aware that the "nation" is created or imagined. But the movement toward the nation is not at all questioned. In such a paradigm, which can be seen in some works more than in others, the urge to nationalize is deemed the primary *cause* of change.9 The formulaic discussions that seemingly trace the nation-building process often end up self-fulfilling prophecies.

What is important is that the language reformers of the first few decades of the Meiji period did not yet know what the "nation" was. Given that the nation is assumed, however, the many reforms that preceded those of Ueda are situated in scholarship as a preparatory phase.[10] At the core of Meiji discursive space is a very simple yet often forgotten linguistic condition: the Meiji literati did not have a shared notion of "the language we speak" that helped to constitute an imagined national community, nor a shared notion that "the language we speak" was indeed their goal. What I seek to highlight in this part of the book is precisely this *lack* of a goal. In so doing, I seek to liberate the discussion of linguistic reform from the "national" so as to analyze how the "national" itself became possible.

Such perspective is important for several reasons. The first is to reevaluate the role of *kan* in the production of linguistic modernity. Recent scholarly focus on the nation aligns with an urge to emphasize the de-Sinification of the "Japanese" language. More often than not, these scholars construe *kan*—be it *kanji, kanbun,* or *kangaku*—as a manifestation of "China," for "Asia" to be left behind in Japan's efforts at modernization.[11] As such, scholars treat *kan* as a negative reference point against which to posit a new "national" form of prose. Of course it is true that many Meiji intellectuals designated *kan* as the other to the modern, but that certainly does not mean that *kan* was not appropriated.

This is not to say that all forms of *kanbun* have been undervalued in recent scholarship. The importance of *kanbun kundokutai* (*kanbun* in "Japanese" or local syntax), for example, has been emphasized by many scholars, especially those who have focused on its role in the political arena, as well as its crucial role in translations of Western philosophy and materials.[12] Interestingly, however, some of the same critics who see the importance of *kanbun kundokutai* take up the Meiji intellectuals' claims for de-Sinification and uncritically link these to colonialist/imperialist tendencies. These critics call such acts manifestations of the "colonial unconscious," which refers to the act of seeking out "Asia" as the "more barbaric other" in the urge to "identify with the West."[13] The aim of this argument is to criticize Meiji intellectuals for their imperialist tendencies—an important aim, certainly—but such an argument tends to identify *kanbun* as "Asian," thereby essentializing the process of de-Sinification. Such overemphasis on de-Sinification conceals the critical role that *kan* indeed played in the production of a new language. Much work has been done recently by scholars, such as the literary critic Saitō Mareshi, to reassess the importance of *kan* in the Meiji period, and my study clearly follows this trend.[14]

In discussing the linguistic reform movements of the Meiji period, the use of the categories "Chinese" and "Japanese," terms which in our vocabulary designate "national" languages, is quite problematic. Given that we are dealing with a time when the "national" had yet to take form, these categories appear anachronistic. This is especially true when we translate. *Kanji, kanbun*, and *kangaku* are often translated as "Chinese" characters, "Chinese" writing, and "Chinese" classics, but such regionally and culturally specific designations, in our post-national age, seem to indicate that *kanji, kanbun*, and *kangaku* all belong to this entity called "China" and are hence "foreign" (indicating that they are merely "borrowed"). The designation "Japanese" for such words as *kokubun* ("Japanese" writing), *kokugo* (the "Japanese" language), and *kundoku* (the reading of *kanbun* in "Japanese" syntax and with "Japanese" suffixes) must also be used with caution, as it, too, assumes an "untainted" realm of "Japanese," a rhetoric that many Meiji intellectuals used when they suddenly discovered that their language was "tainted" by "Chinese." As painful as this may be for readers, I will retain the original terms without translating them to avoid the anachronism, and will qualify every translation of "Chinese" and "Japanese" when I need to revert to them.

In Part I, I also seek to shed light on the epistemological shift that occurred in the understanding of language (*gengo*), especially in its relationship to literature (*bungaku*), a shift that has yet to be addressed in any significant way. Scholars of national language have stressed that there was no unified sense of "the language we speak," focusing instead on how such language came into being. What they fail to note is that the category of *gengo*, the equivalent of what we now call "language," had yet to be discovered in the early Meiji period. *Bungaku*, or what we translate as "literature" today, constituted "language"; it is thus not a coincidence that *kokugo* textbooks featured literary histories.[15] In discussing *gengo* and *bungaku*, contemporary scholars tend to impose current notions of "language" and "literature" onto their supposed Meiji equivalents, unable to challenge such categories.

Take, for example, the following passage where Lee Yeounsuk describes the efforts of scholars of *kokubungaku* (national literature):

> In such efforts, [scholars] did not adhere to the ideals of *genbun'itchi*, according to which the written language was to be unified with the spoken language. This signifies that *kokugo* was still subjugated to *kokubun*. Even Sekine Masanao, who argued that 'today's commonly used language' was the 'core of *kokugo*,' stated that the purpose of '*kokugo* study' was to 'standardize a *kokubun* of authentic elegance.' This was because he, too, could not see the clear boundaries between *kokugo* and *kokubun*. For this hurdle to be overcome, we had to wait for Ueda Kazutoshi.[16]

I owe a great deal to Lee's work, and among the national language scholars of the 1990s, she is perhaps the most sensitive and insightful. However, Lee here resorts to a retrospective narrative and posits a division between *kokubun* and *kokugo* that had yet to exist at that time. She faults Sekine for not being able to see the boundaries between *kokugo* and *kokubun*, but such a view is contingent upon the production of *kokugo* as an independent entity from *kokubun*. Only when we recognize the existence of *kokugo* as an entity separate from *kokubun* can we say that it was subjugated to *kokubun*.

Lee then credits Ueda for going beyond *bungaku* = "language," the idea to which *kokubun* scholars were bound. She naturally assumes that Ueda, when he introduced the division between *kokugo* and *kokubun*, produced *gengo* as "language." This is a process that she traces back to his encounter with the theories of Bopp and Schlegel. Here Ueda claims, "Schlegel mixes *literature and history* in his study of *gengo*, but Bopp goes against such tendencies and studies *gengo itself*, offering a *dry but clear* explanation."[17] In essence, at the core of Lee's understanding is the idea that *gengo* is *langue* (in the Saussurian sense); that *bungaku* is one manifestation of it; and that it was Ueda who was able to finally see this difference. As we shall see in detail in chapter 4, however, Ueda's use of *gengo* and *bungaku* does not coincide with Lee's understanding. For Ueda, *kokugo* was equivalent to the language of "voice," and *bungaku* or *kokubun* was equivalent to the language of *moji* (letters). In other words, for Ueda, *gengo* (*kokugo*) and *moji* (*kokubun*) constituted two separate modes of expression, one via voice and the other via letters.

Both *kokubun* and *kokugo*, and hence the understanding of "language" and "literature," constituted something entirely different from what they mean in our current interpretive scheme. This difference is too often glossed over in a narrative that focuses on the processes of nationalization, which posits *kokugo* as an entity that developmentally emerged from the *kokubun* movement (given the attention to the establishment of the shared sense of nation). An examination of the Meiji period language reform betrays the fact that our perception of "language" and "literature" is quite limiting. Inscribed in the many arguments for reform, especially those in the early Meiji period, are various "languages" that are incompatible with our own. I seek to underscore such paradigms while paying attention to the categories of "language" and "literature."

With such aims in mind, the first three chapters examine the linguistic terrain that historically preceded the Ueda-led *kokugo* reforms. My first chapter analyzes calls for a different orthography, such as the adoption of indigenous syllabic scripts (*kana*), the use of the Roman alphabet, the rejection of *kanji* characters, and the call to adopt the English language. This chapter seeks to highlight the competing "languages" inscribed in the claims for a different orthography that formed the discursive space of the 1870s. The second chapter looks at the early to mid 1880s, with a special focus on *kanbun kundokutai*, the main style of language of the intelligentsia at the time, a form that enjoyed the status of "common language" (or *futsūbun*). I analyze the many arguments against *kanbun kundokutai* and the seemingly contradictory proliferation of the same style, and argue that it was precisely the proliferation of this style that opened up a space for *kokugo* to later claim. The third chapter examines the realm of *zoku* (often translated as the "vernacular"), with a specific focus on the intersection of prose and poetry. The late 1880s and early 1890s featured an increasing focus on *zoku* both by fiction writers and national literature scholars, a tendency that is often integrated in the teleological narrative of *kokugo*, given the appearance of *kokugo* as reflecting a "populist" choice. I show that *zoku* was in fact an aesthetic category for these groups of writers and that it was mobilized in ways that did not signify the vernacularization of language.

In Part II of the book, entitled "Race and Language Reform," I address one major issue that has not been studied in the prior scholarship on language reform: race. Meiji was a race war. And it is crucial to inscribe race in our examination, since no analysis of imperialism or nationalism is possible without race.

When Japan entered the world order in the nineteenth century, the world was of course already racialized. Most importantly, this racialized world order was considered "scientific knowledge." It is not a coincidence that Japanese intellectuals began to obsessively translate world maps early in the Meiji period to disseminate this form of "knowledge." Fukuzawa Yukichi's *Sekai kunizukushi* (*The Countries of the World*, 1869) and Uchida Masao's *Yochi shiryaku* (*An Abriged Account of the World*, 1870) were two prominent texts that were used as school textbooks to teach world geography and disseminate the mode of categorization of the world inscribed within it. Relying heavily on Social Darwinian rhetoric, these texts designated Europe as the center of enlightenment and the most "civilized" geographical region, while portraying Africa and such Asian countries as India as full of ignorant "barbaric" people. Japan, in this framework, was designated as "half-civilized."[18]

It was within such a worldview that Japan was forced to identify itself. In short, Japan's relationship with the West and hence the modern is always already a racialized relationship, one that necessitated a process of self-colonization, which manifests itself as an urge to become the West. But this desire to become the West can only be frustrated, as the West is never fully accessible. How can this frustration be alleviated? Only through emulating the model that is the West and becoming a colonizer. Japan was one such example, and such actions are inscribed in Ueda Kazutoshi's language reform. Introducing race in the second part of this book thus presents a critical foundation through which nationalism and imperialism operated. The choices Ueda made, for example, were integral to such structure. In this way I will further complicate the imperialist nationalist narrative that envelops the scholarship on language reform.

It is curious that scholars of nationalization do not touch upon race, as race scholars have repeatedly shown the slippery slope that exists between nationalism and racism. At the same time, however, lack of references to race in Japan studies is not limited to the scholarship of language reform. Of course, race has been problematized in Japanese literary studies, but it is typically through the representation of "blackness" or "whiteness" in modern Japanese media such as literature, film, or visual culture. While such works have reinscribed race in an otherwise silent scholarly realm, they in many cases do not avoid the trap of biologism precisely because they typically take as their object the physical skin color of a character. When we think of modern Japanese literary studies, many scholars have discussed Japanese imperialism, colonialism, ethnocentrism, but it is very rare to discuss race. Of course there are definite exceptions—Naoki Sakai, for example, has consistently written on race. I would like to follow his lead and try to inscribe race in places that are not often discussed.

As Sakai has pointed out very succinctly in an essay entitled "Reishizumu sutadīzu e no shiza" ("Perspectives on Racism Studies"), racialization needs to be understood as a system of social categorization by which a given individual's physical traits, chosen selectively yet dogmatically, define his/her place in the community to which he/she belongs.[19] Race, in other words, is fabricated—in the double sense of deception and construction. It is imagined or constructed and yet appears to be real, as if it existed somewhere. "Whiteness," for example, only appears to exist and is in fact constructed as an object of desire, a vehicle for belonging to the most "civilized" community by which the modern order is defined. It is important to keep in mind that indexes of identity, such as the national community, national language, or race, must be constantly reconstructed. As with the notion of "authentic citizens" I discussed earlier, the boundaries that determine the indexes of identity are constantly in flux, and hence in need of repeated reinforcement. Furthermore, any index of identity is in itself insufficient; it needs to depend upon other indexes in order to be what it is. In effect, race is not something that can be separated from the categories of ethnicity or nationality. It is impossible to say that race is biological or physical, that ethnicity is cultural, and that nationality is political, despite the fact that many scholars have attempted to distinguish these categories.[20] These notions are all conflated, contaminated, and mutually invasive. The basic premise of this gesture to inscribe race in Japan studies is that racism is integral to our understanding of modernity, with all its slippages into ethnocentrism and nationalism. It is crucial to note that my primary interest is in the process of racialization, which occurs discursively in realms that on the surface appear to have nothing to do with race. As Balibar reminds us: "racism has nothing to do with the existence of objective biological 'races.'"[21]

Furthermore, it is important to understand that civilization, hence race, involves at its core a teleology, a movement toward "whiteness." "Whiteness," constructed as a telos, is intimately related to privilege, including, but not limited to, the "West" in all its incarnations, wealth, social status, "cultivated taste," and the "proper" use of language—such as pronunciation, grammar, and so forth. Frantz Fanon suggests this in *Black Skin, White Masks* as he discusses the "Negro of Antilles" as being "proportionately whiter—that is, he will come close to being a real human being—in direct ratio to his mastery of the French language."[22] He continues:

> Every colonized people—in other words, every people in whose soul an inferiority complex has been created by the death and burial of its local cultural originality—finds itself face to face with the language of the civilizing nation; that is, with the culture of the mother country. The colonized is elevated above his jungle status in proportion to his adoption of the mother country's cultural standards. He becomes whiter as he renounces his blackness, his jungle.[23]

The many "cultural standards" of the civilized, including the proper use of language, are means to racialize and hierarchize people within the global order of modernity. Without conceptualizing race in this manner, we cannot begin to understand how racial categories have changed throughout history. We do not have to look too far back in American history to see when Italians and Jews, for example, were not considered "white."

Such a view of race is vital to understanding the complexity of race that lies at the core of modernity. I suspect that part of the silence on race in Japan Studies (or, for that matter, in East Asian Studies in general) is based on biologism. Race is often disregarded, as discussions of Japanese imperialism and colonialism address Koreans, Chinese, and Taiwanese, for example, all of whom are currently categorized as the "yellow" race. But such an understanding essentializes the racial categories that are by definition fluid. If we do not consider race as "fictive" and inscribe race in areas that appear on the surface to be unrelated to race, we can only reify the categories themselves.

To highlight this importance of race, I specifically take up Ueda Kazutoshi and Natsume Sōseki in chapters 4 and 5, respectively. My analyses of these two figures are designed to complement each other. Ueda, as I have mentioned, has long been deemed the evil imperialist. In contrast, Sōseki has long been seen as a progressive, anti-imperialist figure whose genius was beyond his time. I address these figures in my discussion of race specifically to show that the overt demonization of one individual or the overt deification of another do not do justice to the structural nature of race. Such a tendency is extremely reductive, as it excessively empowers an individual—either as an aggressive imperialist or an ardent resister—and refuses to consider modernity in a structural sense. Imperialistic tendencies cannot be attributed to the monstrosity of an individual or group of individuals, nor can they be completely resisted by an individual or group of individuals. Such tendencies are inherent in modernity itself, and no one exists outside of this framework.

It may appear strange to include Sōseki in a book about language reform. The primary reason for this is that critics view Sōseki as a writer of fiction who experimented with literary prose, while they see advocates of language reform as concerned specifically with language for daily use. However, as I mentioned previously, the categories of "literature" and "language" were then still in flux, and it can only be a retrospective projection on our part to separate them. Furthermore, it is vital in any study of language reform to examine various views of language, and Sōseki's theoretical works, most notably *Bungakuron* (*Theory of Literature*, 1906) and *Bungaku hyōron* (*Literary Criticism*, 1907), provide a unique alternative to those of Ueda and the other advocates of reform. We shall see that the title *Bungakuron* is rather deceptive, as it appears to limit its scope to "literature." The entire work, as well as the notes Sōseki meticulously took as he prepared his monumental work, in fact show that his conception went well beyond the narrow domain of literature. The titles of his notes, such as "The View of the World" and "Enlightenment and Civilization," should give us a clue as to the scope of his thought.[24] Moreover, Ueda and Sōseki were the same age, as counterintuitive as that may seem, and thus invariably responded to the same discursive space.

This section thus attempts to restore these writers to the space in which they are situated, without succumbing to the desire to place them outside of the ideological structure of modernity. In chapter 4, I examine how Ueda, for example, mobilizes the fictive ethnicity that is *yamato minzoku* as the most "authentic" users of *kokugo*. Through an analysis of his writings, I highlight the manner in which he attempted to mark varying boundaries of *kokugo* by mobilizing the logic of equality and naturalization. Following previous scholarship, I further argue that *kokugo* had yet to exist. What I seek to show is that *kokugo* was an idea that was posited to embody "whiteness," an object of desire. In addition, I continue to highlight the fluidity of the categories *gengo* and *bungaku* that shape Ueda's theories. In chapter 5, I explore the fluidity of race in Sōseki's works, such as "Mankan tokoro dokoro" ("Travels in Manchuria and Korea," 1909) and *Sanshirō* (1908), in addition to his theoretical works. I show that his works oscillate between two poles, demonstrating various markers of vulgar racism as well as examining the ways in which he destabilizes racial biologism. I then explore how he attempted to define language at a universal level by consistently erasing the regionality of languages in his theoretical works. At the same time, however, I also illustrate the manner in which he occasionally falls back into racial hierarchies. Such a double move is necessary, I believe, since no text is ideologically monolithic.

PART I

"Pre-Nation"

Linguistic Chaos

A BRIEF OVERVIEW OF LANGUAGE REFORMS in the early meiji period will perhaps be helpful to contextualize the discussions that follow. In the mid-to late-1800s, the literacy level in Japan was extremely low, while written and spoken languages existed separately from one another.[1] Multiple dialects proliferated, making basic communication difficult among the inhabitants of the Japanese archipelago. Meiji intellectuals were faced with the threat of Euro-American nations, which were equipped with the International Law of Sovereign States and its view of uncivilized countries as "lands with no possessor." These intellectuals had to do everything in their power to educate the illiterate masses. They proposed various reforms to standardize the Japanese language, thus facilitating the new forms of knowledge imported from the West. This was an extraordinarily chaotic moment in the history of modern Japan.

As with arguments for any reform, various ideas were raised and debated. The key issues ranged from the choice of orthography—that is, whether to employ indigenous *kana* or Romanized scripts—to how to simplify grammar (or, perhaps more accurately, how to produce standardized grammar). As surprising as this sounds, some intellectuals even argued for the adoption of English as the national language. Proponents of *kana* scripts, such as Shimizu Usaburō (1829–1910) and Miyake Yonekichi (1860–1929), argued that use of *kana* would produce a form of language close to the "spoken" language. Nishi Amane (1829–97) and Nanbu Yoshikazu (1840–1917) each advocated Romanized script for very different reasons; the former argued that the Japanese people would be able to access "everything Western" by employing Romanized script, while the latter reasoned that Romanized script would help standardize Japanese grammar. Mori Arinori (1847–89), the first Minister of Education, criticized the unsystematic nature of the Japanese language and proposed the adoption of simplified English. Other than the issue of orthography, there was no sense of systematicity in the various languages then in use. Fukuchi Gen'ichirō (1841–1906), a strong proponent of linguistic reform, criticized contemporary prose that employed "Western grammar" in its combination of *kanbun* and *wabun*-oriented words and phrases. He famously referred to this usage as *nuebun*, a metaphor based on the mythical *nue* monster that possessed the head of a monkey, the body of a badger, and the arms and legs of a tiger.[2]

Among these disparate arguments for reform, one common denominator was the rejection of *kanji* for both practical and ideological reasons. Such a view is represented by the works of Maejima Hisoka (1835–1919), notably in his "Kanji onhaishi no gi" ("On the Abolition of *Kanji*," 1866) and "Kokubun kyōiku no gi ni tsuki kengi" ("A Proposition for *Kokubun* Education," 1869). Many advocates of reform, like Maeijima, claimed that *kanji* was an inefficient medium to educate the masses, an argument that was fueled by anti-Chinese sentiment. In the 1880s, Toyama Masakazu (1848–1900), who later became the president of Tokyo Imperial University, wrote many essays promoting the abolition of *kanji*. As Toyama remarked, "It is crucial that we jettison the Chinese odor as quickly and thoroughly as possible so as to adopt the culture of Euro-America. Since *kanji* reeks of China, it is impossible to sever ourselves from China insofar as we cling to *kanji*."[3] Ironically, however, his essays were composed in the *kanbun kundokutai* (*kanbun* style language with local "Japanese" grammar). In effect, he was not free of the trap into which many Meiji intellectuals fell: the argument against *kanji* in a sinified style, written in the very form it objected.

The anti-*kanji* reforms in the first decade of the Meiji period leaned toward more practical rather than ideological solutions. Initially, it was imperative that these reforms produce a language that could raise literacy rates and educate the people. The inefficiency of *kanji* was thus the main target. By the second decade, however, the ideological and emotional resistance to *kanji* and its apparent affiliation with China were foregrounded, as foreign relations with China began to worsen given Japan's relation with Korea.

One of the most dominant tropes in language reform was *genbun'itchi* (commonly translated as the "unification of spoken and written languages"). Many Japanese intellectuals mistakenly believed that the strength of European languages rested in precisely this unification, despite the fact that all languages possess distinct written and spoken forms. It is perhaps thus more accurate to say that Japanese intellectuals *discovered* that their spoken and written languages were disparate and so felt the need for their unification. This division, as we shall see in more detail, was ideologically construed. Many felt that, while the spoken language was "Japanese," the written language was "Chinese." Anti-Chinese sentiment that grew in light of the slogan "Westernization and de-Asianization" (*datsua nyūō*) fueled such rejection. Despite the misidentification of *kanji* as "Chinese" and hence "foreign" (no one who uses the Roman alphabet believe that alphabets are Roman and hence "foreign"), we see many references in this period to the written language as "foreign" and hence not "natural" to the Japanese.

Although the history of linguistic reforms typically highlights the contributions of literary figures like Yamada Bimyō (1868–1910) and Futabatei Shimei (1864–1909) to the development of *genbun'itchi* prose, the advocates of such reform were certainly not limited to literary writers. Without falling into the facile dichotomy of aesthetic prose and practical prose, we need to keep in mind that literary writers were much more concerned with producing a stable narrator to posit behind the *genbun'itchi* prose, while advocates of language reform emphasized the "naturalness" and efficiency of *genbun'itchi*.[4] As I will show, the "unification" of the spoken and written languages meant different things for proponents of *genbun'itchi*, but perhaps the most representative essays on this subject were written by Mozume Takami (1847–1928) and Basil Hall Chamberlain (1850–1935). Although both emphasized the need for simple prose, the former used *dearu* and *dearimasu* (suffixes associated with "oral" presentation), while the latter used Romanized script and common "spoken" language.[5]

In the late 1880s, we begin to see a new set of intellectuals take center stage in the advocacy of linguistic reform. These included such scholars of national literature trained at Tokyo University as Sekine Masanao (1860–1932), Ochiai Naobumi (1861–1903), and Hagino Yoshiyuki (1860–1924). They departed from the earlier discourse by determining that *kanji* and *kanji* compounds were in fact "Japanese." Hence they never advocated orthographical reform, except perhaps for the quantitative reduction of *kanji* in actual use. They began to compile *kokubun* textbooks, which focused on literary history from the classical to Edo periods. Their aim was to standardize grammar, primarily the *te ni o ha* particles, conjugation, tense, and suffixes. They extended their reforms beyond prose to include poetry as well.

These scholars of national literature were contemporaries of Ueda Kazutoshi (1867–1937), the so-called founder of *kokugo*. The emergence of Ueda and the establishment of Hakugengaku (Department of Linguistics) coincided with Japan's triumph in the first Sino-Japanese War, a result that established Japan's position as the leader of East Asia. Ueda then became the central figure in the promotion of *kokugo* reforms both within and beyond the Japanese archipelago.

It is very important to remind ourselves that these reformers did not possess a systematic view of what the "Japanese language" should be. They rarely agreed on what constituted "spoken" and/or "written" languages or indeed the meaning of "literature" or even "language." In examining their arguments, it is thus important to suspend our notions of what these categories signify so as to better grasp the meaning of their ideas.

1

Competing "Languages"

"Sound" in the Orthographic Reforms of Early Meiji Japan

This chapter focuses on the calls for orthographic reform that shaped the 1870s. A cursory look at early Meiji discourse shows that there was a general tendency to argue for script reform in order to unify the "spoken" and "written" languages and to reject *kanji* (and by extension *kanbun* and *kangaku*). Take the four reformers that I address in this chapter: Maejima Hisoka sought to abolish *kanji* and adopt *kana* scripts (phonetic alphabets indigenous to Japan) in an effort to produce "a language that, once uttered becomes spoken language (*danwa*) and once written becomes written language (*bunshō*)."[1] Mori Arinori, arguing against "useless Chinese" (referring to *kanji* and *kanbun*), "contemplated" the use of "Roman letters" in turning "the spoken language of Japan" into a written form "based on pure phonetic principles."[2] Nanbu Yoshikazu, too, sought to adopt the Roman alphabet instead of "inconvenient *kanji*" to reform "grammar" so that the new language could be understood whether it was "heard" or "seen."[3] Nishi Amane similarly argued for the use of the Roman alphabet in his effort to "establish rules for spelling and pronunciation" so that "writing and speaking would follow the same rules."[4]

On the surface, therefore, their calls for reform intersect in their efforts to bring about the unification of "spoken" and "written" languages. However, they varied greatly in what they promoted. This was inevitable since, as I suggested in the introduction, there was no agreement on what constituted "spoken" and "written" languages.[5] This, too, was inevitable, given that the reformers catered to (and mobilized) different "languages" in positing their "spoken" and "written" languages. As we shall see throughout this chapter, their reforms included the system of language inscribed in Western linguistic theories, the system of language latent in *kangaku* learning, or the system of language linked to the "fifty-sound syllabary grid" (*gojū-on zu*), traceable to nativist thought. These "languages" do not constitute additives, nor are they ontologically equal to one another; they are very much in tension with one another. Concealed in a narrative that lumps together the first two decades of the Meiji period as a preparatory stage for *kokugo* is precisely this complex intersection of "languages" that I seek to show in this chapter.

This chapter thus takes up varying arguments for a new orthography to make manifest these "languages." Key to this is the focus on the varying notions of "sound" with which the reforms engaged. Whether the reformers were arguing for the abolition of *kanji*, the use of the Roman alphabet or *kana*, or even the adoption of English, they all sought to privilege some kind of "sound," most often defined against *kanji* and *kanbun*.[6] In what follows, I first examine Mori's call for the adoption of the English language and identify the nascent trend of Western linguistics, focusing on what he referred to as "phonetic principles," which had a large impact upon language reform in general. I then move on to Maejima's call for the abolition of *kanji* and show that an orality latent to the study of *kangaku* governs his proposal to adopt *kana* phonetic scripts. In this section, I accordingly extend my discussion to the manner in which literati studied *kangaku* in the late Edo period, since it is particularly pertinent to the manner in which the early Meiji intelligentsia, all invariably educated in *kangaku*, viewed "language." I then turn to works written by Nanbu, who, despite his advocacy of the Roman alphabet, in fact sought to systematize grammar by engaging with the fifty-sound syllabary grid of *kana* scripts, a syllabic representation of existing sounds. Finally, I address essays written by Nishi, who also advocated the Roman alphabet. We find many different "languages" inscribed in his argument, as he sought to produce a system of agreement between pronunciation and spelling.

Such an inquiry into the reforms will show that what we typically assume to be manifestations of Westernization and de-Asianization (*datsua nyūō*) needs further scrutiny. We shall see how the many efforts to adopt phonetic letters, too often considered efforts at Westernization, in fact engaged not only with Western linguistic theories but also with the fifty-sound syllabary grid and the study of *kangaku*. Despite the reformers' rejection of *kanji*, the system of language integral to *kangaku* learning looms strong in the arguments for reform. This does not mean that I seek to undervalue the forces of Westernization present in early Meiji; indeed, I begin my inquiry with the discourse of Western linguistic theories that shape Mori's call for reform and later examine how they intersected with the study of *kangaku*. Such an inquiry will show that it is essential to go beyond the surface layer of orthography and decipher the underlying system of languages that compete and collide in these reforms.

"PHONETIC PRINCIPLES" OF WESTERN LINGUISTIC THEORIES: MORI ARINORI'S PROPOSAL FOR THE ENGLISH LANGUAGE

It goes without saying that the encounter with the West and the Roman alphabet made a huge impact on language reform movements in Japan. Even before the Meiji period, scholars of Dutch studies had often referred to the superiority of the Roman alphabet to *kanji*.[7] In the Meiji period, Western linguistic theories, which had only recently joined the ranks of "science," further reinforced such views.[8] Although it was not until the second decade of the Meiji period that Western linguistic theories became influential in the language reform movements in Japan, we can already see their nascent form, for example, in Mori Arinori's essays and speeches advocating the use of the English language:

> The spoken language of Japan being inadequate to the growing necessities of the people of that Empire, and *too poor to be made, by phonetic alphabet, sufficiently useful as a written language*, the idea prevails among us that, if we would keep pace with the age, we must adopt a copious and expanding European language. The necessity for this arises mainly out of the fact that Japan is a commercial nation; and also that, if we do not adopt a language like that of the English, which is quite predominant in Asia, as well as elsewhere in the commercial world, the progress of Japanese civilization is evidently impossible. Indeed a new language is demanded by the whole Empire. . . . All the schools the Empire has had, for many centuries, have been Chinese; and, strange to state, we have had no schools nor books, in our own language for educational purposes. These *Chinese schools, being now regarded not only as useless, but as a great drawback to our progress*, are in the steady progress of extinction. . . . The only course to be taken, to secure the desired end, is to start anew, by *first turning the spoken language into a properly written form, based on a pure phonetic principle*. It is contemplated that Roman letters should be adopted . . . It may be well to add, in this connection, that the written language now in use in Japan, has little or no relation to the spoken language, *but is mainly hieroglyphie*—a deranged Chinese, blended in Japanese, all the letters of which are themselves of Chinese origin.[9]

This passage, originally written in English, is from an 1872 letter Mori wrote to William D. Whitney, an American linguist at Yale.[10] It engages with the highly ideological view of language that dominated Western linguistics in the nineteenth century. Such an ideological view is most clearly apparent in the theory advanced by Friedrich von Schlegel (1772–1829). Indo-European languages, according to Schlegel, were "inflectional languages," which, he noted, could express "complex ideas through a single word: the root contains the main idea, the syllables that serve to form derived words express accessory modifications, and the inflections express variable relations." For Schlegel, these languages, as the most advanced form of languages, were the only medium that could bring about "any improvement of the human spirit."[11] In contrast, the "isolating languages," among which he classified "Chinese," showed no inflection and were "made up of monosyllables that we cannot even call roots," and could only be "lifeless," hence the least advanced and an impediment to progress.[12]

Schlegel may not have been the major influence behind Mori's proposal, but such an ideological view was present in Mori's argument when, for example, Mori noted that "Chinese schools" in Japan "are now regarded not only as useless, but as a great drawback to our progress."[13] Mori was certainly not the only one to adopt such a view. Katō Hiroyuki, the president of Tokyo University, attempted to define "our language" (*hōgo*) as being as far away from "Chinese" (*shinago*) as possible when establishing the Department of Linguistics (Hakugengaku) in 1880: "According to the theories of linguists, our language is completely different from *shinago* in type and instead shares a root with Manchurian, Mongolian and Korean."[14]

Predictably, such an ideological view of languages extended further into scripts in Schlegel's theory, as Roman alphabets were considered the most advanced and ideographic characters like *kanji* less so. In order to sever itself from classical philology, Western linguistics took as its object of study the phonetics of a given language as opposed to "dead" texts. Therefore, the criteria by which Indo-European languages were considered the most superior were drawn from many studies on "sound." In such a paradigm, the Roman alphabets, given their phonetic nature, as well as their ability to express "complex ideas" with the mere twenty-six letters of the alphabet, were deemed most civilized.[15] In contrast, *kanji*, as script, were seen as not representing their phonetic aspect, and were hence equated with "hieroglyphie," a view that Mori clearly adopted.

Mori, however, did not blindly adopt such views. To scrutinize what he ultimately advocated with his reference to the "phonetic principle," important in our line of inquiry, let us look at how he appropriates the dichotomy between "phonetic" and "hieroglyphic" scripts in his argument. Perhaps surprisingly, Mori deployed the criticism of "hieroglyphie" not only against "Chinese" but also against the English language. Such a claim was not unique to Mori. As Seth Jacobowitz shows in *Writing Technology in Meiji Japan*, Mori was also engaging with arguments of Anglophone reformers like Noah Webster, who sought a "national tongue based on an American rather than British vernacular, which would be vouchsafed by a simplified spelling system" and would jettison "unnecessary silent letters and multiple-letter combinations representing the same phonetic values."[16] Similarly, Mori proposed that the English language be changed to what he referred to as "simplified English" for adoption in Japan; in addition to substituting "seed" for "saw" and "seen," "speaked" for "spoke" and "spoken" to regulate the irregular verbs, Mori also suggested systematizing irregular spelling, such as "though" to "tho" and "bough" to "bow," which he claimed would be a "recast of English orthography—making the language actually what it claims to be—phonetic—instead of hieroglyphic on a phonetic basis, which is what it now really is."[17]

Two things ought to be highlighted here. First, what this criticism shows is that by "hieroglyphie," he was not simply referring to *kanji*-like figures or characters. In his understanding, phonetic letters did not necessarily produce phonetic language, and "hieroglyphie" was not limited to the "non-West." Mori was thus not blindly advocating the ideological view, as his argument here has the implication of questioning the Social Darwinist paradigm that situates "Chinese" (or "Asia" and its non-phonetic letters) as backward and English (or the "West" and its phonetic letters) as the most civilized. He of course did nothing to defend "Chinese" (which, for Mori, included *kanji* and *kanbun*, including the *kundoku* style), as he assumed that its infiltration into what he called "Japanese" had caused the demise of "language in Japan."[18] But he certainly did not uncritically cater to the dichotomy of a phonetic West vs. a non-phonetic Asia put forth by linguistic theories and those around him.

Second, his idea of "phonetic language" was one that privileged pronunciation over spelling. He sought to change "though" to "tho" to achieve commensurability, but did not attempt to change the pronunciation to match "though." This is precisely why adopting "phonetic letters" would not constitute reform for Mori. He sought a language in which the spelling would perfectly adhere to pronunciation; adopting phonetic letters would be insufficient to implement such reform. This privileging of pronunciation is on a par with theories of Western linguistics, which had discovered itself as a discipline through the study of phonetics by severing the study of language from classical philology.[19] The focus on phonetics, therefore, was its *raison d'être*.

What Mori thus sought was a simplified and "perfected" English as the language of Japan. This, at least, was his explicit goal. This does not mean that he did not seek reform to the "spoken language" of Japan. Although his arguments to do so only appear implicitly in his arguments for simplified English, he gives us a hint as to how he would have carried out the reform if he had implemented it.[20] The analysis of his ideas for the reform of the "spoken language" would further clarify how he conceptualized the "phonetic principles" by which he sought to bring reform.

It would be recalled that Mori lamented the current state of language in Japan in the following manner: "the only course to take . . . is to start anew, by first turning the spoken language into a properly written form, based on a pure phonetic principle." Here he is not discussing the adoption of "simplified English," but how he would reform the spoken language of Japan if he were to "start anew." In his introduction to "Education in Japan," he further suggests that the language itself needs to be reconfigured: "There are some efforts being made to do away with the use of Chinese characters by reducing them to simple phonetics, but the words familiar through the organ of the eye are so many that to change them into those of the ear would cause too great an inconvenience and be quite impracticable."[21] The new language, by virtue of being defined by "a pure phonetic principle," would thus be endowed with a system by which "words familiar through the organ of the eye" would be replaced by "those of the ear." Mori does not discuss how he would go about implementing this, but it is not too hard to imagine that he was, for example, thinking about increasing the variety of syllable structure to reduce homonyms, or the introduction of some kind of a phonetic system to mark the variety of existing homonyms, thereby defining the new language via "a pure phonetic principle." It was, in effect, a way to introduce a new phonetic structure to the "spoken language of Japan." Without such reform, he deemed the "spoken language of Japan" to be "too poor to be made, by a phonetic alphabet, sufficiently useful as a written language." In other words, merely adopting a phonetic alphabet and transcribing "the spoken language" without bringing reform to the language itself was not going to be enough.[22] He sought to alter and rearrange the sound system as a way to establish a new *écriture*, one which privileged pronunciation (rather than its scriptural equivalent), to completely alter what Mori called "deranged Chinese, blended in Japanese."[23]

What this unattempted reform shows is that Mori's use of "phonetic principle" was prescriptive. This interestingly reformulates what is at the core of Western linguistics. The central focus of linguistics was a descriptive study of multiple aspects of "sound"; it devised a phonetic system by which to describe languages focusing on, for example, phonological change, articulatory phonetics, and so forth. Mori, instead, sought to use these phonetic principles prescriptively, as a means to redefine and restructure the language. He saw in linguistic theories a way to reform the language, not simply a means to describe its limitations.

The phonetic focus by which linguistics defined itself as a discipline, deployed in the framework of comparative linguistics, produced an influential albeit fundamentally invalid dichotomy of the "phonetic West" and "hieroglyphic Orient."[24] Mori questioned this dichotomy, but he was one of the few intellectuals to be able to do so. This dichotomy in fact haunted the linguistic reform movements for decades to come. Partly as a result of this, the privileging of "sound" we see in the early Meiji period has too often been monolithically attributed to the "West." Of course, the existence of Indo-European languages and Western linguistic theories had a large impact upon language reform movements. And, as we shall see in the following chapter, the phonetic focus of Western linguistic theories became a more influential force in the 1880s, shaping the reforms, as arguments to adopt the Roman alphabet increase in number. However, Western influence alone cannot completely explain this "phonetic" focus we see in early Meiji. The following section will show that there were in fact other forces at work that compelled the Meiji literati to advocate phonetic scripts and insist on phoneticizing texts (which are otherwise written in "hieroglyphic" *kanji*).

THE ORALITY OF *SODOKU*: MAEJIMA HISOKA AND THE ABOLITION OF *KANJI*

Mori was certainly not the only one to see the need for an entirely new language. In fact, most proponents of language reform in the first decade of the Meiji period sought a new medium. Maejima Hisoka, who is perhaps more famous for his contribution to the establishment of the Japan's postal system, was also a strong advocate of language reform; his 1866 "Kanji onhaishi no gi" ("On the Abolition of *Kanji*") has often been identified as the beginning of modern orthographic reform. The main gist of his proposal is to abolish *kanji* altogether and employ *kana* scripts, but at one point in the essay, Maejima gives us a glimpse of an idea of the "new language" he sought:

> In establishing *kokubun* and its grammar, I don't mean that we need to return to the ancient forms of writing (*kobun*) and use suffixes such as *haberu* and *kerukana*, but rather I mean that we should employ the common language of today (*konnichi futsū no gengo*) like *tsukamatsuru* and *gozaru*, and apply some rules. That language changes with time is something I believe holds true both in our country and abroad. But I propose a language that once uttered becomes spoken language (*danwa*) and once written becomes written language (*bunshō*). I thus propose a language in which there is no disparity in style between spoken or written.[25]

This is the passage often referred to as one of the first references to *genbun'itchi*.[26] However, as literary critic Kamei Hideo has argued, Maejima was certainly not conceptualizing the "spoken" language as we have it now, nor the *genbun'itchi* that was later established. Kamei contends that Maejima had in mind a language that was very similar to *sōrōbun*, a style of language that was used in official documents, especially toward the end of the Edo period.[27]

To further scrutinize what Maejima means by "common language of today," I wish to identify the governing system of language that shapes Maejima's argument for reform. Rejecting *kanji* as a "hindrance to progress" and promoting the use of *kana* (which is likened to the Roman alphabet), Maejima appears to engage with the ideological view of Western linguistic theories. He emphasizes the amount of time people waste learning the means to knowledge and not knowledge itself, to the extent that critics like Lee have argued that Maejima's argument is shaped by a "utilitarian perception of language" typical of "practical knowledge" (*jitsugaku*).[28] His anti-*kanji* sentiments, as well as his conscious effort to identify *kana* with Roman alphabets, may lead us to think that his view is largely influenced by Western learning. However, take the following passage in Maejima's "Kokubun kyōiku no gi ni tsuki kengi" ("A Proposition for *Kokubun* Education"), which he wrote in 1869:

> The issue of enlightening the people is about providing education. . . . By 'providing education' I refer to abolishing *kanji* and taking *kana* (i.e., *hiragana*) as the national

> script, changing the conventional methods of education and, with new methods, educating people with subjects that range from ethics, physics, political science to law as well as daily things, all in simple national script like *kana*. . . . When we rely on old methods of education by using *kanji*, or even when we change the methods of education but use *kanji, kanji* would not only be trying for students' brains (*shin'nō*) and interfere with their intellect, but would also interfere with the development of the students' physical constitution (*taishitsu*) and weaken their physical frame (*taikaku*). There would be no hope to equal the physically and intellectually well-equipped people of Euro-America.[29]

This is a strong criticism against *kanji* and "the old methods of education." But notice the inextricable relationship Maejima draws between orthography and the physical makeup of those who study it. Such statements have not been scrutinized beyond the significance of emotionally-charged metaphors that express anti-Chinese sentiments. I do not doubt that Western linguistic theories reinforced anti-Chinese sentiments in Maejima. However, perhaps ironically given his strong criticism of *kangaku* in this essay, this link between orthography and the students' physical composition replicates the manner in which *kangaku* was studied in the mid- to late Edo period, the very education that Maejima and his generation had.

The study of *kangaku*, which was predominantly a study of its classics, had roughly three stages of learning: "raw-reading" (*sodoku*), reading (*dokusho*), and instruction (*kōgi*).[30] In the late Edo period, the practice of *sodoku* was foregrounded as one of the most important training practices in *kangaku*. This is significant, because the practice emphasized the physical characteristics of learning. *Sodoku* was a form of learning in which students declaimed words and phrases without knowing their meaning. Students verbally repeated their teachers, who read the texts orally and used pointers to indicate the characters and sentences they were reading. This process was repeated until the students had memorized the texts.[31] In effect, the body memorized the texts through the rhythm and sound of the sentences.[32] *Dokusho*, in which meaning was attributed to the language they memorized, followed; this was then supplemented by the third phase, *kōgi*, in which the meanings/interpretations of the texts were sought, debated, and discussed.[33]

The physical posture with which students practiced *sodoku* was extremely important, and the need for proper posture was carried over to later stages of *kangaku* studies and beyond. There is a famous anecdote about Nishi Amane, who, upon falling ill, began to read works by Ogyū Sorai, which Neo-Confucianism (Shushigaku) had categorized as "heretical studies" (*igaku*), because he thought he could read them in bed without worrying about proper posture. Nishi was pleasantly surprised to find them interesting, a discovery that would not have been possible had he not fallen ill. It had been engrained in him that appropriate posture was absolutely necessary in reading "proper" *kangaku* texts.[34]

The emphasis on the need for proper physical posture continued well into the Meiji period. *Kaisei kyōjujutsu* (*On New Strategies of Teaching*), written as late as 1883 and apparently governed by the new "Western" pedagogical method of J. H. Pestalozzi, describes the teaching of *sodoku*. The importance of posture is repeated again and again, with the text outlining the specifications for students' practice of *sodoku*:

1. The legs must be bent sixty degrees, and both feet must be perfectly still on the floor.
2. The student must sit as deeply as possible, and his lower back must slightly touch the chair.
3. The knees must be at a right angle.
4. The entire body should be slightly tilted forward.
5. The student ought to hold out his chest.[35]

The list continues to detail thirteen posture specifications for when one is sitting and another fourteen for standing. It was with such rigid physical posture that students experienced the rhythm and sound of the sentences. *Sodoku* was, as intellectual historian Tsujimoto Masashi claims, a process through which the entire body consumed the text of recitation.[36] It was a process of learning that required one's full physical attention until the memorized sentences were engrained in the body.

Such a relationship between the body and learning is derivative of Neo-Confucian ethics, the implication of which is beyond the scope of this chapter. Suffice it to say that *kangaku* education, *sodoku* being one of its important components, sought both moral and physical development, one integral to one another.[37] In effect, Maejima's criticism of *kanji* betrays the fact that he had internalized the physical training inscribed in *kangaku* education, especially in the *sodoku* practice. For Maejima, language was inextricably linked to the physical component, which affected the growth of the mind.

Note that this system of *sodoku*, though practiced for a long time in the Edo period, was only institutionalized in early nineteenth century. A *sodoku* exam (*sodoku ginmi*) was set up and attracted students from all over the country when passing this exam became a goal for students not only at Shōheikō, the official school of the Bakufu, but also in the provinces and non-Bakufu sponsored private schools (*shijuku*). *Sodoku ginmi* played an important role in standardizing the reading of the *kangaku* classics. It served to authorize the "correct" way of reading, regulating the variations that existed. Prior to such standardization, there were different methods devised by different masters or schools in reading *kanbun*, which determined how certain characters were read, how certain words were conjugated, where to place which of the *te ni o ha* particles, and when to employ the *on*-reading (phonetic approximation of the "original" sound or *kaon* 華音) or the *kun*-reading ("indigenous" pronunciation) of *kanji*. There were, in other words, "plural" readings of a single work, as different masters made different decisions; these decisions were not merely interpretive, but also grammatical.[38]

However, once standardized, it was as if the "right" way of reading preceded the *kanji* texts. In effect, the *kanbun* texts were no longer open to structural interpretation; the *te ni o ha* particles, conjugation, whether or not to employ *on*-reading or *kun*-reading for a given *kanji* compound, and so forth, were all determined by the authorized reading. There was, in other words, a "right phonetic reading" *behind* the characters. Once the structural ambiguity had been erased, it was no wonder that *kanji* came to appear as a hindrance. As a result, it was not a coincidence that the entire focus went to the phoneticizing of the text.[39] This explains the unconditional valorization of phoneticizing *kanji* scripts we see in Maejima and for that matter in many others in the early Meiji period. Once a *kanbun* text had been phoneticized, it was then easy to vocalize it. In effect, the institutionalized practice of *sodoku* created a space in which the main aim was to vocalize the authorized reading, which was a crucial means to learn and access "knowledge." We can now see that what has been taken as an adoption of Western "phonetic" languages and the impact of Western linguistic theories also grew out of *sodoku*, the first goal of which was to vocalize (hence phoneticize) the written script.

One of Maejima's arguments against *sodoku* was the length of time a student wasted in mastering the medium of knowledge, time better spent on knowledge itself, which is precisely why Lee characterizes his argument as utilitarian.[40] Now we can see that the institutionalization of *sodoku*, and hence the standardization of "knowledge," is behind such a positing of the problem. This may have been further reinforced by the ideological view promoted by Western linguistic theories, in which phonetic alphabets were considered more superior and "hieroglyphic" *kanji* less so, but it is also clear that *sodoku* played a large part in structuring Maejima's proposal in the first place.

Additionally, *sodoku ginmi* standardized the *kundoku* reading, which converts the syntactical order of the *kanbun* to "Japanese-local" grammar by inserting diacritical marks, particles, and suffixes, and conjugating words as necessary. The focus on the *kundoku* emerged out of an anti-Ogyū Sorai movement, as Sorai, in his "discovery" of the ancient texts, criticized the *kundoku* as "a barrier that stood between the reader and the language of Confucian texts," suggesting that "the ancient way" could only be accessed through *chokudoku* (literally "direct reading," referring to a reading in pure *kanbun* syntax) via *kaon* (in the "original" sound).[41] In criticizing such a view, Neo-Confucian scholars tried to show that it was in fact in the *kundoku* that "accurate" reading could be offered.[42] What *sodoku ginmi* did, in other words, was to disseminate and standardize the *kundoku* form of reading. What is important to remember, then, is that this institutionalized practice of reading, the core of *kangaku* study, was the orality of *kundoku* reading.

There are two things that ought to be highlighted here. First, we must remember that there was an orality integral to the learning of *kanbun*. We often lose sight of this orality given the prevalent dichotomy of phonetic and "hieroglyphic" letters, frequently used to compare *kanji* to the Roman alphabet or *kana* scripts.[43] Second, the orality associated with *kanbun* was that of the *kundoku* reading. With this in mind, we need to revisit Maejima's use of *danwa*—which is typically translated as "spoken" language—because not all utterances are necessarily "spoken."

In "Kokubun kyōiku no gi ni tsuki kengi," Maejima says the following: "The new *kokugo* will accommodate Western words and *kanji* compounds. Its structure ought not cater to classic elegance but to *zokubun* of contemporary times (*kintai*)."[44] The typical translation of *zokubun* is "vernacular prose," but we must not uncritically equate *zokubun* here with our sense of the vernacular. *Zokubun* here aligns with Maejima's earlier use of "common language of today" (*kyō futsū no gengo*) as it opposes "classic elegance." As Saitō Mareshi has shown, references to "common language" did not mean "vernacular" *per se;* they signified the *kundoku* order (as opposed to the *kanbun* order).[45] In fact, "common" (*futsū*) and "contemporary" (*kintai*), both of which are used by Maejima to denote *zokubun*, are terms used to characterize writing that were *not* pure *kanbun*, referring to the *kundoku* style of writing.[46] Recall that Maejima was critical of a language in which there was a discrepancy between "spoken" and "written" languages. Given the *sodoku* practice, it is not too farfetched to say that the disparity of *danwa* and *bunshō* languages that he saw was the disparity between *kanbun* and its *kundoku* reading. In effect, the language he promoted by using the term "common" or the phrase "the *zokubun* of contemporary times," was first and foremost a language in *kundoku* syntax. This is on a par with his decision to retain *kanji* compounds, despite his rejection of *kanji*, given that *kundoku* syntax strings together the *kanji* compounds. Whether written or spoken, his new language thus was to follow the *kundoku* order.

The practice of *sodoku* and its institutionalization played a large role in shaping the views of language that Meiji literati harbored. But as they intersected with the view of language offered by Western linguistic theories, which reinforced anti-*kanji* sentiments, the phonetics of *kanji* and the orality of the *sodoku* practice were concealed. If we characterize all such anti-*kanji* movements as manifestations of de-Sinification (and Westernization), we would further reinforce such concealment. For Meiji literati, anti-*kanji* sentiments may have manifested themselves as the desire to de-Asianize and Westernize, as many expressed. However, we simply replicate their views if we turn a blind eye to the role that the study of *kangaku* played in fostering anti-*kanji* sentiment.

In the following section, we will see a yet another notion of "sound" that shaped the arguments for reform, one that is inextricably linked to the development of the fifty-sound syllabary grid (*gojū-on zu*). Given that this development is often linked to nativist learning, it is perhaps ironic that this appears most tellingly in arguments to adopt the Roman alphabet.

ASSIGNING THE "CORRECT" SOUND: NANBU YOSHIKAZU AND THE FIFTY-SOUND SYLLABARY GRID

It is easy to imagine how advocates for reform who valued the phonetic nature of *kana* might take it a step further and argue for the use of the Roman alphabet. The call for the use of the Roman alphabet took off primarily in the second decade as Western linguistic theories became more influential. However, Nanbu Yoshikazu's proposals for the Roman alphabet, to which we will now turn, were not grounded in Western linguistic theories, and thus ought to be considered independently from what developed later. Nanbu was the first ever to make an argument for the use of the Roman alphabet, in works entitled "Shūkokugoron" ("On Learning *Kokugo*"), in 1869, and "Moji o kaikaku suru gi" ("On Reforming the Scripts"), in 1872.

After arguing how inconvenient *kanji* is for memorization and promoting instead the use of the Roman alphabet, Nanbu argues the necessity to first do the following:

> In order to change the script and establish grammar, we must first decipher the correct sound (*oto o tadasu*) and designate appropriate script. Our country has fifty sounds, in fact, seventy-five including voiced consonants (*dakuon*), and all words are produced with these sounds. As such, we must first of all identify the correct sounds; in order to do so we must designate appropriate scripts to them.[47]

Nanbu was certainly not alone in arguing for script reform as essential component to standardizing language; we saw that Mori sought the same in his call for simplified English. Yet what is unique to Nanbu is the way in which he associates script, grammar, and "correct" sounds. There are two points of focus here: the inextricable link he sees between script and grammar, which will be addressed later in this section, and his use of the phrase "*oto o tadasu*" (literally, "to correct sounds"). Perhaps the first reaction to "*oto o tadasu*" is to equate it with correcting pronunciations and standardizing dialects. This is understandable, because many dialects divided the nation in the early years of the Meiji period. Yet, among three essays Nanbu wrote between 1875–77 on adopting the Roman alphabet, he does not once mention dialects or, for that matter, the actual spoken language. Dialects were not taken up as a central issue among the advocates of linguistic reforms until the 1880s, when they began to talk about standardizing Japanese through the Tokyo dialect.[48] The sound Nanbu refers to here does not appear to have any link to actual uttered sounds or spoken language.

If it is not spoken language or dialects, what then constitutes the "*oto*" of "*oto o tadasu*"? Just as with Maejima, the system of language that shapes Nanbu's proposal is evident from what he criticizes, namely *kana*. One of the main reasons that Nanbu advocates the Roman alphabet is because the vowels and consonants are separate, a convenience which, he argues, is non-existent in *kana*. Moreover, Nanbu contends that *kana* scripts need to "improvise" when representing "contracted sounds" (*yōon*) like *ja* (じゃ) and *kya* (きゃ), which require two *kana* characters, as well as "voiced sounds" (*dakuon*) like *da* (だ) and *ga* (が), which need two additional dots for *ta* and *ka* respectively. Both of these methods of representation are too unsystematic for Nanbu. With the Roman alphabet, he suggests, "equal" value would be assigned to each sound of the syllabary grid.

Nanbu, like Mori, sought a language that could be understood equally well either when "seen" or "heard." Yet Nanbu certainly did not propose to adopt English, nor did he cater to Western linguistic theories in the way Mori did. Nanbu instead subscribed to a view of language inscribed in the syllabary grid, which is latent in his use of *oto o tadasu*. *Oto o tadasu* is a phrase used with regard to *kanazukai* (uses of *kana*) in the history of writing.[49] It is used in reference to rendering *kanji* as *kana*, that is, assigning *kana* to respective *kanji* characters. With *oto o tadasu*, Nanbu was thus referring to the act of assigning alphabetical letters to each *kana* sound. It is these sounds of the fifty-sound syllabary grid, which he at other places calls *koe* (or *kowe* to be exact, because he opts to use classical orthography, both denoting "voices"), that he seeks to systematize in adopting the Roman alphabet.[50]

Let us delve further into the "sounds" of the syllabary grid and *kanazukai* in order to explore the perception of language that Nanbu harbored.[51] The development of the syllabary grid and *kanazukai* in the Edo period engaged with nativists' study of ancient texts, all of which were written in *kanji*.[52] The nativist Keichū, for example, attempted to recover the "original" sounds inscribed in the *Man'yōshū* (*Collection of Ten Thousand Leaves*). Motoori Norinaga, in seeking indigenous "Japanese-ness" (defined in opposition to what he called *karagokoro*, or the "Chinese heart") in ancient texts, too, sought the words of the ancients expressed in *Kojiki*. Both sought to access the "sound" *behind* the *kanji*, the "voices" that logically preceded the *kanji* that mediated them. There is a clear inversion at work here: it is the practice of reading that posits the sound *behind* the *kanji*, but it is as if that sound had always been there, waiting to be excavated.[53] The implications of such inversion are beyond the scope of this chapter. Suffice it to say that, through such a scholarly turn, "sound" had become a central medium by which to access the ancient texts. Only by focusing on these sounds could the readers access the ancient voices.[54] Within such a scholarly trend, the syllabary grid became not only a means to represent sounds manifested in ancient texts, but the embodiment of ancient voices themselves. For the nativists, the syllabary grid signified a meaningful system of sounds that embodied the voices of the past.[55]

"Sound" in such a paradigm is an abstract sound, made manifest only textually. It may have been uttered in the past, but it is not linked to a "living" sound. It is, for example, very different from the phonographic *kana* system (*hyōonshiki kanazukai*) that appeared in the second decade of the Meiji period, which sought to represent *kana* in ways closer to contemporary pronunciation. It is also very different from how Mori conceptualized the unification of sound and script. Instead, it features a prescribed system of sound that is linked to past texts and not an actual pronunciation. In effect, Nanbu sought commensurability between two systems of script, *kana* and the Roman alphabet.

Nanbu may have appropriated the syllabary grid in conceptualizing his idea of reform, but this does not mean that he adhered to the nativist ideology. Far from it. He saw it purely as a phonetic system and a practical medium to systematize language. He was certainly not alone in this. That the utilitarian value of the syllabary grid was being discovered in the early years of the Meiji period as an appropriate medium to educate young children is evident in its inclusion in many school textbooks.[56] Many Meiji intellectuals promoted its use in education, more so than the other well-known syllabary sequence, *iroha*.[57] This was precisely because the syllabary grid was seen to embody a system of sounds, while *iroha* (which constitutes a poetic sequence) was considered to be a system of writing.[58] *Iroha* was usually the first to be taught in the Edo period in private calligraphy schools (*tenarai juku*), schools for elementary education in which writing was prioritized over reading, given its practical link to letter-writing and other daily chores.[59] In effect, the fifty-sound syllabary grid as a phonetic system was thus being brought to the forefront in the early Meiji period. And Nanbu was clearly on a par with such a general trend.

For Meiji intellectuals, the practicality of the syllabary grid lay not only in its ability to represent the existing sound system but also in its link to a system of grammar.[60] Katayama Junkichi, in his textbook for elementary education (*Shōgaku tsuzuriji hen*, 1873), says the following:

> The fifty-sound syllabary grid . . . vertically represents the five vowel sounds and horizontally represents the variation of *a, i, u, e, o*. It also represents *shōzengen* [the old way of saying *mizenkei* or irrealis], *ren'yōgen* [adverbial], *setsudangen* [the old way of saying *shūshikei*, conclusive], *rentaigen* [attributive], and *izengen* [realis]. It embodies rules for adjectives, adverbs, and verbs, which also show past, present, and future forms. It is orderly and convenient, and surpasses anything that China or Europe has. To educate our children, we must therefore use the fifty-sound syllabary grid as the foundation for education and teach them rules of sound and grammar. The forty-seven letters of the *iroha*, in comparison, do not offer a system of sounds, nor a system for conjugation.[61]

What does Katayama mean when he suggests that the syllabary grid embodies grammatical rules? Take, for example, the word *kaku* or "to write" (for convenience, I will here use our contemporary orthography): *kaku* conjugates into: *kaka*(*nai*) (irrealis, to denote the negative), *kaki* (*masu*) (adverbial), *kaku* (conclusive), and *kake*(*ba*) (realis, to denote hypothetical), thus following *ka, ki, ku, ke* sequence. In effect, when the word's column is identified, hence identifying the "correct sound," so is its conjugation. Katayama does not account for the many types of verbs that do not conjugate in accordance with the syllabary grid, but it is clear that Meiji intellectuals saw the grid as a means to standardize grammatical rules.

It is worth recalling here that, for Nanbu, "sound" was inextricably linked to grammar. Nanbu clearly saw the grid's value in its ability to teach the grammar necessary for standard conjugation. Identifying the proper column for conjugation was especially important for the historical *kana* system, which Nanbu sought to reflect in his system of Romanization.[62] Take, for example, the verb *tohu* 問ふ or "to question." In the irrealis form, *tohu* becomes *toha* (*nai*), hence showing us that it conjugates in the *h*-column. Its adverbial and realis equivalents, in the historical *kana* system, are *tohi* and *tohe* (問ひ・問へ), although they were pronounced with /i/ and /e/, like its contemporary conjugation, namely *toi* and *toe* (問い・問え). Nanbu clearly valued the systematicity thus inherent in the syllabary grid. It is not a coincidence that, after giving up on the Roman alphabet in the second decade of the Meiji period, he joined the historical *kana* faction of the advocates of *kana* scripts (as opposed to *hyōonshiki kanazukai*, those who advocated the use of *kana* that reflected contemporary pronunciation).

It is perhaps difficult to fathom a discursive site in which such a system of language lay "hidden" behind a proposal to adopt the Roman alphabet. In catering to such a system, however, Nanbu sought a way to use the existing system of *kana* and grammar, very unlike, say, Mori, who sought to alter the phonetic structure as a whole. The paradigm of language inscribed in the fifty-sound syllabary grid that Nanbu sought to deploy has not been scrutinized enough in the study of language reform. This is, in part, because the choice of *kana* is often likened to the Roman alphabet as opposed to "hieroglyphic" *kanji*. Such a triangular scheme treats *kana* purely as a phonetic system and relegates *kana* to a status secondary to the words and concepts that it presumably represents, inevitably divorcing *kana* from its grounding in the syllabary grid; this further reinforces the severance between the syllabary grid and its ideological link to the voices of the past espoused by the nativists. The idea that *kana*, because of its "phonetic nature," is like the Roman alphabet, therefore, is very limiting.

We will now turn to Nishi Amane's proposal that also argued for the adoption of the Roman alphabet, a proposal that engaged with the many "languages" we have seen so far. Nishi and Nanbu were similar in that both sought to establish a system of grammar by adopting the Roman alphabet. But Nishi did not draw on the syllabary grid to systematize grammar; he instead attempted to create his own system of grammar by focusing on the relationship between pronunciation and spelling, drawing on Western linguistic theories and other paradigms of language.

RECONCILING PRONUNCIATION AND SPELLING: NISHI AMANE AND THE ROMAN ALPHABET

As a strong advocate of the Roman alphabet, Nishi Amane wrote “Yōji o motte kokugo o shosuru no ron” (“On Writing *Kokugo* in the Roman Alphabet,” 1874) for the inaugural issue of *Meiroku zasshi* (*Meiroku Journal*), perhaps the most famous of his writings advocating language reform. Among the many calls for reform in the 1870s, this work is one of the most complex, because it combines many of the “languages” we have looked at in this chapter and challenges the normative understanding of “language” and “unification of spoken and written languages” that we in the contemporary times harbor. As such, even a sophisticated critic like Lee Yeounsuk sees it as a manifestation of a blind pursuit of the West.[63] Yet let us not hastily dismiss Nishi’s claims, and first identify the logic behind his choice of the Roman alphabet. He lists ten advantages of adopting the Roman alphabet; here are numbers one and three:

> By adopting the Western alphabet, we shall establish grammar (*gogaku tatsu*). This is the first advantage. . . .
>
> Since writing and speaking will follow the same rules, what is written is what is spoken. Lectures, toasts, speeches before assemblies, and sermons by preachers may all be recited as they are written and written as they are read. This is the third advantage.[64]

What he is claiming is not immediately obvious. “Establishing grammar” was one of the goals that Nishi, along with many others like Nanbu, had in devising his arguments for the use of the Roman alphabet. Yet the link Nishi saw between his orthographic choice and grammar is nothing like what we examined in Nanbu’s work. It is inextricably linked with the third advantage, namely that “writing and speaking” follow the same rules. What does this mean, specifically? Some critics see Nishi’s proposal as one of the early arguments of *genbun’itchi*, only to criticize it for not pushing the ideals of unification far enough.[65] Yet, if we look at the examples he provides carefully, his proposal appears very practical. Here are his examples:

・denotes characters that are not read
～denotes a change in sound
The top line shows spelling, and the bottom line shows pronunciation
For adjectives that end with *ku, si,* and *ki*:

1. Spelling　　イカサマヲモシロシ (omosirosi)
　　ikasama　omosirosi
　　•
   Pronunciation:　イカサマヲモシロ・イ(omosiro.i)

2. ヲモシロキ コト (omosiroki koto)
omosiroki koto
•
ヲモシロイ コト (omosiro.i koto)

3. コレハ ヨロシシ (kore wa yorosisi)
kore wa yorosisi
•
コレハ ヨロシイ (kore wa yorosi.i)

To make nouns modifiers:

4. キタイ ナル ヒト (kitai naru hito)
kitai naru hito
••
キタイナ ヒト (kitai na.. hito)

Verbs :

5. イマ キカム ユワム (ima kikamu yuwamu)

6. キルル (kiruru) ima kikam yuwam kiruru
~ ~ ~
イマ キカウ ユワウ (ima kikō yuō) キレル (kireru)[66]

What Nishi has devised here is a system of agreement for "uniting" the written and spoken languages. Take the first example. We may write "*omoshirosi*" but say "*omoshiroi*." As long as we *agree* to read *omoshirosi* as *omoshiroi*, then the written and spoken languages follow the same rules. By writing in the Roman alphabet, it becomes clear it is the "s" that is a silent letter, which ought to be skipped; *kana* would not be as convenient in this sense. Like Maejima before him, Nishi advocated a new language in which the "spoken" and "written" languages followed the same structure, but he did not aim to use the same language for both spoken and written like Maejima did in proposing to use the "common language." He sought instead to take the divergence of spoken and written languages and reconcile it by devising a new system of pronunciation and spelling. This is slightly different from Mori's proposal to establish commensurability between pronunciation and spelling. In proposing simplified English, Mori sought to relegate script to reflect pronunciation, hence proposing to change "though" to "tho." Nishi, however, sought to retain the spelling "*omoshirosi*" but in pronunciation skip the "s." The idea may seem absurd on the surface, but any written language features a system of agreement with its reading equivalent. According to Mori's set of evaluative criteria, Nishi's system would be considered "hieroglyphic," but Nishi's was a practical way to devise a systematic unification.

Despite the seeming originality of his ideas, Nishi's proposal drew on many languages we have seen so far. This is evident from the following list he provided of what ought to be done to adopt the Roman alphabet:

1. Determine the relationship between the ABCs and our sounds (*hōon*).
2. Our sounds have four voices. Establish rules for them.
3. Determine the characteristics of words and categorize them accordingly.
4. Determine what is intrinsic and extrinsic in the language.
5. Decide rules for spelling.
6. Decide rules for pronunciation.
7. Decide rules for inflection.
8. Decide tenses and conjugation of verbs.
9. Decide rules for employing sounds of *kanji*.
10. Decide rules for employing Western words.[67]

The first two points evoke *kanazukai*, as he proposes to assign letters of the alphabet to "our sounds." He was clearly adopting the prescribed system of sounds represented by *kana* scripts. Thus, this is similar to Nanbu, who promoted the *kana* sounds, and dissimilar from Mori, who sought to introduce an entirely new phonetic structure. Moreover, Nishi's interest in *kana* was not spontaneous. He had in fact once advocated the use of *kana*, as evident in his experimental work on grammar entitled *Kotoba no ishizue* (*The Foundation of Language*, 1870), which he wrote entirely in *kana*. He opens the work with his discussion on what he calls "Kowe no manabi" ("On Learning Voices") and argues the superiority of the syllabary grid over the *iroha* sequence, showing that his notion of "our sounds" (*hōon*) is clearly derivative of the former.

"Our sounds," according to Nishi, have "four voices" (*shisei*). The exact meaning of "four voices" is unclear, as editors and the translator of *Meiroku zasshi* claim.[68] However, the "four voices," which typically refer to four tones in Chinese, refer to the pitch accent pronunciation that was used in systematizing a version of *kanazukai* by Fujiwara Teika (1162–1241) before *kanazukai* was altered and "corrected" by later nativists.[69] Teika apparently assigned *kana* based on the varying pitches of the "four voices." Such *kanazukai*, however, had long been criticized by the Edo nativists as "inconsistent," because it did not properly adhere to the ancient usages (the "pure voices" of the past). Why did Nishi choose to evoke this, in many ways considered "invalid," *kanazukai* in systematizing the use the Roman alphabet? It was because his focus was on pronunciation, or more specifically, phonological changes that would account for the discrepancy between pronunciation and spelling. As his examples showed, Nishi was interested in deciphering the relationship between pronunciation and spelling, which was more closely reflected by Teika's system of *kanazukai*.

This focus on pronunciation is where his engagement with Western linguistic theories, in which he was very well informed, comes into the picture.[70] Even in *Kotoba no ishizue*, after he argues the superiority of the syllabary grid, he discusses how these sounds are produced in the mouth, drawing on articulatory phonetics. In a section called "Kotoba to aya to no koto" ("On Words and Sentences"), he includes what looks like a vowel chart, something he learned when he studied in Europe.[71] Drawing on studies of phonological changes in Western linguistics, he sought to establish a system by which to unite pronunciation and spelling. Take the earlier example of "*omoshirosi*" and "*omoshiroi*" again. Nishi was interested in deciphering the process behind the elision of the "s" sound. If he could see the system that enabled the elision of such sounds and hence understand the phonological change, he would be able to establish his new grammar.

Yet Western linguistic theory was not the only realm he drew on to decipher phonological change. To explore this issue further, it is important to note that the phonological changes in his examples only occur in inflection. That is to say, he offers examples of verb and adjectival conjugation—such as "*yorosisi*" to "*yorosii*," "*kikamu*" to "*kikau*"—but not of nouns or other words in which inflections do not occur. Had he been drawing on Western linguistic theories, he would have shown interest in all words, not just inflected forms. We could, of course, say that phonological changes occur most often in inflection, but this does not seem to be a satisfactory explanation for Nishi's curious focus. I sense something quite deliberate in his choice to limit his inquiries into phonological change (and hence the rules to "unite" pronunciation and spelling) to inflected forms.

What is behind such a choice? Number nine on his list, "Decide rules for employing sounds of *kanji*," may give us some clue. Here, we can see Nishi's urge to represent "*kanji* sounds" as such in his new language. In other words, he seeks to distinguish *kanji*-based renderings even in the Roman alphabet. One of Nishi's earlier orthographic experiments may shed light on his proposal. When studying in Europe, he had been involved in a project to romanize *Great Learning* (*Da xue*), one of the *kangaku* classics, in the *kundoku* form.[72] Here is an example:

> 物有本末。事有終始。知所先後。則近道矣。
>
> Mono *hon-batsu* ari; waza *siu-si* ari. *Sen-kou* suru tokoro wo sireba, sunavatsi mitsi ni tsikasi.[73]

Notice how he italicized the *kanji* compounds as if to retain the orthographic difference in the Roman alphabet. Despite his rejection of *kanji*, Nishi was never against the use of *kanji* compounds in the new language he sought.[74] In effect, in "employing sounds of *kanji*," it is likely that he was looking for a way to represent *kanji* compounds as a unit, whether by italicizing them or by devising something else to mark their "*kanji*"-ness. This was the same for what he called "Western words" in item number ten in his list.

These units, represented as such, would remain free of phonological change in his new language, and hence their pronunciation and spelling would not deviate from one another. In effect, a system of agreement between pronunciation and spelling only had to be devised for inflected forms. This structure inevitably replicates the *kundoku* structure, which links a series of *kanji* and *kanji* compounds by making inflectional changes, conjugating, and adding tenses to the original *kanbun*. As Saitō Mareshi has shown, *kundoku* offers a system of grammar by which to link and make sense of *kanji* compounds.[75] Despite Nishi's rejection of *kanji* and his strong inclination to Western linguistic theories, the *kundoku* reading played an important role in his arguments for reform.

The idea of a unification of "spoken" and "written" languages that Nishi proposed is nothing like we saw in the other reforms. Nishi's call for reform presented itself as a combination of the languages we have seen throughout this chapter. While he sought to deploy the existing system of sounds, he devised ways to "translate" them into the Roman alphabet by drawing on theories of Western linguistics and *kundoku* reading.

CONCLUSION

Despite an apparent similarity in the urge to unify the "spoken" and "written" languages, the proposals for linguistic reform in early Meiji Japan varied from each other in their methods and goals, probably more so than at any other time in the history of modern Japan. This shows the multiple directions in which reforms could have developed before being "standardized" as "national language." Moreover, it also shows that a clear path had yet to be defined. The only thing that these advocates knew was that a new medium had to be produced, be it through the adoption of English, *kana* scripts, or the Roman alphabet. In effect, what marks the first decade of Meiji period language reform is intellectuals' search for "languages" that could regulate the new medium they sought.

Choices of orthography did not limit these thinkers. Although we often attribute a given orthography to the paradigms of knowledge that support it, the call for the Roman alphabet did not necessarily signify a pursuit of Western learning, nor did the argument for *kana* signify a longing for nativist learning. These advocates freed their orthographic choices from their apparent foundations in grappling with the many complex issues they faced in producing their own system of language. From our perspective, too, such a link between orthography and knowledge, often made in studies of linguistic reforms, can only be a hindrance in the attempt to see the complex ways in which varying perceptions of language intersected and were made manifest in arguments for reform.

The rejection of *kan*, too often treated as a given in the early Meiji period, also needs further analysis. Even as *kangaku* was rejected as a "hindrance to progress" not only by the four reformers but by many early Meiji intellectuals, the institutionalization of *sodoku* was firmly behind the Meiji reformers' urge to phoneticize scripts. Many intellectuals may have been against *kanji* as script, but *kanji* compounds and *kanbun* grammatical structure (especially in its *kundoku* form) were appropriated to produce a new language, as we saw in Maejima and Nishi.

As we saw throughout this chapter, the notions of "sound" that shaped the first decade were many, none of which ought to be conflated with one another. The "phonetic" principles of Western linguistic theories, the orality of *sodoku*, the "sound" inextricably linked to the syllabary grid, and *kanazukai* systems all offered themselves as a means to regulate the styles that were available in the discursive site in question. These varying "languages" manifested differently in the way the reformers sought commensurability between "spoken" and "written" languages. In Mori's idea of commensurability, on a par with the idea of phonetics in Western linguistic theories, the pronounced sound was privileged; it was thus up to spelling to reflect the pronunciation (hence the proposal to change "though" to "tho"). Maejima's concern centered on phoneticizing (and hence vocalizing) *kanji* scripts, seeking commensurability between the oral "reading" (*kundoku*) and "writing" (*kanbun*). Nanbu privileged the textual sound represented in the fifty-sound syllabary grid, which was perfectly translatable to Romanized script; the commensurability that he sought was technically via one set of script (*kana*) to another set of script (the Roman alphabet), divorced entirely from pronunciation. With Nishi, commensurability between pronunciation and spelling was achieved by a system of agreement, not relegating either mode of expression to a position secondary to the other.

As we shall see in the following chapter, the competing "languages" that were foregrounded through these "sounds" continued to shape the calls for reform in the 1880s, which were marked by the emergence of *kanbun kundokutai* as "common language." An inquiry into *kanbun kundokutai* will not only allow us to reassess the role of *kan* in the production of linguistic modernity, but also to see how the "languages" changed form as linguistic reforms entered a new era with the appearance of a "common language."

2

Sound, Scripts, and Styles

Kanbun kundokutai and the National Language Reforms of 1880s Japan

This chapter explores the popularity of *kanbun kundokutai* (*kanbun*-style language in "Japanese" syntactical order with "Japanese" suffixes), which proliferated as a "common language" (*futsūbun*) in the second decade of the Meiji period, as well as the anti-*kanji* reforms and discourses that co-existed with this popularity. As I mentioned in the introduction, the issue of *kanbun kundokutai* is compelling, given that *kan*, too often uncritically equated with "China," is treated as a negative reference point against which to posit *kokugo*, a "national" form of prose.[1] The focus on de-Asianization (*datsua*) in the Meiji period, which has become especially strong given the postcolonial trends in recent literary studies, reinforces the desire to retain *kan* as the other to the "modern." As if to supplement such a narrative, much work has been done on the link between the new national literature (*kokubungaku*) scholars and the Edo nativists (*kokugaku*), focusing on what Meiji *kokubungaku* scholars rejected *and* inherited in their efforts to produce *kokugo*. However, without exploring the relationship between *kokugo* and *kanbun kundokutai*, existing scholarship presents *kokugo* as if it emerged from a vacuum (or from a *kokugaku* lineage that had somehow remained dormant until the 1890s). Perhaps to offset such a narrative, critics tend to posit nationalism as that which preceded and hence prompted the emergence of *kokugo*. This is part and parcel of the teleological narrative, because it once again posits nationalism as the primary motivation. This chapter inquires into the manner in which *kokugo* negotiated with the proliferation of *kanbun kundokutai* before the Ueda-led *kokugo* reform era, and shows how the emergence of *kokugo* in fact appropriated the realm of *kanbun kundokutai*.

I will first briefly define *kanbun kundokutai* and then discuss the fertile space it occupied in the early Meiji period. I will then turn to the many arguments for reform that shaped the second decade of Meiji and inquire into the forces that governed those arguments in an effort to highlight how Meiji literati situated *kanji* characters and compounds, and ultimately *kanbun kundokutai*, in their arguments for new language. Not only will this discussion provide a general background to the historical period in question, but it will also serve as an important context for one of the primary texts I take up in the subsequent section, Yano Ryūkei's 1886 *Nihon buntai moji shinron* (*A New Theory of Style and Orthography in Japan*, hereafter *New Theory*), one of the few texts that advocated a style of *kanbun kundokutai* as the most appropriate language to "foster learning among the Japanese people" amidst the many movements against it.[2]

Situating *New Theory* as the backdrop to the linguistic reform movements, I will show how it engages not only with varying arguments for orthographic reform, but also with a shift that occurred in *kanbun kundokutai* as it began to claim autonomy from *kanbun*.[3] As we shall see in more detail later, the domain of *kanbun*, too, shifted in the first two decades of the Meiji period, providing a fertile ground upon which linguistic reforms were discussed and made possible. *New Theory*, I contend, steps into the possibilities opened up by *kanbun kundokutai* and, at the same time, helps to create the possibilities themselves.

All this prepares for the final section of this chapter, which explores the works of national literature scholars of the late 1880s and early 1890s, with a specific focus on their silent negotiation with *kanbun kundokutai*. I will show that national literature scholars appropriated the realm of *kanbun kundokutai* that laid the groundwork for the purportedly nationalist choice they made, a process that is effaced by scholarship that essentializes the nation as a preexisting telos.

THE POPULARITY OF *KANBUN KUNDOKUTAI* AND ANTI-*KANJI* REFORMS AND DISCOURSES

Kanbun kundoku was initially devised to read *kanbun*, or classical "Chinese" writing; hence it was a style of language that was initially a translation of the *kanbun* text. "*Kanbun*," to use Benedict Anderson's language, constituted the "sacred language" which was "imbued with impulses largely foreign to nationalism."[4] *Kanbun kundoku* was thus a method that was devised to access this "sacred language" in "local" translation. This then developed as a separate style, although the rhythm, rhetorical effects, and, to a large extent, grammar were bound to the *kanbun* text. Strictly speaking, therefore, *kanbun kundokubun* (*kundoku* writing, with *kundoku* referring to "local" syntactical order) and *kanbun kundokutai* (*kundoku* style) ought to be differentiated, given that the former is a "translation" of the original *kanbun* text while the latter is a style of language that developed from the translated prose.[5]

As we saw in chapter 1, different masters or schools devised different rules for reading *kanbun*, which determined how characters were read, how words were conjugated, and where to place the *te ni o ha* particles. The types of reading that derived from such practice were many. For example, the most popular among late Edo and early Meiji literati was called *issaiten*, devised by the Confucian scholar Satō Issai (1772–1859). In comparison to other forms of reading, its defining characteristics were 1) fewer supplemented words/phrases (*hodokugo*); 2) more readings in *ondoku* of *kanji* characters, with *ondoku* referring to the phonetic approximation of the original pronunciation; and 3) reading as many *kanji* characters as possible, hence fewer "dropped characters" (*ochiji*).[6] This is probably the style that linked up to what was later known as the "plain gloss" style (*bōdokutai*) of *kanbun kundokutai*, which used a bare minimum of suffixes and used primarily *ondoku*. This "plain gloss" style was predominant, especially in the 1880s.

In addition to the "plain gloss" style, however, there was another form of *kanbun kundokutai* popular in the early Meiji period; this was known as the "translated" or "elaborated" style (*yakudokutai*). This style sought to adjust even the honorific language and use *kanbun*-oriented renderings of polite language that did not exist in *kanbun* itself.[7] It was used by literate peasants and townsmen, who, as a result, had the ability to read and compose *kanbun*, even if they were less familiar with the full corpus of *kangaku* classics.[8]

These two types of *kanbun kundokutai* existed side-by-side in the early Meiji period. But the "plain gloss" style began to predominate among Meiji literati, especially as new *kanji* compounds and phrases began to increase through the translation of foreign words. This had two somewhat contradictory effects. On the one hand, *kanbun kundokutai* proved to be extremely functional and versatile in absorbing new knowledge, but, on the other hand, this very versatility alienated less-literate townspeople and peasants, because it introduced many new terms and phrases that were beyond the scope of their literacy.[9] It produced an ironic situation in which the very literati who were concerned about disseminating new knowledge increased the difficulty of the language, leading them to further lament the fact that too many people in Japan were uneducated.[10]

In effect, *kanbun kundokutai* enjoyed the status of "current language" (*kintaibun*) and "common language" (*futsūbun*) among Meiji literati, as the style proved versatile in adopting new forms of knowledge and translating newly imported materials. The contemporary literary critic Saitō Mareshi states that one way to look at *kanbun kundokutai* is to see the style as a schema that offers a system of grammar by which to link and make sense of *kanji* compounds.[11] The "plain gloss" style allowed for the bare skeleton of grammar. As long as such a system was in place, adding new *kanji* compounds—necessary in translating new concepts and ideas imported to Japan—was not a problem. The practicality of *kanbun kundokutai* in the Meiji period is often attributed to the *kanbun* background literati had acquired in the Edo period, but, as Saitō claims repeatedly, it is in the *kanbun kundokutai* that such practicality was taken to its fullest potential.

Newspapers were one of the primary media that did much to foster the popularity of *kanbun kundokutai*, not only as the dominant style used in newspaper reports and columns, but also as a means to disseminate many translations of scholarly works, not to mention the newly established laws and declarations.[12] In addition, many fictional works popularized *kanbun kundokutai*, such as *Karyū shunwa* (*Romantic Stories of Blossoms*, 1879) (Oda Jun'ichirō's abridged translations of Bulwer-Lytton's *Ernest Maltravers* [1837] and *Alice* [1838]), Yano Ryūkei's *Keikoku bidan* (*Illustrious Tales of Statesmanship*, 1883), and Tōkai Sanshi's *Kajin no kigū* (*Chance Meetings with Beautiful Women*, 1885–97), to name a few examples. These texts were widely read by Meiji literati, which undoubtedly contributed to the proliferation of *kanbun kundokutai*.

Furthermore, we begin to see a great number of composition (*sakubun*) textbooks produced in the 1870s and 80s that centered on *kanbun kundokutai*, designed for different levels of literacy. In addition to those that focused on letter writing and other forms of "practical" composition, *kanbun kundokutai* textbooks were produced in response to the growing need for *kanbun kundokutai* in Meiji, which in turn further increased its popularity.[13] Journals and periodicals that specialized in compositions such as *Eisai shinshi* (*A New Journal for the Talented*) appeared, soliciting compositions from their young readership.[14] The main styles of composition published in these journals were *kanbun kundokutai* and *sōrōbun* (epistolary style). To be published in *Eisai shinshi* was considered a great honor among the youths of the time, as seen from records of reminiscences by Meiji literati like Uchida Roan (1868–1929).[15] In short, *kanbun kundokutai* was everywhere apparent, rightfully named the "current language," and hence offered a legitimate choice as the means for standardization.[16]

Perhaps ironically, the more popular *kanbun kundokutai* became, the more anti-*kanji* sentiment grew. The popularity of *kanbun kundokutai* posed a threat to the advocates of language reforms, whose primary goal was to produce a language that would provide not only a basic education to the heretofore uneducated, but also offer easy access to newly imported knowledge. The "impracticality" of learning *kanji* was one of the primary criticisms that motivated the movement for reform. As we saw last chapter, Maejima Hisoka wrote as early as 1866, in "Kanji onhaishi no gi" ("On the Abolition of *Kanji*"), that "by abolishing *kanji* from the education of the public, we will reduce the amount of time spent on reading and writing, that is to say, on memorizing the pronunciation and figures of ideographs."[17] Such criticism of spending too much time on the *means*, and not the *content*, of knowledge, was reiterated again and again throughout the Meiji period.

The desire for language reform was, moreover, motivated by not only practical but also emotional resistance to *kanji*, which increased in intensity as foreign relations between China and Japan (via Korea) produced great anxiety about Japan's position in East Asia.[18] Toyama Masakazu (1848–1900) wrote the most essays promoting the abolition of *kanji* in the 1880s and stated the following in his 1884 "Kanjiha" ("Destruction of *Kanji*"):

> I am in support of any group that seeks to abolish *kanji*, whatever conjugation system said group advocates in promoting *kana*. I will support any group with the most people. Actually, I will support any group—whether the *Tsuki* or the *Yuki* factions,[19] whether advocates of *kana* or the Roman alphabet—as long as they seek to abolish *kanji*. I will not hesitate to give my support. There is nothing I hate more than *kanji* these days.[20]

The rest of the speech, as well as the series of essays he wrote for *Tōyō gakkai zasshi* (*Academic Journals of Japan*) clearly indicate that anti-Chinese sentiments were behind such an emotional reaction against *kanji*. For someone like Toyama, the popularity of *kanbun kundokutai* must have been unbearable. However, interestingly, the very language in which he wrote his argument against *kanji* was *kanbun kundokutai;* this was true even when he wrote in the Roman alphabet.[21] This was a common contradiction harbored by many advocates of language reform who, perhaps ironically, contributed to the dissemination of *kanbun kundokutai*.

Taguchi Ukichi (1855–1905), a well-known historian and economist of the Meiji period, took a different approach in arguing against *kanji* in his 1884 essay "Nihon kaika no seishitsu shibaraku aratamezaru bekarazu" ("On the Path to Enlightenment in Japan"), criticizing the inevitably "aristocratic" nature of *kanji* and *kanji* compounds (*kango*). Claiming that it is a luxury to be able to immerse oneself in learning letters, he writes:

> There are many *kanji* compounds that are hard to understand through sound [alone]. If they are simply spoken as such, they will not be comprehensible to many. The language will only be comprehensible to those above middle class and hence those with luxury, necessarily becoming aristocratic in character.[22]

This is one of the first class-based criticisms of *kanji* and *kanji* compounds we see in the Meiji period. It of course presents what is by now a clichéd understanding of the length of time that is necessary to study *kanji*, but it further caters to the discourse of the Freedom and People's Rights Movement prevalent at the time, forces of which were quite strong in mid-1880s Japan.[23] The elitist nature of the ruling class was equated with the language they employed, and such an argument had a significant impact upon the promotion of the vernacular language to raise the overall literacy rate in Japan.

As we saw last chapter, the status of *kanji* and *kanbun* was further threatened by Western linguistics. Theories of Western linguistics found their way to Japan in the early years of the Meiji period as comparative linguistics entered the realm of the natural sciences, empowered by Social Darwinism. This development of Western linguistics owes much to Friedrich von Schlegel, said to be the first to coin the term "comparative linguistics," who employed methods of anatomy in the study of language in order to take it closer to the natural sciences. To remind ourselves of the highly ideological view of languages that Schlegel promoted, here are his categorizations: "Inflectional languages," as many Indo-European languages were categorized, "are eminently capable of expressing complex ideas through a single word: the root contains the main idea, the syllables that serve to form derived words express accessory modifications, and the inflections express variable relations. . . . Only these languages bear in themselves a principle of fecundity, of progressive development, and can guide the way in any improvement of the human spirit."[24] As such, Schlegel argued, inflectional languages present themselves as the most advanced form of languages. In contrast, he likened "isolating languages" like Chinese, which do not show any inflection and are "made up of monosyllables that we cannot even call roots," to a lifeless organism and hence a reflection of barbarity.[25] Strictly speaking, it was the Chinese language and its grammar that was object of attack, but the attack further provoked the anti-Chinese sentiments that *kanji* themselves invoked. Many factors thus contributed to the rejection of *kanji* and *kanbun* in 1880s Japan: practicality, anti-Chinese sentiments, the anti-elitist trend of People's Rights Movement, and Western linguistic theories.

The renunciation of Chinese as a "lifeless" language was certainly not the only way that Western linguistics affected the language reform movements in Japan. One crucial element was the focus of linguistics on phonetics, as we saw in Mori's proposal in the last chapter. As the study of Western linguistics tried to establish itself as a part of the growing body of natural sciences in the nineteenth century, scholars sought to focus on "living," as opposed to "dead," languages, presumably the object of study of classical philologists from which linguistics sought to differentiate itself. The "living" language referred to the language "currently in use," and precisely because of this, it privileged sound and the pronunciation of words and phrases. It was, in a post-Saussurean manner of speaking, the production of *langue* via sound. "Living" language did not necessarily refer to spoken language; rather, it featured a way of defining language through sound—how it *would* be pronounced—and not necessarily how it was actually spoken by the people.[26]

How did such a privileging of sound become translated in the many language reforms in 1880s Japan, and what effect did it have on the status of *kanji* and *kanbun*? Let us look at some arguments for the use of Roman alphabets. In "Rōmaji o mote Nihongo o tsuzuru no setsu" ("On Writing Japanese Language in the Roman Alphabet," 1882) and *Rōmaji hayamanabi* (*The Learning of the Roman Alphabet*, 1885), Yatabe Ryōkichi (1851–99) argued that sound should be the main criterion by which to define a language.[27] His argument for the Roman alphabet was based on its ability to transcribe as accurately as possible the many sounds in the Japanese language that *kana* apparently could not account for. In his paradigm, therefore, the sound of a given word becomes privileged over script, which, as a means to transcribe that sound, is thereby secondary. He posits the following rules: "1) In writing in the Roman alphabet, the words should be transcribed not based on *kana* but based on pronunciation; 2) We must do our best to use the Tokyoite's pronunciation as the standard."[28] Critics have been quick to note the centrality of the Tokyo dialect and its importance in the standardization of the spoken language in a statement like this, but we should not immediately assume that Yatabe is promoting the transcription of "the spoken." The example he gives in *The Learning of the Roman Alphabet* is quite revealing: in transcribing "Ari to kirigirisu no hanashi" ("The Ant and the Grasshopper"), the opening passage reads:

> Natsu mo sugi aki mo take, yaya fuyugare no koro ni narite, aru atataka naru hi, ari domo ōku uchiatsumari, natsu no hi ni toriosametaru e wo hi ni hosu tote, ana yori hikiidashi itari.[29]

Despite the fact that it is rendered in the Roman alphabet, this passage, with its 5–7 rhythm and grammatical structure, features written prose reminiscent of classical tales (*monogatari*). His text therefore may transcribe the pronounced "sound" (and that may very well be the Tokyo sound) of the chain of words that constitute his prose, but it does not necessarily transcribe the "spoken." Such a view was quite faithful to the manner in which Western linguistics defined "living" language via sound.

There were, however, many arguments that conflated the "living" language with the spoken. Many Meiji intellectuals thought that the advantages of the Western languages lay in their alleged unification of the spoken and written languages, which was inevitably traced to the phonetic nature of the Roman alphabet. As such, many argued that Japan ought to adopt the Roman alphabet or *kana* in order to move their written language closer to the spoken. Taguchi Ukichi's "Nihon kaika no seishitsu shibaraku aratamezaru bekarazu" is one such example. Rejecting *kanji* and *kanji* compounds as aristocratic, he claims, "I am a supporter of the use of the Roman alphabet. I believe that adopting the Roman alphabet to write our own language will allow the spoken and the written to unify completely."[30] As flawed as this logic is—because phoneticizing the written language does not automatically produce the spoken language—he argues that *kanji* and *kanji* compounds interfere with the unification of spoken and written languages. This notion was quite prevalent among the advocates of language reform. Many anti-*kanji* arguments held that *kanji*, given its "hieroglyphic" nature, was entirely divorced from the spoken, an idea further supported by the view that *kanbun*-style composition was the medium furthest from the spoken language.[31] Those who advocated such a stance often lost sight of the fact that there is also a phonetic element to *kanji*. In effect, we can identify in this period two binary oppositions that align with each other, namely "spoken/written" and "phonetic scripts/'hieroglyphie.'" The privileging of sound, inextricably linked to the Roman alphabet and Western linguistic theories, reinforced the idea that *kanji* and *kanbun* constituted "dead" languages.

Yet this privileging of sound was not limited to those advocating the Roman alphabet. In fact, one group of *kana* advocates promoted the phonographic *kana* system (*hyōonshiki kanazukai*), which attempted to transcribe and hence reproduce the pronunciation of a given word in *kana* spelling. Arguing against the other dominant group of *kana* advocates, who promoted the historical *kana* system (*rekishiteki kanazukai*)—which refers to an older system of spelling that presumably reflected how the words were pronounced in the Heian period and was thus already in discord with the Meiji pronunciation—*hyōonshiki* supporters sought to transcribe the sounds and to relegate writing secondary to sound.[32] Just like the supporters of the Roman alphabet, they too had many debates on whether to use the Tokyo or Kyoto dialect as the basis for standardizing spelling.[33] The privileging of sound was thus everywhere apparent, governing the many arguments for reform.

In 1880s Japan, therefore, we had, on the one hand, the popularity of *kanbun kundokutai* in newspapers, textbooks, fictional works, and compositions. Yet, on the other hand, the arguments for language reforms—be they for the Roman alphabet, *kana* scripts, or *genbun'itchi*—almost always targeted *kanji, kanji* compounds, and *kanbun* for criticism. As a result, it appears that the forces supporting *kanbun kundokutai* and language reforms were not only separate, but worked against each other. The privileging of sound in Western linguistic theories, moreover, further reinforced the binary oppositions ("spoken/written," "phonetic scripts/'hieroglyphie'") that supported such seemingly opposing forces. This is the contradictory background that nation-centered stories of *kanbun kundokutai* perhaps inadvertently reinforce. However, as I will show in the next section, they in fact worked together to create a new space for reform. This will be evident as we look at Ryūkei's *New Theory*, which bridged the two realms by mobilizing the discourse of Western linguistics and arguing for the superiority of *kanji, kanji* compounds, and ultimately *kanbun kundokutai*. By seeing how he responded to the many criticisms against *kanji* and *kanbun*, we can gauge the commonality that these two apparently opposing forces actually shared.

YANO RYŪKEI'S *NEW THEORY* AND THE SHIFT IN *KANBUN KUNDOKUTAI*

Published in 1886, *New Theory* was conceptualized and written (or, more accurately, dictated to his brother Yano Takeo) during Ryūkei's trip to England between 1884 and 1886. *New Theory* is composed of six chapters, titled "Gotai gosei no koto" ("Enunciated Style and Force"), "Bungo oyobi buntai no koto" ("Written Words and Style"), "Nihon ni mochiu beki moji oyobi buntai no koto" ("On the Orthography and Style that Ought to Be Adopted in Japan"), "Kana to kanji no yūretsu" ("Advantages and Disadvantages of *Kanji* and *Kana*"), "Nihon no kana to rōmaji to no yūretsu" ("Advantages and Disadvantages of *Kana* and the Roman Alphabet in Japan"), and "Zenpen no yōryō oyobi hoi" ("Summary and Supplemental Points"), respectively. As these chapter titles show, Ryūkei's focus revolves primarily around orthography rather than grammar or style. Chapter 3 is often taken up as the most important chapter, since Ryūkei here discusses the five different styles available in Japan.[34] Among them, he chooses what he refers to as *ryōbuntai* (a twofold style)—a *kanbun kundokutai* with *kana* glosses on all *kanji*—as the most appropriate style "to promote people's learning." However, Ryūkei's engagement with contemporary reforms is more apparent in other chapters. Given the limited space available here, it is not my intention to provide a comprehensive analysis of the text, but rather to highlight the manner in which the text engaged with the contemporary reforms to show how Ryūkei evaluated *kanbun kundokutai* and argued for its superiority.

The first two chapters show Ryūkei's awareness that the spoken and written languages were fundamentally different and hence had different needs and functions. As we have seen, the unification of the spoken and written languages had been heralded as one of the key ways to bring about language reform, which constituted one of the main arguments for the Roman alphabet and *kana* scripts. Thus, Ryūkei's stance that the spoken and written languages ought to be treated differently sets him apart from his contemporaries.[35]

Chapter 1 begins with the following: "In order to identify the most beneficial orthography and style that we need to adopt in order to best develop the people's level of learning, we must look at enunciated style (*gotai*) and enunciated force (*gosei*)," referring to the forms of spoken words and their brevity.[36] In effect, he agrees with his contemporaries that speech forms are important for language reform. What is decisively different, however, is his focus on the phonetics of *kanji*. His discussion compares the number of syllables between what he refers to as *dogo* ("native" language) and *shinago* (language originally from China), which roughly align with *kun-yomi* (the "*kun*"-reading or "indigenous" pronunciation) and *on-yomi* (the "*on*"-reading or phonetic approximation of original characters) of *kanji*, respectively.[37] In discussing the advantages and disadvantages of the respective languages, Ryūkei provides several examples, including these two:

神罰思ヒ知タルカ kami no togame omoi shittaruka

(Do you now see the power of divine punishment?)

神罰思ヒ知タルカ shinbatsu omoi shittaruka

(Do you now see the power of divine punishment?)

如是我聞 wa re ka ku ki ku (Thus I have heard) 6 syllables

如是我聞 nyo ze ga mon (Thus I have heard) 4 syllables

In both cases, he claims that the latter examples are superior, because they are "convenient for the movement of the mouth" given the smaller number of syllables. To substantiate his claim, he argues: "That which relates the most meaning in the smallest amount of oral movement is considered the best language, and that which tells the least meaning with the most oral movement is considered lowly."[38] Accordingly, he argues that *shinago*, which has fewer syllables, is superior to its *dogo* counterparts.

Whether or not we agree with him is not the issue here. What he is trying to do is to argue for the superiority of *on-yomi* and ultimately *kanji* compounds based on their economy and conciseness, which clearly draws on theories of linguistics dominant in nineteenth-century Europe. Ryūkei's argument, for example, engages with the theory of natural selection applied to articulatory phonetics, which argued that change in speech sound develops based on simplicity of pronunciation relative to easy movement of the muscles.[39] August Schleicher (1821–68), who insisted on the importance of articulatory phonetics, claimed that words requiring less muscle movement survived linguistic evolution; such, he claimed, was the natural order of things. Ryūkei mobilizes Western linguistic theories that were in most cases used to promote the superiority of the Roman alphabet to argue for the superiority of *kanji* and its compounds.[40] In light of contemporaneous anti-*kanji* arguments, this is an important move on Ryūkei's part, because he is giving a *phonetic* reason for the existence and durability of *kanji* compounds. Unlike advocates of the Roman alphabet and *kana* scripts who rejected *kanji* as "written" ideographs that were furthest from the "spoken" and hence "living" languages, Ryūkei refuses to relegate *kanji* to such a status. He reminds his readers that, although *kanji* may be ideographic, it still retains its phonetic value, which is precisely where its strength lies.

Ryūkei reorients his argument as he begins to show the advantages of *kanji* and its compounds as written scripts. In chapter 4, arguing for the superiority of *kanji* over *kana*, he says the following:

> In the world of vision, the language that relates the most meaning in the smallest amount of time is considered superior, while the language that tells only little in the most amount of time is considered inferior. In other words, the language that evokes the most meaning in the quickest possible glance is the superior language.[41]

What is foregrounded here is no longer the phonetic value of *kanji*, but its ideographic nature. This logic also appropriates elements from the linguistic and rhetorical theories that I referred to earlier, clearly invoking the authority of such theories. Ryūkei's logic, however, is not necessarily correct. Once we recognize the fact that a word written in the phonetic alphabet is a unit, our vision does not necessarily read the phonetic syllables individually before recognizing it as a word. But this does not take away the advantages of ideographic scripts that embody more meaning efficiently, in fewer characters, as Ryūkei describes. As contemporary critic and literary scholar Komori Yōichi argues, the print media chose the mixture of *kanji* and *kana* as the economic winner from among the many claims for different orthography, because *kanji* compounds could more concisely and economically pass along necessary information than *kana* or the Roman alphabet.[42] In arguing for the superiority of *kanji*, Ryūkei pinpointed one of the main reasons for the popularity of *kanbun kundokutai*, the form that he was advocating: its efficacy for print media.

Seeing his logic in both phonetic and ideographic selection helps explain Ryūkei's preferred style of language in chapter 3, the most-often cited chapter of the book. Here Ryūkei sets out to describe the five styles of language that are in use in Japan. The first is *kanbun*, referring to "the pure *kanbun*" used from the time when *kanbun* first entered Japan: in other words, a form of writing in *kanji* that strictly follows the original classics. The second is *kanbun hentai* (a variation of *kanbun*), which is a "Japanized" *kanbun* that employs words and phrases that are not in the original *kanbun* texts. The third is *zatsubuntai* (an assorted style), which, according to Ryūkei, is a style of *kanbun kundokutai* that began toward the end of the Tokugawa period. Accordingly, *zatsubuntai* is based on translated word order, and hence, unlike the first two styles, avoids the inconvenience of moving back and forth to read the sentences. He valorizes this style by saying, "[T]he emergence of this style signified a great advance in the world of letters in Japan, which multiplied the convenience of spreading knowledge among the people."[43] According to Ryūkei, this style can be traced back to the thirteenth-century *Heike monogatari* (*The Tale of the Heike*) and the c. 1370 *Taiheiki* (*Chronicle of Medieval Japan*), but it was further developed by Edo literati like Arai Hakuseki and Kaibara Ekken. This, Ryūkei adds, is also the medium used for translating Western writings. The fourth style he discusses is *ryōbuntai* (the twofold style), which is a *zatsubuntai* with *kana* glosses added to the *kanji* characters.) Finally, the fifth is *kanatai* (the *kana* style), which is a style that uses only *kana;* he includes the *Genji monogatari* (*The Tale of Genji*, eleventh century) and *Ise monogatari* (*The Tales of Ise*, mid-tenth century) as prime examples. What he ultimately advocates is *ryōbuntai*, which is basically *kanbun kundokutai* with complete *kana* glosses. The rest of the chapter elaborates the superiority of *ryōbuntai* by employing the logic used in the other chapters, namely the superiority of *kanji* compounds and *kanji* as concise orthography, and ultimately proposes to reduce the number of *kanji* characters to around 3000.[44]

It is easy to question Ryūkei's categories. For example, the primary difference between *zatsubuntai* and *ryōbuntai* is whether or not there are *kana* glosses; surely, that cannot be considered a stylistic difference.[45] These categories are also far from exhaustive, since the tradition of *kanbun kundokutai* prior to the end of Tokugawa period is not accounted for. *Kanatai* is also rather vague; it appears to be a purely orthographic categorization, but the difference between the *kana* style of the *Genji monogatari* and *kanbun kundokutai* is much more than a simple matter of orthography. However, it is futile to criticize Ryūkei for being wrong or selective in his categorization. Rather, it is best to question what he gains through such categorizations.

The categorizations in *New Theory* are inextricably linked to orthographic styles. The focus on orthography is consistent throughout *New Theory*, as his discussion of any given language is quite narrowly limited to orthography—that is, *kanji*—and not that of thematics or its rhetorical effects. Perhaps a better way to say this is that Ryūkei deliberately severs the language he wants to promote from its rhetorical or content-oriented effects. Even as he discusses the styles of language in chapter 3, and mentions some classical works with them, his defining characteristics of a given style are either the order in which a given sentence is written (that is, whether it follows *kanbun* or *kundoku* grammar), or the existence of *kana* glosses. Throughout the text, he does not discuss the rhetorical effects of language, whether those effects be the number of syllables or the conciseness of *kanji* compounds for reading.

Perhaps his decision to classify the available styles in this manner is more compelling when we think about the categories he used in his earlier attempt at theorizing styles in "Buntairon" ("On Styles"), which he wrote in the second volume of his famous work of fiction, *Keikoku bidan*, serialized in the newspaper *Yūbin hōchi* between 1883 and 1884. He categorized the four available styles in Japan as the following: *kanbun* style, which is appropriate for "tragic elegance"; *wabun* (indigenous "Japanese" writing) style for "weakness and calmness"; ōbun chokuyakutai ("direct-translation style" of Western language) for "precision and accuracy"; and *zokugo rigentai* (local vulgar style) for "comic twists and turns."[46] They are, in effect, styles that define the content of narration, with clear attention paid to the rhetorical effects of a given style. Such categories, in other words, allow the writer to mobilize the prior literary tradition that is inscribed in a given style as these styles maintain a dialogic relationship with past literary discourse. With *New Theory*, Ryūkei is, in effect, making a break with his own past categories, which were primarily rhetorical. The discussion in *New Theory* thus signifies an attempt to institute a clear severance between what he calls *ryōbuntai* and its predecessors.[47]

This gives us a new perspective from which to see Ryūkei's discussion of *kanji* and *kanji* compounds. His discussion not only implicitly criticizes his contemporaries, who uncritically argued for the superiority of the Roman alphabet and *kana* scripts for their phonetic nature, but also aims to give a new life to what he refers to as *ryōbuntai*. His use of Western linguistic theories contributes to this aim in several ways, by introducing an entirely new way to theorize language and style. Furthermore, his argument to reduce *kanji* to 3000 characters ultimately shows his focus on the *current* use of *kanji*. He claims that among the 80,000 or so *kanji* characters available, many are from classical literature and had become obsolete in later periods. He therefore proposes to reduce the number of characters to those in current use.[48] We should not think of this as a reduction in mere number, as Ryūkei might like us to believe. There is another rhetorical manipulation at work, which is evident in his constant use of the word "*futsū*" (glossed with the English word "popular" in *katakana* to refer to characters currently in use). "Popular" writing—which includes official pronouncements, school textbooks, and newspapers—is differentiated from *bungakusho* (the English phrase "literary work" is provided in *katakana*), which includes fiction, specialized writings, history, and biography.[49] The division between the "popular" writings and *bungakusho* is certainly neither clear-cut nor even valid; for example, newspapers featured many fictional works, as well as other "specialized writings." Hence, this is better situated as a prescriptive division. Popular writings, in other words, are genre-specific; they are anti-literary and anti-rhetorical. The characters that ought to be used in those popular writings, therefore, should be limited to those that do not invoke literary or rhetorical effects.

This brings us to another commonality between *New Theory* and the orthographic reforms. What is particularly noteworthy in the desire for new orthography is not only the anti-Chinese sentiments and pro-Western perceptions of language—which are, of course, very obviously there—but the strong desire to sever the present from its past. There were many "practical" arguments for the use of the Roman alphabet and *kana*, but they cannot entirely account for the strong desire to completely alter the linguistic landscape. While some sought to bracket the issue of orthography and first reform the style of languages (which seems much more prudent and "practical"),[50] the arguments to adopt new orthography remained firmly present, integrated into varying attempts at language reform. Even the arguments for *kana*, the foundational ideology of which is often traced to the Edo nativist movement, included calls for an entirely different transcription of words, one that was based on pronunciation (*hyōonshiki kanazukai*) rather than the more conventional historical *kana* system (*rekishiteki kanazukai*) that followed classical orthography, which would have significantly altered the visual representation of language. The urge to erase the linguistic traditions of the past existed in almost all of the language reform movements, and the adoption of a new orthography simply offered the most dramatic break with the past. Ultimately, what better way to erase the linguistic traditions of the past and start anew than to adopt a new orthography, which brings change not only in content or in style, but in the very representation of its own language?

Just like the other arguments for new orthography, then, *New Theory* embodies the urge to sever itself from the past. The question we must address is: What "past" did Ryūkei want to sever *ryōbuntai* from? Since *ryōbuntai* is *kanbun kundokutai*, its natural ancestor was *kanbun*.[51] In effect, not only was Ryūkei seeking a new way to promote *kanbun kundokutai*, but a way to sever the connection between *kanbun* and *kanbun kundokutai* and to take *kanbun kundokutai* out of the genre of *kanbun*. Let us explore this severance a little further, especially in the context of *kanbun kundokutai* and its development. In so doing, we will see that Ryūkei's advocacy of *ryōbuntai*, and ultimately the severance of *kanbun* and *kanbun kundokutai*, was not unique to him or unbefitting of the discursive conditions of the time. In fact, it was on a par with a movement in *kanbun kundokutai* that was occurring in the general media.

Given that *kanbun kundokutai* grew out of a method of reading that was initially devised to interpret *kanbun, kanbun kundokutai* was secondary to the original *kanbun*. However, when it was appropriated to meet the needs of the new world, *kanbun kundokutai* began to take on a life of its own.[52] There were, of course, many reasons for this. As I discussed above, one was *kanbun kundokutai*'s ability to accommodate many new *kanji* compounds; there were also the many changes made to *kanbun kundokutai* as it accommodated new grammar in translating Western languages, such as the introduction of relative clauses and other formulaic expressions. There were also various efforts on the part of individuals to depart from the rules and literary conventions of *kanbun*. One well-known example is Fukuzawa Yukichi; when he first wrote a draft of *Seiyō jijō* (*Conditions of the West*, 1866), he was told that he ought to have it checked by a Confucian scholar because it lacked "authentic elegance" (*seiga*). Responding that his main aim was "communication" (*tatsui*), he left his prose as it was.[53] To "communicate" his ideas, he felt it necessary to break the mold of "authentic elegance," which was undoubtedly based on the literary conventions of *kanbun*.

In addition, in the realm of *sakubun*, or composition, a parallel discursive movement in the 1880s further facilitated *kanbun kundokutai*'s shift away from *kanbun*. This shift in composition is perhaps most telling, because most intellectuals equated composition with *kanbun* writing, and hence it constituted a domain often considered to be the most conservative. As such, a dichotomy is repeatedly posited between the realms of composition and linguistic reforms in recent scholarship: while "old-fashioned" composition continued to teach *kanbun*, linguistic reforms sought to jettison *kanbun*. Despite such characterizations, the realm of composition too, however indirectly, contributed to the shift in *kanbun kundokutai* and hence in the relationship between *kanbun* and *kanbun kundokutai*.

The complexity and the sheer variety of composition textbooks that were available in the early Meiji period is certainly not a topic to which I could do justice in this chapter. Yet a quick review of publishing changes supports the argument that the relationship between *kanbun* and *kanbun kundokutai* changed in this period. Consider, for example, the form of model sentences (*bunpan*) composed by distinguished or well-versed men, many of which were published by scholars presumably upset by the increase in students who lacked the knowledge of *kangaku* classics. Such model sentences were pure *kanbun* and hence not rearranged according to familiar syntax, and these textbooks included a list of model phrases, grammar (sentence structures), vocabulary, rhetorical devices such as *shōō* or *fukusen* (both denoting different forms of foreshadowing), and so on. Many had the original *kanbun* in big letters, followed by the *kundoku* reading in small letters. On the surface, therefore, such *bunpan* replicated the hierarchy between an original *kanbun* and a derivative *kanbun kundokutai*. However, in the 1880s, we see such composition textbooks being published without the original *kanbun*. *Kiji ronsetsu: shūbun kihan* (*Practice Book of Model Sentences*, 1884) is one such example. This textbook was published not only in fully conjugated form with the word order following the *kundoku* reading, but with glosses on how to read the characters, as well as the clear placement of *te ni o ha* particles. (Predictably, Confucian scholars were extremely critical of such a style and rejected the textbooks as vulgar renderings of *kanbun*).[54]

Such a practice was further supported by the publication of *kanji* compound dictionaries in the Meiji period. Saitō Mareshi notes that dictionaries of *kanji* compounds began to be published in great number in the Meiji period, while the dictionaries of the previous era catered more to the writing of *kanshi* or Sinified verse. In effect, Saitō concludes, these dictionaries were specifically composed to read *kanbun kundokutai* and not *kanbun*.[55] The dissemination of such textbooks and dictionaries clearly reinforced the "original" status of *kanbun kundokutai*, thereby robbing *kanbun* of its primary status.[56]

The effect of such a shift can easily be imagined. *Kanbun kundokutai* divested itself of the *kanbun* rhythm, a decisive element of the "authentic elegance" associated with *kanbun*. The rhetorical effects associated with such rhythm also disappeared. Ryūkei's *New Theory*, with its focus on orthographic efficacy rather than rhetoric, is thus very much a product of its time, as it clearly engaged with the shift in *kanbun kundokutai* by focusing on the current use of *kanji* and their compounds. His arguments for the superiority of *kanji* and *kanji* compounds, just like in the realm of composition, also severed their positions from the literary conventions, rules, and "authentic elegance" to which *kanbun* was subject. *New Theory* therefore not only constitutes a criticism of the contemporary arguments for orthographic reform, but also embodies the many discursive movements that shaped the very reforms Ryūkei criticized.

THE DEVELOPMENT OF *KOKUBUN*

As *kanbun kundokutai* became "liberated" from its secondary status, a space opened up for another system of language to claim authority and "primary" status. This was "national letters" (*kokubun*). It is not a coincidence that criticisms of *kanbun kundokutai* as a style that "destroy[ed] the Japanese grammar" emerged in great number around this time. As long as *kanbun kundokutai* was relegated secondary to *kanbun*, whether or not it adhered to "Japanese" grammar was not an issue. But toward the end of the 1880s, as scholars of "national literature" began to take center stage, such criticism emerged, suggesting that *kanbun kundokutai* had begun to achieve primary status by that time.

In characterizing the *kokubun* movement that emerged in the late 1880, typically scholars trace it to the Edo nativist movement; its attempt to produce *wabun*-oriented "common language" (*futsūbun*) by incorporating *kanji* compounds in *wabun* is characterized as an effort to counter the popularity of *kanbun kundokutai* (and ultimately to supplant its status as "common language"), which is likened to the efforts of the Edo nativists.[57] It may thus be easy to say that *kokubun* scholars took after Edo nativists as they criticized *kanbun kundokutai* for destroying Japanese grammar. But it is also easy to imagine how the significance of such criticism changed when *kanbun kundokutai* was no longer treated as secondary to *kanbun*.

Let us examine how the *kokubungaku* scholars of the late 1880s and early 1890s position *kokubun*. See, for example, the following passage from Ochiai Naobumi's "Shōrai no kokubun" ("The Future of National Letters," 1890), which criticizes the grammar of the "current language" as "unsystematic" and "unruly":

> As long as we call a given style *kokubun*, there must be a standard system of grammar and usage. Looking at today's letters, many err in the conjugation of verbs and use of particles, and violate the relationship between verbs and particles, as well as the relationship between particles. There are too many careless usages of *kana* suffixes, confusion between transitive and intransitive forms, and mistakes in tenses.[58]

Notice what Ochiai focuses on in this passage: particles, conjugation, tense, and suffixes. These are the grammatical elements that are needed to convert *kanbun* to *kanbun kundokutai*.[59] Ultimately, he seeks to systematize the very rules used to adopt *kanji* compounds in the *kundoku* form and situate them as the defining characteristics of *kokubun*. Rather than a critique that follows in the footsteps of Edo nativists, this effort is better situated as an attempt to redefine and reorient the "current language" as *kokubun* by focalizing these structures of "Japanese" language as defining characteristics of *kokubun*. Simply put, Ochiai used *kanbun kundokutai*'s status as the "current language" and designated it as the imperfect *kokubun*. I do not mean to imply that these scholars did not incorporate any *wabun*—they clearly did, especially in the early 1890s as the *kokubun* movement ripened. The point is that their definition of *kokubun* relied heavily on *kanbun kundokutai*, the form by which *kanji* compounds were processed in the *kanbun kundokutai* tradition. In defining *kokubun*, they thus appropriated the fertile space opened up by the shift in *kanbun kundokutai* in the early Meiji period. That is, such a definition of *kokubun* became *possible* as "current language" claimed autonomy from its ancestor.

The focus on "current language" as an object of critique does not stop here. Here is a passage from Sekine Masanao's "Kokugo no hontai narabi ni sono kachi" ("The Basis of *Kokugo* and Its Value," 1888). After he focuses on *te ni o ha* particles and verb conjugation to define the "Japanese-ness" of *kokugo* (national language) and criticizes the current style of language as "unsystematic" just as Ochiai did, he continues:

> An erudite man has sought to adopt *wabun*—the old language used about a thousand years ago—as the language of the present. Accordingly, he designated the study of classical writings (*kobun*) and vocabulary (*kogo*) as the main aim of our "national language" study (*kokugogaku*). . . . In my humble opinion, I believe that the basis of *kokugo* lies in the language that is in use today. And the main goal of *kokugo*

> scholarship is the study of the structure and rules of today's language based on rules specific to our country, so as to correct the unruliness of the spoken and written languages, and write a systematic language so that it can be easily understood without confusion.[60]

Sekine, too, redefines the "language of the present" as *kokugo* by promoting "rules specific to our country." His argument, however, goes a step further than Ochiai's by implicitly associating the *kokugo* lineage with *wabun*, citing works like *Ise monogatari* and *Genji monogatari* later in his essay. This has two important effects. First, it legitimates *kokugo*'s "*current* practicality," because it is posited in opposition to impractical "old words that are unfamiliar to our ears" (*kikinarenu kogen*).[61] Second, the dichotomy of *kokugo* versus *kobun/kogen* (as *wabun*) replaces the most obvious dichotomy—*kanbun kundokutai* versus *kanbun*—which is deliberately effaced in this discussion. In effect, Sekine effaces *kanbun*'s original status and situates *wabun* as the rightful ancestor to the "current language" (which is renamed as *kokugo*).[62] Such a rhetorical operation is not unique to Sekine. We see similar arguments by other national literature scholars of the late 1880s, such as in Hagino Yoshiyuki's "Wabun o ronzu" ("On *Wabun*," 1887).

This erasure of *kanbun* as origin extends to other national literature scholars, who compiled many textbooks of model compositions to disseminate their *kokugo*. As the models for *kokugo*, these textbooks selected not only works considered *wabun* or even those written by the Edo nativists like Motoori Norinaga, but also pieces by Edo writers such as Arai Hakuseki and Kaibara Ekken, men that Ryūkei chose as the models for his *zatsubuntai*. Haga Yaichi, in his 1890 *Kokubungaku tokuhon* (*Anthology of Japanese Letters*), praises Arai's narrative and says he prefers this mixed *wa-kan* style (*wakan konkōbun*) to the neoclassical prose (*gikobun*) developed by the Edo nativists.[63] In other words, *kokugo* clearly absorbed texts that had *kanbun* ancestry, while erasing *kanbun*'s originary status. This further reinforces the severance of "current language" from its *kanbun* "ancestor." Or rather, such a rewriting of the "origin" was made possible by the shift in *kanbun kundokutai* and its severance from *kanbun*.

Though *kokubun* advocates were effacing the primacy of *kanbun*, they, like Ryūkei, embraced the efficacy of *kanji* and sought to incorporate them as "Japanese." Since *kokubun* advocates did not inherit the anti-*kanji* sentiments of the second decade of the Meiji period, they did not promote orthographic changes.[64] Here is another section of Sekine's "Kokugo no hontai narabi ni sono kachi," wherein he discusses *kungo* (indigenous words) and *ongo* (referring to *kanji* compounds, "Chinese" in origin):

> *Kungo* and *ongo* were initially different in character, but [*ongo*] have since changed and adopted our sound and speech forms (*onchō gosei*) over several hundred years. *Ongo* have thus been assimilated naturally by *kungo* and have since become one with them. As such, it is not easy to rid ourselves of *kanji* compounds. If we forcefully

resist the use of these compounds, *kungo* will become deficient and inadequate not only in writing but also in speech.[65]

This is a logic on a par with Ryūkei's argument in *New Theory*. It evaluates *kanji* compounds in terms of their phonetic value instead of their ideographic character. It further assimilates the *kanji* compounds as "Japanese" based on their very phonetic value. In fact, this is a departure from the Edo nativists' view that constantly designated *kanji* as a "foreign" medium that interfered with the "Japanese-ness" of language. Instead, in Sekine's paradigm, it is assumed that *kanji* is pronounced, and the sound—the manner in which it is read—is privileged over the written script. It is, in other words, a logic that ties in with Western linguistics; it is not a coincidence that *onchō gosei*, a phrase used in Sekine's passage, is also used to translate the term "phonetics" in linguistics. Sekine's view seems to endorse the idea that it is the pronunciation of a word that makes it a word, and this is precisely what the discourse of linguistics promotes.

CONCLUSION

On the surface, the many arguments for reform that proliferated in 1880s Japan and rejected *kanji, kanji* compounds, and *kanbun* appear incongruous with the increasing popularity of *kanbun kundokutai*. As we have seen, however, the orthographic reforms of the second decade constituted a parallel discursive movement to the shift in *kanbun kundokutai*, as both sought to sever the past from the present. Their relationship may not be causal, but the focus on the "current" linguistic terrain is predicated on the proliferation of the "current language," a space opened up through a multitude of forces that shaped the discursive site in question: the many translingual practices that shaped the early Meiji period, the development of print media, anti-Chinese sentiments that resulted from growing anxiety vis-à-vis Japan's status in East Asia, the People's Rights Movement and the proliferation of "democratic" discourse, the prevalence of Western linguistic theories, and so forth. Although in appearance they differ in their goals, it is not a coincidence that both *New Theory*, which promoted *kanbun kundokutai*, and national literature scholars, who promoted *kokubun*, sought out this discursive space in which to posit their own means toward standardization. Without seeing the development of *kanbun kundokutai* as an integral part of *kokugo* reform, we lose sight of the fact that it was developments in *kanbun kundokutai* that made such reform possible.

The *kokubungaku* scholars' emphasis on the "current language" is too often attributed to their sense of nation, and hence the idea that a national community ought to have one common language.[66] However, we must not forget that such an idea needs a linguistic terrain that can accommodate and hence make possible such views. It is much more convincing to say that such a positing of *kokugo* became possible through the space opened up by *kanbun kundokutai*, which allowed *wabun* to supplant *kanbun* in its "ancestral" status and hence the retrospective gaze that discovered *wabun* as the rightful lineage of (*kanbun*) *kundokutai*. The scholarly focus on the production of the nation has undoubtedly brought much needed perspective on language reforms by highlighting their political nature. However, there is a kind of inversion at work in how this scholarly work posits the nation, unnecessarily empowering the nation as an entity that motivates the movements that created it. It features, in many ways, an anachronistic projection of a Japanese national identity that necessarily excluded *kanbun*—whether it be *kanbun* or *kanbun kundokutai*—as a means of achieving language reform. This scholarship also obscures the fact that the conception of national language that ultimately prevailed after the Sino-Japanese war should actually be traced back to the reform of *kan*. More attention to the pre-Ueda Kazutoshi era, not simply as an "imperfect" preparatory phase for *kokugo* reform, but as a space in which the varying forces of linguistic encounters struggled with one another, can help expose what recent focus on the nation and nationalism conceals.

APPENDIX

Kanbun: 当是時臣唯独知有韓信不知有陛下也

Two types of *kanbun kundokutai* derivative of the above *kanbun:*
bōdokutai: 是時ニ当リ臣唯独韓信アルヲ知ル陛下アルヲ知ラザル也
yakudokutai: 是時に当りて臣は唯独り韓信あるを知りて陛下の<u>ましますを知り奉らざるなり</u>(underlined portion showing the honorific language absent from *kanbun*). [These examples were taken from Kamei Hideo, *Kansei no henkaku* (Tokyo: Kōdansha, 1983), 32–34.]

The following are examples Ryūkei raises for *kanbun hentai, zatsubuntai*, and *ryōbuntai* in *New Theory:*

Kanbun hentai:
恒例之祭祀不陵夷如在之礼奠令怠慢因茲於関東御分国々並荘園者地頭神主等各各存其趣可致精誠也(437). From *Goseibai shikimoku* (*The Formulary of Adjudications*, 1232).

Zatsubuntai:
宇都宮公綱千余人ヲ以テ来リ援ヒ急ニ攻テ柵ヲ抜キ城趾ヲ鑿ル正成、機ニ応ジテ之ヲ拒グ敵竟ニ抜クコト能ハザリキ (439). From Rai Sanyō, *Nihon gaishi* (*An Unofficial History of Japan*, 1827).

Ryōbuntai:
キセイリョウトウ　ヨキ　ヨセテ　クワワリ　イマ　キ　クツ　アラテ
紀清両党千余騎寄手ニ加テ未ダ気ヲ屈セザル荒手ナレバ（云々）(440).
From *Taiheiki* (*A Chronicle of Medieval Japan*, late fourteenth century).

Kanatai:
ミダノ、ツルギノ、トナミヤマ、クモヂハナカス、ミコシヂノ、クニノユクスエ、サトトヘバ、イトド、ミヤコハ、トウザカル、サカイガハニモ、ツキニケリ (440). From *Yōkyoku: Yamanba* (*Noh lyrics: Mountain Hag*, 1840).

3

Zoku as Aesthetic Criterion

Reforms for Poetry and Prose

The rise of the *kokubun* movement coincided historically with the efforts by fiction writers Tsubouchi Shōyō (1859–1935) and Yamada Bimyō (1868–1910) to produce a new language. Critics often seamlessly link these two movements, suggesting that their emphasis on *zoku*[1] reflects a common goal to produce a "shared language" through a medium most familiar to and easiest to understand for the widest readership.[2] This is not entirely unwarranted, as *kokubungaku* scholars sought to adopt what they referred to as "common conversation" (*tsūjō no danwa*) and "everyday language" (*nichiyō no bun*), while Shōyō sought to embrace "the spirit of *zokugo*" (*zokugo no seishin*), and Bimyō argued strongly for *zokubun* in his fiction. In fact, Bimyō himself supported such a view; he recalled in his 1910 memoir that he had been inspired by, for example, the *kokubungaku* scholar Mozume Takami's famous call for *genbun'itchi* (typically translated as the "unification of spoken and written languages") and the advocacy of the spoken language.

However, Kamei Hideo, in his *Meiji bungakushi* (*History of Meiji Literature*) provocatively claims that the efforts at *kokugo* and the *genbun'itchi* movement (in a discussion of which he included works of Shōyō) had nothing to do with each other.[3] I am not entirely convinced that they are unrelated, but I agree they did not share the same agenda, clearly differing from one another in their views of what constituted an ideal language. An uncritical equation of the *kokubun* scholars' call for "common conversation" with Shōyō and Bimyō's advocacy of *zoku* ignores too many differences. While *kokubun* scholars sought what they called authentic or "correct" elegance (*gasei*) in the current language, a language that would constitute a manifestation of a "pure original voice" of the past, fiction writers embraced *zoku* as a means to inject the vigor of *zoku* into the current language in order to break with the past. In this sense, Ueda Kazutoshi's *kokugo* (national language) reform interestingly resonates with the fiction writers rather than the *kokubun* scholars with which he is associated. In this chapter, I will thus bracket the notion that these writers were searching for a "shared" or "popular language" and examine the specific goals and agendas inscribed in their efforts at reform. I will identify areas in which they in fact converged, as well as those in which they differed, and further reveal areas in which they inadvertently replicated each other, hence supporting each other even when they did not have a shared objective.

With such an aim in mind, I wish to engage with reforms that addressed the intersection between prose and poetry. These shed important light on the ways in which the terms *ga* and *zoku* were mobilized in the evaluation of prose and poetry, and we shall see that *ga* and *zoku* were first and foremost aesthetic criteria for these writers. This is often forgotten in the study of language reforms, because there is an assumption that the realm of aesthetics is reserved for "literature" and does not apply to "language." However, we must remind ourselves that we are dealing with a time when such a division had yet to exist. *Bungaku* constituted language: the understanding of *bungaku* as one artistic manifestation of "language" as *langue* had yet to emerge.

In what follows, I will offer a brief prelude to *kokubungaku* scholars' references to *tsūjō no danwa*. I will then look at the prevalent *waka* poetic reform movement of the late 1880s and early 1890s, which was led by many of the same *kokubungaku* scholars who were involved in the *kokubun* movement, such as Hagino Yoshiyuki, Takatsu Kuwasaburō, Ochiai Naobumi, and Mikami Sanji. I examine the calls for *waka* reform by focusing on the manner in which they sought to appropriate the space of new-style poetry (*shintaishi*) and how that affected the definition of *zoku*. I then turn to works of Tsubouchi Shōyō and Yamada Bimyō, the leading advocates of *zokugo*/*zokubun* in their search for fictional prose, such as "Bunshō shinron" ("New Theory of Writing," 1886) and *Nihon inbunron* (*Theories of Japanese Poetry*, 1891).

A PRELUDE: THE *KOKUBUN* MOVEMENT AND "*TSŪJŌ NO DANWA*"

In the previous chapter, we saw that the *kokubun* movement designated *kanbun kundokutai* as "imperfect" *kokubun* and sought to take over the linguistic terrain opened up by the popularity of *kanbun kundokutai*. That was, however, but a part of the story. *Kokubungaku* scholars further sought to rename this "imperfect" *kokubun* the "commonly spoken language." Here is an example from the "Gengo torishirabejo hōhōsho" ("Guidelines of the Office of Language Inspection," 1888). After repeating a by-then clichéd narrative of *kanji* and *kanbun* as the origin for the disparity between the written and spoken languages, it claims that it must identify "the most commonly used linguistic style of our country": "What we refer to as the commonly used linguistic style is what the Japanese people now in the Meiji period use in common conversation; we will use that as the base and correct any deviations and supplement any shortcomings to standardize it."[4] We must not essentialize the use of "common conversation" and assume that *kokubungaku* scholars are referring here to actual spoken language. It is much more likely that it is on a par with Mozume Takami's famous call for *genbun'itchi*. Mozume has been considered one of the most radical of the *kokubungaku* scholars in terms of the advocacy of "writing as we speak" (*kuchi de iu tōri o kaku*). He claims, "It would be best to write the lively spoken language that naturally and purely spills out of one's mouth."[5] What lies at the core of his argument is the dichotomy between the "spoken" ("Japanese") and the "written" (the foreign, that is to say, *kanbun*). He consistently defines the spoken language, which "*naturally* and purely spills out of one's mouth" (emphasis added), in opposition to what he calls "borrowed language." The "spoken language" to which he refers is not the actual spoken language, but one that is specifically defined in opposition to the invariably *foreign* written language. In the 1890s, however, *kanji* and *kanji* compounds were no longer considered "foreign" for *kokubungaku* scholars. "Foreign written language," therefore, refers to *kanbun* syntax, while "spoken language" refers to *kundoku* syntax, which had been deemed more "natural" and hence closer to "our own."

If these *kokubungaku* scholars did not advocate the transcription of the spoken or a use of the current language "as is" in spite of their arguments for the "spoken" language and "common conversation," what, then, did they advocate? Take, for instance, the following from a bulletin published by Nihon bunshōkai (the Society of Japanese Letters), a group made up of prominent *kokubungaku* scholars such as Hagino, Ochiai, Sekine, Mozume, Ōki Fumihiko, as well as Nishimura Shigeki and Nishi Amane, the original Meirokusha members.[6]

> It goes without saying that the spoken and written languages of a nation represent its independence and hence they must be standardized. The language must be based on the natural language of the nation's people that is easiest to understand for all. . . . This does not mean that we ought to employ classical or elegant language (*kogen, gagen*). But neither should we limit ourselves to current language (*kingen*) or *zokugen*. We ought to strike a balance and avoid excessively vulgar current language, as well as remote classical language. . . .[7]

Reiterating the need to develop a new language based on "natural" wording and grammatical structure (that is, *kundoku*), they sought to "strike a balance" between *ga* and *zoku*.[8] This statement is typical of *kokubungaku* scholars. See, for example, Sekine Masanao's "Kokugo no hontai narabi ni sono kachi" ("The Basis of *Kokugo* and its Value," 1888). Despite his insistence that the "basis of *kokugo*" is in "language currently in use today," he advocates a standardization of the language based on what he calls "authentic or 'correct' elegance" (*gasei*).[9] Yet "striking a balance" between *ga* and *zoku* certainly did not mean balancing numerically; it signified a process of identifying so-called *gasei* in the "current language" and using that as the standard by which to "correct" the "imperfect *kokubun*." The "Gengo torishirabejo hōhōsho" that I quoted earlier will help us understand this further. It claims that its goal is to produce two types of language, one "common language" and one "lofty style":

> The lofty style is the language of our imperial country, used by all the people of this land before foreign language entered. It has changed over the years, but it is still correct (*tadashii*). . . . The common language of the present is fundamentally derivative of this lofty language).[10]

What *kokubungaku* scholars called "lofty" was an ideal form of language retrospectively posited as that which existed prior to the intervention of the "foreign."[11] Given that the common language—or what would be *kokugo* once reform was complete—was posited as derivative of the lofty language, such language in effect signified the "standard" (the authentic elegance) as a manifestation of the "pure" voice of the past.[12]

The seeming contradiction between advocating "common conversation" and "writing as we speak" on the one hand, and arguing to "strike a balance" between *gagen* and *zokugen*, on the other, can now be put to rest. Such a contradiction is but the result of an essentialized understanding of "common conversation."[13] Yet such a narrative of contradiction, inevitably resulting in an overemphasis on the *zoku*, helped to conceal the fact that the "standard" (authentic elegance) was in itself in the making. They had to invent this "standard" underlying the "current language": a supposed manifestation of a pure voice that existed prior to the introduction of the "foreign" (*kanbun*). Thus, the main aim of *kokubungaku* scholars was not to reform *zoku* (the "imperfect" common conversation), but to establish the standard language, which could only putatively be constructed by designating the realm of *zoku* as that which needed reform.

WAKA POETIC REFORM: APPROPRIATING *SHINTAISHI*

Kokubungaku scholars did not limit their discussions of *ga* and *zoku* to prose, but also applied them to *waka* reform, which began in the late 1880s. There had been, of course, earlier attempts at poetic reform, most notably that of new-style poetry (*shintaishi*), which is considered to be the origin of modern Japanese poetry. The *shintaishi* reform played a large role in the *kokubungaku*-led *waka* reform, as *kokubungaku* scholars inherited the reforms started by *shintaishi* poets and made them their own to institute reform in *waka*.[14]

Debates on *waka* reform began with Hagino Yoshiyuki's "Kogoto" ("Trivial Renderings," 1887), which appeared in *Tōyō gakkai zasshi* (*Academic Journal of Japan*), the main outlet for the publication of many *kokubungaku* scholars' works. In it, Hagino called for poetic reform in the following manner:

> The language for the portrayal of the many things in the world that arouse emotions differs with any given historical time. The *Kojiki* was written in the language of its

> time, as was the *Man'yōshū*. This is so not only for works of our country, but also with regard to the old poetic forms of China and the West. . . . Our emotions ought to be portrayed in the current language. With this in mind, we ought to break the mold of our old practices and embark on a new path.[15]

In addition to this call for a new poetic language, Hagino sought to push poetic boundaries by exploring new topics for *waka*, stating that love and ephemerality ought not be the central themes; he further advocated the structural reform of *waka*, claiming that thirty-one syllables only limited the poetic form.[16] Perhaps predictably, these ideas for reform provoked much criticism in *kokubungaku* circles. Hattori Motohiko, for example, specifically targeted Hagino's call to incorporate the "current language," claiming that *waka*, which ought to be "composed with elegant language," would not be *waka* anymore if composed in the current language; it would only be "local folk songs" (*zokuyō*) or "wild poetry" (*kyōka*).[17] A series of essays on the topic followed. Emphasizing the limited scope of *waka* diction, theme, and form, Mikami Sanji, another *kokubungaku* scholar, stated that *waka* ought to use the "elegant language" of the day (as opposed to the "elegant language" of the past) and agreed with Hagino that it was crucial to "pay attention to poetic diction and theme, not to mention the length of poetry" so that Japan could produce works like "Dante's *Divine Comedy* and Milton's *Paradise Lost*."[18] The central issues of the debate, therefore, revolved around the use of "current language," the length of verse (beyond thirty-one syllables), and poetic themes.

Very similar calls for reform had begun five years before, when *Shintaishishō* (*An Anthology of New-Style Poetry*, 1883) was compiled by Toyama Masakazu, Inoue Tetsujirō, and Yatabe Ryōkichi, all of whom were scholars of "Western learning."[19] Take for example, Yatabe's following passage in his preface: "There were several of us who lamented that our countrymen rarely used commonly used language to compose poetry; we thus decided to produce new-style poetry (*shintaishi*) by imitating our Western counterparts."[20] Inoue argued the same in his call for a poetic form that used "current language."[21] Toyama, in his preface, criticized existing poetic forms, be they *tanka* (short verse, typically composed of 5–7–5–7–7 syllables) or *chōka* (long verse, composed of a series of 5–7 syllables and ending with 7–7), as "quite shallow in theme" and charged that that "a theme that can be expressed within [*tanka*'s] thirty-one syllables is something like a small sparkling firework or a falling star; [*tanka*] cannot express a continuous thought."[22] *Shintaishishō* thus employed a series of 7–5 metrical structure in all their verses. With regard to theme, too, we find, for example, Toyama's "Shakaigaku no genri ni daisu" ("On the Principles of Sociology") attempting to push poetic boundaries.[23] The three compilers' criticisms of existing poetry and Hagino's later criticism of *waka* are strikingly similar. All focus on the limitations of poetic theme and syllabic length and seek to incorporate "current language" to expand poetic horizons.

Despite such similarity in their calls for reform, many *kokubungaku* scholars looked down on *shintaishi* and sought instead to develop *chōka* (long verse), which belonged to the *waka* tradition. Ochiai Naobumi says the following in the preface to *Shinsenkaten* (*New Collection of Poetry*, 1891):

> Recently there are an increasing number of compositions in *shintaishi*. The authors' claim is that it is impossible to portray complex thoughts and emotions in *tanka* (short verse). I do not disagree. They are right. But they do not realize that we also have *chōka*. What we seek is to develop *chōka* and reject the tasteless and primitive *shintaishi*.[24]

As the contemporary literary critic Shinada Yoshikazu has convincingly shown, however, whether it was the adoption of a 7–5 metrical rhythm as opposed to the 5–7 metrical rhythm of *chōka*, or the willingness to expand the range of poetic theme and diction, what the *kokubungaku* scholars sought for *chōka* was exactly what *Shintaishishō* had proposed.[25] Without openly admitting this, *kokubungaku* scholars forcefully situated *shintaishi* as an extension of *chōka*.[26] Moreover, such an appropriation of *shintaishi* also allowed the *kokubungaku* scholars to locate an "imperfect" *chōka*. In essence, the main objective was not to denigrate *shintaishi*, but to posit a "standard" poetic form (which the *kokubungaku* scholars sought to name *kokushi*, that is, national poetry) by representing *shintaishi* as a deviation from the "standard."[27] This parallels the manner in which the *kokubungaku* scholars designated *kanbun kundokutai* as an "imperfect" *kokubun*, then posited the "standard" by which to "correct" it.

What is important for our purposes is how *zoku* was reconfigured as *shintaishi* and appropriated in *waka* reform, as well as what *waka* reform perhaps inadvertently inherited in this process. Two things warrant special attention: how the *kokubungaku* scholars redefine *shintaishi*'s use of "*heijō no go*" and "*ima no go*" and their adoption of the 7–5 metrical rhythm (instead of reverting to the 5–7 metrical rhythm of *waka*).

While two of the compilers of *Shintaishishō*, Inoue and Yatabe, advocated the use of "current language," the third compiler, Toyama, reiterates their position as follows: "Instead of using elegant language and stiff Chinese expressions[28] to display poetic skill, we have decided not to differentiate between the new and the old, or *ga* and *zoku*, and have decided to mix up words from *wa*, *kan*, and the West, with the main aim of making it easy for people to understand."[29] For many *shintaishi* poets, *zoku* signified a medium that was "easy to understand." In this sense, *zoku* was not something that *shintaishi* poets sought to disparage; it was in fact something they wanted to embrace.[30] In contrast, *kokubungaku* scholars—to whom such mixture of *wa*, *kan*, and Western words signified *zoku*—sought to "strike a balance" again, this time between the styles of language used in *waka* and *shintaishi*. Take a look at the following passage from Hagino's "Waka oyobi shintaishi o ronzu" ("On *Waka* and *Shintaishi*"), where he discusses the disadvantages of both forms of poetry. While criticizing *waka* for being too "old-fashioned" and reasserting the need to use "existing 'living' language," he says the following:

> There are, however, *ga* and *zoku* in today's language. One must not uncritically use *zokugen*, vulgar diction, regional dialects, and the like and produce poems of *genbun'itchi*. . . . Poetry is a lofty form. It ought not be vulgar. In order for a poem to be lofty, poets must use correct and elegant diction. . . . *Shintaishi* does not use correct grammar. Where there is language, there are rules. Certain rules should not be broken.[31]

The "current language" that had been embraced by *shintaishi* were thus relegated to the realm of *zoku* (as that which needed reform), and "today's elegant language," the contemporary manifestation of the "pure original voice," was privileged as the "correct" medium for *waka* poetry.

However, the problem with this argument becomes apparent when we examine the 7–5 metrical rhythm they adopted, because the 7–5 metrical rhythm is inextricably linked to the very "current language" the *kokubungaku* scholars relegated to the realm of *zoku*. First, the 7–5 metrical rhythm was linked to Bakin-esque prose, rampant in the mid-1880s, especially as Bakin was being rediscovered in the political arena, where political fiction (*seiji shōsetsu*) was being written in such prose.[32] Such rhythmical prose in effect carried the energy of the Freedom and People's Rights Movement, and was hence heavily reliant on *kanbun kundokutai*, the primary language of the politically oriented intellectuals. As Sugaya Kikuo claims in his *Shiteki rizumu: onsūritsu ni kansuru nōto* (*Poetic Rhythm: Notes on Meters*), *shintaishi* poets specifically catered their poetry to the political arena.[33] It is not a coincidence that someone like Yano Ryūkei referred to Bakin's prose as *zokubuntai*.[34] In addition, *shintaishi* poets also integrated "folk songs" (*zokkyoku*) as they incorporated rhythmical stereotypical phrases like "ame no furuhi mo kaze no hi mo" (even on rainy and windy days) and "kane no otosuru tasogare ni" (at dusk one hears the temple bells), both of which are fixed expressions prevalent in *zokkyoku*, making them "easy to understand."[35] These expressions invariably were in 7–5 metrical rhythm. In short, what the *kokubungaku* scholars rejected—*zoku* diction and "incorrect" grammar—were integral to the 7–5 metrical rhythm they adopted. The 7–5 metrical rhythm of the *shintaishi* thus introduced an entirely new discursive dynamic to *waka* poetry.

There were several reasons that *kokubungaku* scholars adopted the 7–5 metric structure despite its inextricable link to the very *zoku* diction and grammar they sought to reject. First, the 7–5 metrical rhythm allowed them to push poetic boundaries. *Waka*, with its 5–7 metrical rhythm, was often criticized for "lacking energy" and its inability to represent concepts like "gallantry" and "strong resentment," prevalent in prose in the 7–5 metrical rhythm.[36] Moreover, as the literary critic Kamei Hideo aptly stated, 7–5 rhythm was "haunted" by "pivot words" (*kakekotoba*) and "associated words" (*engo*) integral to the *waka* tradition, from which 6–8 metrical rhythm would have been free.[37] In effect, because of such advantages, the use of another metrical rhythm would have been unthinkable.

Kokubungaku scholars clearly faced a dilemma, given that the 7–5 metrical rhythm inevitably brought in the *zoku* they sought to eradicate from *waka* to retain its elegance. To resolve this, they sought to emphasize "tone" (*onchō*) or "rhythmical tone" (*chōshi*) as an *aesthetic* principle. The *kokubungaku* scholar Takatsu Kuwasaburō, in his "Shiika o ronzu" ("On Poetry," 1888), begins his definition of poetry with *chōshi*, designating it as one of poetry's defining characteristics. According to Takatsu, poetry is something that is chanted; as such, he argues, *chōshi* has to retain its elegance: "If the *chōshi* is bad, even when the ideas and things portrayed are lofty and elegant, no one will be impressed . . . but if the *chōshi* is good, people will be impressed even when the ideas and things that are portrayed are not that lofty or elegant."[38] Here, he carefully divorces *chōshi* from the poetic theme and makes it an independent characteristic that makes poetry elegant. Such an argument seeks to define poetry formally through *chōshi* and not through the ideas or themes it expresses. In this definition, the 7–5 rhythm is a sheer meter; it putatively (and logically) sanitizes the 7–5 rhythm of the Bakinesque prose and the folk song expressions that came along with it. In this manner, *kokubungaku* scholars sought to downplay the difference between the 5–7 and 7–5 rhythms.[39]

What *kokubungaku* scholars inherited by appropriating *shintaishi* was perhaps more than they had anticipated. They sought to assert the superiority of "authentic elegance" over *zoku*, but they adopted the metrical structure that invariably activated the very *zoku* they sought to reject. Yet the 7–5 metrical rhythm was necessary not only to reform *waka* but to retain continuity with past discourse, given its link to techniques in the *waka* poetic tradition. "Authentic elegance," after all, was a link to the "pure original voice" of the past, and its poetry, for it to have the rightful status of national poetry, needed to retain that continuity. It was, in effect, vital that the 7–5 metrical rhythm be severed from *zoku*. Surprisingly, perhaps, the *kokubungaku* scholars' endeavor found support in the works of Bimyō and Shōyō. In an entirely different context and with different agendas, these fiction writers, too, sought to sever the connection between what they referred to as "*zoku*" and the 7–5 metrical rhythm.

ZOKUBUN AND READING PRACTICES: SHŌYŌ'S AND BIMYŌ'S LINGUISTIC EXPERIMENTS

In *Shōsetsu shinzui* (*The Essence of the Novel*, 1885–1886), Shōyō explains the reasons to embrace *zokugo* as such: "Speech is spirit; writing is form. Emotions are expressed with complete frankness in *zokugo*, whereas in writing they are overlaid with a veneer that to a certain extent camouflages their reality."[40] Designating *zokugo* as the language that best represents emotions, Shōyō here posits *zokugo* (equated with speech) in direct opposition to writing.[41] Writing, he claims, takes away the "frankness" of *zokugo.* Although Bimyō does not emphasize the link between *zoku* and emotions as Shōyō does, he too posits *zokugo* and "everyday conversation" in opposition to writing when he discusses the need for reform. Such an understanding of *zoku* differs from that of *kokubungaku* scholars, because the latter sought to define their "common conversation" against *kanbun* (and hence the "foreign"), rather than against written language in general. This difference appears slight, but it has great implications. While *kokubungaku* scholars emphasized the "naturalness" of common conversation, with its link to "our own" (which manifests itself as "authentic elegance") vis-à-vis the "foreign," the fiction writers' definition of *zoku* was speech vis-à-vis writing. This greatly expanded the horizon of *zoku*. For Shōyō, for example, *zokugo/zokubun* included many words and phrases that were yet to be "textually registered." In other words, it included not only regional dialects, but also words and phrases that had yet to be introduced to a system of agreement in which writing became possible. Such a realm of *zoku* was, in more ways than one, uncharted territory, severed from earlier forms of writing. Shoyo's criticism of *zokugo*'s verbosity, appearing in several of his essays, in part arises from the need to explain these words when textualized.[42] In this *zoku* he saw "animated qualities" of "vigor and passion" that were capable of expressing emotions and the seeds for his artistic language.

This is, in effect, a decisive difference. While *kokubungaku* scholars, through their identification of *zoku*, sought to posit authentic elegance as the contemporary embodiment (and hence continuous extension) of the "pure voice" of the past, Bimyō and Shōyō sought to embrace *zoku* for its power, the energy and animated vigor that earlier writing lacked; thus they aimed for a rupture with the past. In the realm of *zoku*, therefore, we find two contradictory impulses at work. As we shall see below, these contradictory impulses also appear tellingly in the "tone" (*onchō*) they seek to promote in their reforms.

Despite this difference in their definitions of *zoku*, we find that *kokubungaku* scholars and fiction writers deployed similar logic in addressing the issue of the 7–5 metrical rhythm. We see that both Shōyō and Bimyō also sought to treat the 7–5 metrical rhythm as a simple matter of rhythmical tone (*chōshi*). Look at Shōyō's statement in "Bunshō shinron" ("New Theory on Style," 1886):

> Those who prefer Chinese poetic verse or those engrained in rhythms inscribed in syllables of fives and sevens compose not for the meaning but for the language itself. That is why they value verse even if it means bending the idea, privileging a fluent flow.... Kyokutei Shujin, the founder of Bakin-esque writing, can be said to embody a fluent flow; however, [although he skillfully hides this,] we can see a trace of him bending the idea for the sake of flow, to say nothing of the recent novices. I, too, was a slave to rhythm until recently.[43]

The object of criticism here is Bakin-esque prose, which dominated the realm of the *shōsetsu* in the mid to late 1880s.[44] In Shōyō's argument, the metrical rhythms of fives and sevens or of Chinese poetic verse, which constitute the "fluent flow" of the sentence, exists independently of the "idea" presented—just as *kokubungaku* scholars defined rhythmical tone. The difference is that Shōyō defines these rhythms as a structural *restriction* that interferes with the expression of the "idea," rather than an aesthetic principle by which to judge a given verse.

While Shōyō's primary target was the 7–5 metrical rhythm, Bimyō went so far as to argue against metrical rhythm altogether, at least in prose. In response to the critics of *genbun'itchi*, who denounced the new prose as "inelegant," Bimyō claims that their characterization is based on "tone" (*onchō*), which should not be applied to prose. There is, he asserts in "Genbun'itchiron gairyaku" ("On the Theories of *Genbun'itchi*," 1888), "a *waka*-like tone" that is inscribed in the classical language by which the critics evaluate *zokubun:*

> That which takes *onchō* as its defining characteristic is poetry, but that which does not is prose. . . . Poetry is something that is chanted. Prose, however, is not. In order to recite a verse, it is necessary to have *onchō*. For something that is not chanted, *onchō* is useless. It is unfortunate that even Bakin lacked such a perspective. He disseminated language with a 7–5 metrical rhythm. It is then that the difference between poetry and prose was erased.[45]

Bimyō is in fact referring to two types of *onchō* here, one of *waka* (a 5–7 rhythm) and the other of *shintaishi*/Bakin-esque prose (a 7–5 rhythm), but he does not distinguish between them. In light of what we saw earlier in the works of *kokubungaku* scholars, his logic has two contradictory implications. On the one hand, he is arguing against the idea that his new language—the adoption of *zokubun*—is "inelegant," a typical criticism by *kokubungaku* scholars. On the other hand, he does so by submitting to their view that treats metrical rhythm, be it 5–7 or 7–5, monolithically, hence nullifying the difference between *waka*-like tone and Bakin-esque rhythm, which is exactly what *kokubungaku* scholars argued. Bimyō is instead attempting to define his prose away from any sort of metrical rhythm, making rhythm a quality specific to poetry, the beauty of which ought not be used in examining prose. In short, in criticizing the 7–5 rhythm, both Bimyō and Shōyō most likely inadvertently reinforced the linguistic scheme posited by *kokubungaku* scholars in their call for *waka* reform.

Why this criticism of metrical rhythm by these fiction writers? What lies at the core of this is the existence of *onchō* inscribed in the practice of reading/recitation. Maeda Ai's famous essay on reading practices, in which he brilliantly describes a shift from "oral reading" (*ondoku*) to "silent/solitary reading" (*mokudoku*), will be our guide here.[46] Oral reading practices and communal recitation were dominant forms of reading in the early Meiji period; this was especially so for the many politically oriented *shōsetsu*, which deployed the 7–5 metrical rhythm. Maeda shows that this was a practice governed by a shared rhythm of the sentences, traceable to the practice of *sodoku*, a form of learning of the *kangaku* classics that declaimed words and phrases without knowing their meaning. Maeda contends that such a rhythm constituted a "spiritual language" that fostered solidarity among those who shared it. Such reading practices were, he argues, gradually supplanted by solitary reading, which constituted the modern practice.

Shōyō and Bimyō, in their search for new artistic prose, were trying desperately to leave behind a form of prose integral to such communal reading practices. Bimyō, in "Genbun'itchiron gairyaku," specifically takes up the issue of oral reading in arguing against the use of tone in evaluating the "elegance" of a given style of writing. He claims, "The Japanese have a way of reading that is very different from conversation; it is rather close to singing. This is one of the hindrances to *zokubun*."[47] He thus argues that what is considered beautiful is based on this "reading that is like singing," hence calling into question the set of criteria by which critics of *zokubun* evaluated "beauty."[48] Such criticism of "reading like singing" proved itself a good strategy for differentiating between prose and poetry because of poetry's increasing association with actual singing in the late 1880s.[49] Since many *shintaishi* were adopted as "school songs," many of the compositions were literally sung. This was also a time when many "military marches" were produced through *shintaishi*, further inscribing a music-centered character on poetic composition.

What Bimyō and Shōyō sought, therefore, was to sanitize prose, stripping it of an *onchō* associated with existing reading practices, and to relegate *onchō* to the position of a musicality reserved for the realm of poetry. This *onchō* was precisely what defined the "writing" that they sought to leave behind in their efforts to adopt *zoku* (or "speech"); hence it was vital that they sever the 7–5 metrical rhythm from the realm of *zoku*. In the process, Shōyō and Bimyō replicated *kokubungaku* scholars' solution to the dilemma that resulted from appropriating *shintaishi*. This certainly does not mean that they endorsed or consciously supported the *kokubungaku* scholars' poetic project. Far from it. Bimyō and Shōyō severed the 7–5 metrical rhythm and Bakin-esque prose/*shintaishi* so that they could embrace their *zoku* (and relinquish the past associated with it), while *kokubungaku* scholars sought to sever them so that they could retain the 7–5 metrical rhythm (and the "voices of the past" it made manifest) as an aesthetic form. Nevertheless, whatever their agendas and goals, we cannot deny that Bimyō and Shōyō's search for a new prose form facilitated the severance of the 7–5 metrical rhythm from *zoku* that *kokubungaku* scholars sought to institute.

Bimyō and Shōyō did not seek to eradicate *onchō* completely. In fact, they sought a new *onchō*, one that was free of the 7–5 metrical rhythm that defined past "writing." Note that solitary reading did not signify lack of *onchō*.[50] The clue to understanding the new *onchō* that they sought lies in how they reiterate the term: in *Shōsetsu shinzui*, Shōyō glosses *onchō* as the "voice of reading" (*yomigoe*), while Bimyō refers to a "tone of voice" (*seichō*).[51] With these terms they refer to another orality, vital for their "artistic" prose.

BIMYŌ'S *GENBUN'ITCHI* AND *INBUN*

Bimyō's struggle for reform comprised two seemingly independent endeavors. On the one hand, he sought to produce a new form of prose by adopting *zokubun*.[52] On the other hand, he tackled *inbun* (lit., the "language of rhythm"), the very negative reference point against which he defined his prose. He continued to write fiction and is now better known for his prose reforms, but his theoretical interest began to shift toward *inbun* in the early 1890s.[53] Despite the difference in genre, I believe that a common drive governs his efforts in prose and poetry, linked specifically to the issue of *onchō* as aesthetic criterion. Both of these efforts are marked by the need to produce an alternative *onchō* by which to evaluate both poetry and prose.

In "Ware ware no genbun'itchitai" ("Our *Genbun'itchi* Style," 1891), Bimyō writes:

> When language is recited and its flow interrupted and its true meaning lost, it is "a blockage" (*jūtai*). When it is recited and its flow smooth and true meaning conveyed, it is "non-blockage" (*fujūtai*). *Fujūtai* should be differentiated from melody (*rakuchō*).[54]

Here, Bimyō continues his efforts to differentiate between prose and poetry by introducing a new concept called *fujūtai* or "non-blockage." As Maeda has aptly pointed out, Bimyō's concept of "blockage" here is inextricably linked to how meaning is received by the reader.[55] In other words, if and when a given "flow" introduces breaks where they are not supposed to be (for example, in the middle of a word) and hence interferes with the communication of meaning, then it constitutes "blockage." The flow in "non-blockage" does not interfere with meaning.

Notably, "non-blockage" has an oral component: "When prose is orally read, the best is "non-blockage." When poetic verse is sung, the best outcome is melody."[56] Bimyō, therefore, may have been against recitation (the old form of oral reading), but he did not reject *onchō* in his prose. In 1890's "Bun to gochō no kankei" ("On the Relationship between Language and Tone"), he discusses "spiritual tone" (*seichō* 斎調), which is "the sound of words that brings joy to the ear," and "non-spiritual tone" (*fuseichō* 不斎調), "the sound that brings unpleasantness to the ear."[57] What he has in mind is the sound of a sentence independent of metrical rhythm. Bimyō thus sought a prose with *fujūtai* that would bring "joy to the ear."[58] Such attention to sound is also reflected in his adoption of the suffixes *desu/masu*. Although he first chose to use the suffixes *da/datta* in his prose for efficiency, he reverted to *desu/masu*, he said, because he considered the sound of *da/datta* too "vulgar."[59]

What then constituted the sound of "non-blockage"? For Bimyō, it was none other than the sound of "everyday conversation." In "Genbun'itchiron gairyaku," he says: "Leaving classical language aside, *zokubun* is a language that copies the way we speak, so in reading it, we ought to read it just like everyday conversation" instead of singing it.[60] Yet he knew that such artistic language could not simply be achieved by "transcribing *zokugo*." This is the most evident in Bimyō's response to Uchida Roan (a.k.a. Fuchian)'s criticism of his experimental prose: "If we transcribe our everyday conversation and make it our written language, who—with the exception of some philosophers—would consider that a language of beauty? . . . Is our everyday conversation complete in form? That certainly isn't the case."[61] Bimyō thus implies that "everyday conversation" must be "made complete" in order for it to be a language of beauty. In effect, he was not advocating the "spoken language" as it was; he was clearly seeking to produce a written language that was a *representation* of everyday speech.

His choice of *desu/masu* for suffixes further supports such a view.[62] As Yamada Shunji argues in depth in *Taishū shinbun ga tsukuru Meiji no "Nihon"* (*Meiji "Japan" through Popular Newspapers*), *desu/masu* was an integral part of what was established as the "conversational style." This was prevalent in the miscellaneous section of newspapers at the time; inscribed in it were "the writers' voices" with the result that it was a language that gave the readers the illusion that the reporters were talking to them.[63] This *desu/masu* prose thus clearly mobilized an orality, which, for Bimyō, featured a possibility for a new language. From the time he adopted *desu/masu*, his fictional works increasingly featured dialogue that could be "read as it was spoken," producing a prose that had an orality independent of metrical rhythm.[64]

In "Genbun'itchiron gairyaku" and elsewhere, Bimyō constantly argued against the criticism that *zokugo* style was "unruly" and "ha[d] no system of grammar," a criticism that was repeated not only by *kokubungaku* scholars, but by Shōyō as well.[65] What this shows is that Shōyō and Bimyō did not have the same *zoku* in mind. Despite the fact that they both posited *zoku* in opposition to writing and sought a prose form that severed itself from the past, Shōyō had a broader conception of *zoku* that included "unregistered" language, language that had yet to be textualized. But Bimyō had found a more orderly form of writing—a representation of oral dialogue—already in the making. And this prose, as far as he was concerned, was imbued with an orality of its own that was divorced from metrical rhythm.

Bimyō continued to critique the validity of metrical rhythm as an aesthetic criterion for prose, which, much to his dismay, remained quite dominant. This, I believe, is one of the main reasons that Bimyō sought to treat *inbun* concurrently with prose reform. His project on *inbun* is of particular interest to us, because it reengages the issue of 7–5 metrical rhythm, the criticism of which facilitated the *waka* reform conceptualized by *kokubungaku* scholars. Perhaps not surprisingly, we shall see that Bimyō's criticism of the 7–5 metrical rhythm in the realm of poetry ultimately undermined the efforts of *kokubungaku* scholars at *waka* reform.

In a series of essays he wrote on *inbun*, Bimyō asserted the flexibility of rhythm inscribed in a given verse. The existing metrical rhythm, according to Bimyō, was not the absolute. In order to challenge its dominance, he sought to break up the 7–5 metrical rhythm by introducing an alternate rhythm. In *Nihon inbunron*, he says:

> [In terms of metrical rhythm,] 7 is not necessarily 7; it could be "3 and 4" or "4 and 3." It could also be "2 and 5," or "5 and 2." "2 and 5" could also be "2 and 2 and 3" or "2 and 3 and 2." To say that this is all 7 is very sloppy indeed.[66]

Since there are rarely words that take up 7 syllables, Bimyō suggests, it is possible to mobilize such variation. What he highlights here is the existence of a semantic structure within the metrical structure. For example, "Daichi yōyaku nubadama no" should not be understood as a simple 7–5, but as 3–4–4–1, all of the semantic units having breaks in between. Bimyō's textual experiments incorporated such views, as he visually represented such semantic breaks. Here is an example from his *Shinchō inbun: seinen shōka shū* (*New Forms of Poetry: Anthology of Youth Poems*, 1891).

万象　の　ゆめ　いま　覚めて
大地　やうやく　ぬば玉　の
闇　の　ころも　を　脱ぎ　去りぬ
薄むらさき　の　よこ雲に
誰　が　織りまぜ　の　唐にしき
こがね　の　色　の　目眩さ　よ。

Banshō no yume ima samete
Daichi yōyaku nubadama no
Yami no koromo o nugi sarinu
usumurasaki no yokogumo ni
Dare ga orimaze no karanishiki
Kogane no iro no mabayusa yo

The universe awakens from a dream
The earth finally divests itself
Of blackberry darkness.
On the light-purple clouds
Who quilted the colors of brocade?
How bright the golden colors![67]

The original text would normally have been strung together without being parsed in this manner, the strangeness of which is lost in the Romanized text. Despite the fact that this verse has a 7–5 metrical structure, such visual parsing, as Kamei has rightly noted, allows for the reader to reorient him or herself to the rhythm and to project new breaks.[68] In other words, he or she could read "Banshōno yume imasamete" (5–2–5) or "Banshō no yume ima samete" (4–1–2–2–3) or any other variation he or she chooses. Bimyō thus sought a way to redefine the various breaking points and repetitions and internally undermine the dominance of the 7–5 metrical rhythm. In other essays, he even proposed that metrical rhythm need not be limited to 5–7 or 7–5; it could be 6–8, 8–6, further suggesting that lines could be divided 3–3, 4–4; 4–4–3–2–1.[69]

In addition to undermining the dominant metrical rhythm, Bimyō sought to introduce another aural element to the poetic mixture. This time, it was accent. He attempted to adopt Western poetic techniques such as the iambus, trochee, and anapest in his poetic composition. In effect, the poetic sound, which he called "musical rhythm" in *Nihon inbunron*, was a combination of metrical rhythm (in all its variations, parsed according to semantic units) and accent.[70]

In an instance of iambus from *Nihon inbunron*, he takes the word *yume* (dream) as an example and claims that the accent lies in "*me*"—*yu* is the "low sound" while *me* constitutes the "high sound." Trying to compose a verse with such iambus, he proposes: *yume yume kimi no, tama kura ni* (all of the words that repeat the same iambic structure as *yume*).[71] By highlighting such accent repetition, he thus sought to introduce another set of *onchō* to poetic verse. However, not all such poetic techniques are applicable to the Japanese syntactic structure, which is apparent, for example, in his attempt to adopt anapest, in which "two short sounds are followed by one long one, such as *yanagi* (willow). The high sound is *gi*, while *ya* and *na* have the same tone."[72] Here is an example transcribed in the way Bimyō parsed the verse: "*Yanagi ninemu rerutoho kefuri*," the high sound being "*gi*," "*mu*," "*toho*," and "*ri*," respectively. Such parsing follows the structure of the anapest, but semantically it should be parsed as "*Yanagi ni nemureru tohoke furi*." As such an example shows, the forced use of these methods directly imported from Western languages and their poetic traditions shatters the semantic structure of the Japanese words, making the poem incomprehensible. In this sense, such methodology produced what he earlier called "blockage" in meaning.

Bimyō was therefore successful in some experiments, yet not so successful in others. But one thing is certain. His work on *inbun* was an incessant search for new sets of rhythm that could undermine the dominance of the 7–5 metrical rhythm while also introducing new means to create *onchō*. Predictably, such proposed reforms did not sit well with *kokubungaku* scholars, who sought a use of diction and semantic structure based on "authentic elegance." Bimyō's efforts to destabilize the 7–5 metrical rhythm were a source of much frustration for someone like Ochiai, who wrote in "Kokubun kokushi o ronjite yo no bungakusha ni nozomu" ("On National Letters and Poetry: A Request to Men of Letters"):

> The general consensus among men of letters is that the thirty-one-syllable form must be changed. They also say that the 5–7 metrical rhythm is passé; poetry must now be in a 7–5 metrical rhythm; they generally say [compositions] should not be limited to 5s and 7s; one should compose freely and use 1–2, 3–4, 5–6–7, or 8–9–10. Fine. Change the thirty-one-syllable form, forget 5–7, and even relinquish 7–5. What is the alternative metrical rhythm? What kind of poetry would that be? I'd like to know, I'd like to see it.[73]

This article was published as Bimyō was publishing his series of articles on *inbun*. What is at the core of Ochiai's frustration is the lack of a standard form by which to define poetry, which is precisely what the *kokubungaku* scholars were seeking. Bimyō's proposed reform in poetry obviously ran counter to those of *kokubungaku* scholars, who sought to establish rules based on authentic elegance, or more accurately to project authentic elegance onto the standard, rather than to destabilize them.

In both his work on prose and *inbun*, Bimyō, whether consciously or otherwise, challenged the *kokubungaku* project. His first set of negotiations was to sever prose from what he called a "musical" rhythm, and endow it with an entirely different orality. His works on *inbun* featured his effort to destabilize the dominant 7–5 and 5–7 metrical rhythms and introduce a new set of rhythm and poetic sound as an alternative aesthetic principle. In so doing, he questioned what constituted "elegance" in *onchō*, the concept that firmly governed those "artistic" criteria based on which his *genbun'itchi* and poetic experiments were belittled by *kokubungaku* scholars.

SHŌYŌ AND THE "ELOCUTIONARY" METHOD

While Bimyō busied himself with *inbun*, Shōyō took an entirely different path in his search for a new orality. For Shōyō, the *yomigoe* (lit., "reading voice") with which he glossed the characters for *onchō*) referred to an orality inscribed in the practice of "elocution." Here is a passage from "Bunshō shinron":

> The main goal of language is to represent emotions. Language that fails to do so does not encompass perfect beauty. . . . Then, what kind of language is most appropriate to represent emotions? In answering this question, I would say that a language that applies what in English they call elocution is the most appropriate. . . . Elocution is a method of reading wherein intonation and tempo are based on the meaning of the sentences.[74]

As Maeda has argued, this elocutionary reading that Shōyō proposed in "Bunshō shinron" is the absolute opposite of "raw" reading, through which students recited and memorized the sentences without knowing the meaning.[75] This move, on Shōyō's part, thus aligned with his argument against the Bakin-esque narrative and the practice of communal recitation that prioritized metrical rhythm over content. Yet just like Bimyō, Shōyō was not conceptualizing a form of prose devoid of orality. He sought a new language that had, inscribed within itself, a new orality based on intonations that adhered to meaning rather than formal structure (such as the 7–5 metrical rhythm) and that would replace earlier reading practices. This was on a par with Shōyō's claim that the "elocutionary method" was a type of reading that should not necessarily be adopted when a text was orally delivered. Instead, he described it as "a reading that had to be adopted during solitary reading."[76] In effect, such orality had to be discernible in the language in which the works were written without the oral delivery of the texts themselves.

Shoyo's orality differed from what Bimyō had in mind for his prose. In "Bunshō shinron," Shōyō raises two examples, "*anata Asakusa e ikimasuka*" and "*kono shina wa oyasuu gozaimasu*," and says the following:

> What is most troublesome in our language are the suffixes. We add something so strange, which no other language has, to the end of the sentences. In the above examples, I'm referring to the '*masu*' of '*gozaimasu*' and '*yukimasuka*,' which is utterly unnecessary. We can just say '*yuku ka*' and '*oyasui*,' but we add instead '*gozaimasu*' and '*yukimasuka*.' This is commonly called an honorific and has been our custom for quite some time, but it is entirely unnecessary. When it is used in written form, it especially interferes with the force of the language. In writing in the 'descriptive style' or 'epic narrative,' or even in speech, if we use such suffixes and write exactly like everyday conversation, the language will be unnecessarily long and will lose the refined intonation and tone.[77]

Here, Shōyō targets "honorifics," which form part of the reason that language "becomes unnecessarily long," a criticism he leveled against *zokubuntai* in *Shōsetsu shinzui*.[78] His examples show that his criticism specifically targets the suffix *masu*. Shōyō thus set his new prose against the "voice" of the "oral dialogue" that Bimyō advocated. In effect, he rejected two forms of orality available to him in the mid-Meiji period: that of the 7–5 rhythm and that of the "conversation-style" prose that featured a representation of an oral dialogue.

Shōyō further developed his theory in another essay, "Doppō o okosan to suru shui" ("On the Aim to Popularize Methods of Reading," 1891), which is of special interest, because he consciously differentiated his position via Sekine Masanao, the *kokubungaku* scholar who also advocated elocutionary method in promoting the language of authentic elegance. In the essay, Shōyō first describes three types of reading: mechanical reading (*kikaiteki doppō*), grammatical reading (*bunpōteki doppō*), and logical reading (*ronriteki doppō*).[79] Mechanical reading is the equivalent of "raw" reading, "a reading in which they pay no attention to word/phrase breaks and simply utter the sounds of characters in written order."[80] It is otherwise named "dead reading," devoid of "emotion, warmth, and activity."[81] The grammatical reading is one that Shōyō claims that Sekine advocates, which he describes in his "Kokubun rōdokuhō" ("Elocutionary Methods of *Kokubun*," 1891). In fact, this is seemingly what Shōyō was advocating in his earlier essay, "Bunshō shinron," as it is also referred to as "correct reading," which pays close attention to "pronunciation, rules of grammar, word/phrase breaks," while the intonation and tone adhere closely to the meaning of the sentences.[82]

Before examining the third and final form of reading, which Shōyō dubbed "logical reading," let us first briefly look at Sekine's "Kokubun rōdokuhō." Sekine, like Shōyō, takes as his negative reference point "monotonous reading," the equivalent of mechanical reading, and claims that a reader must pay attention to pronunciation, phrase, elocution, and vocal tone.[83] First, Sekine sought to standardize pronunciation by renouncing regional dialects. In addition, he claimed that this would further standardize spelling, which, according to Sekine, had not been standardized because people tended to follow pronunciation in spelling. As long as people pronounced words incorrectly, he suggested, spelling would also be irregular. The elocutionary method, therefore, would teach not only proper pronunciation but also spelling. Sekine further argued that the reader needed to pay close attention to phrasal units and understand clearly "the grammatical structure prior to enunciation."[84] In promoting elocution, Sekine sought to advocate a reading based on meaning, one that for example used "high pitch to express words of interrogation, suspicion, and excitement" while "naturally using low pitch to express acceptance, conclusion, and interpretation."[85] And finally, with vocal tone, Sekine envisioned a relationship in which intonation and tone adhered closely to meaning.

To the extent that they were arguing against mechanical reading, Shōyō and Sekine appear to be in agreement. However, what is strikingly different is the absolute position that the text intended for elocution occupies in Sekine's essay. Take, for example, Sekine's discussion on pronunciation. In his logic, the chosen text displayed the standard spelling, which, he claimed, was too often irregularized by "mistaken" pronunciation, whether as a result of regional dialects or a faulty memory. It embodied correct grammatical structures and phrasal units. Sekine's essay thus features an unconditional valorization of the text for elocution, which invariably constitutes prose of "authentic elegance" as that which governs "correct elocution." Or, more accurately, in such a scheme, oral delivery is relegated to a position secondary to that of the *gasei* language inscribed in the text for elocution. Elocution thus ought to make manifest the *gasei* prose buried in the passages.[86]

In contrast, Shōyō did not place such emphasis on "correctness" in promoting his "logical reading." Here is a passage from "Doppō o okosan to suru shui":

> I seek to develop what one elocutionist called 'fine reading.' Fine reading does not simply clarify the meaning of the sentences (grammatical reading) nor make it forceful and agreeable (Whately). . . .[87] If the emotion inscribed in the language is beautiful, it ought to sound beautiful, if the emotion inscribed in the language is hurried, it ought to sound hurried. . . . The voice's sound should adhere to the emotions inscribed in the language as closely as possible.[88]

The orality of elocution here adheres not to the text itself but to the "emotions inscribed in the language." To access this "emotion inscribed in the language," Shōyō claims that "even when grammatically it makes sense to read [a given sentence] without any breaks, if, logically speaking, there appears the need to express strong feelings, and one can only do so by introducing breaks, one ought to be flexible and address it accordingly."[89] "Grammatical correctness" can thus be sacrificed to foreground the emotions inscribed in the language.

Perhaps surprisingly, Shōyō further claims that "logical reading" offers "a means to analyze life and human beings and also a means to teach the very thing one has learned."[90] This language, in other words, ought to be imbued with an orality that would assist the interpretation of "life."[91] In other words, the orality of a given text, even read silently, should carry with it an interpretive scheme.

Obviously, such prose had yet to exist. As was the case in *Shōsetsu shinzui*, where his ideas were prescriptive of the *shōsetsu* despite the appearance of being descriptive, the new form of prose with an orality of "logical reading" had yet to be produced. This was in keeping with his adoption of textually unregistered *zokugo* as a means to invigorate fictional prose. The search for a new orality thus marks his attempt to break with earlier forms of writing. The elocutionary language that Shōyō promoted was not a method to access the standard *gasei* language (that linked itself to the past "voice") seemingly "buried" in (or more accurately projected onto) the text of elocution as was the case in Sekine, but first and foremost a language that was discontinuous with the existing practices of reading and writing.

CONCLUSION

We have taken multiple steps to examine the intersections between reforms in poetry and fiction by focusing on works of *kokubungaku* scholars and two leading fiction writers who advocated *zokugo* in their prose. They intersected at unexpected places, and at the same time differed completely at areas of apparent superficial convergence. Despite the seeming similarity in advocating "*tsūjō no danwa*," they differed in what they argued against (*kanbun* for *kokubungaku* scholars and writing in general for fiction writers). The difference, though in appearance minor, was striking. While *kokubungaku* scholars sought to identify authentic elegance, the contemporary embodiment of a pure original voice, in the "current language," fiction writers strove to generate a new language of the present, one severed from the past (a "past" represented by Bakin and the practices of communal recitation through which his works were consumed). This difference, I believe, is at the core of Kamei's statement that *genbun'itchi* and *kokugo* reforms had nothing to do with each other.

Yet this difference produced an unexpected overlap, which facilitated a linguistic turn that both sought to achieve, despite lacking any real shared goal or agenda. The severance of the 7–5 metrical rhythm from what they each called *zoku* was one such example. *Kokubungaku* scholars embraced the 7–5 metrical rhythm as a "standard," the manifestation of the past they sought to recover in the present, while the fiction writers sought to relinquish the past (Bakin-esque prose and communal reading practices) inscribed in the 7–5 metrical rhythm.

In effect, their searches for voices continuous with and discontinuous from the past converge in *onchō*. They shared the conviction that *onchō* was precisely that which defined language and that the past was firmly inscribed in it. To produce continuity with the past, *kokubungaku* scholars could not relinquish the 7–5 metrical rhythm. In contrast, fiction writers—be it in the form of Bimyō's "conversation-style" language or that of Shōyō's "elocutionary" language—desperately sought a new *onchō* that would replace the 7–5 rhythm that defined past practices of reading and writing.

When we deem *zoku* as a populist choice, it is easy to seamlessly link the efforts of the *kokubungaku* scholars and fiction writers. However, once we bracket the notion that these writers were in fact in search of a "shared language," we begin to see the multiple linguistic operations that go into their references to *zoku*. The aesthetic aspect of language is too often glossed over in a narrative that emphasizes *zoku*'s populist character. None of the writers denied that they sought an artistic language; in fact no one even questioned it. Without considering *zoku* as an aesthetic category, we lose sight of the importance that *onchō* played in their arguments.

The typical narrative of *kokugo* reform says that we must wait until the emergence of Ueda Kazutoshi to completely sever *kokugo* from *kokubun*.[92] The assumption is that *kokubun* scholars subjugated *kokugo* to *kokubun*; hence any effort to cater to aesthetics is seen as a lingering attachment to the *kokubun* era. The following chapter will question such a division between *kokugo* and *kokubun*. Such an inquiry will show that the division between speech and writing that fiction writers produced in defining *zoku* came to be appropriated in Ueda's discourse on *kokugo*, wherein he set out to define *kokugo* as a mode of expression via voice, all the while defining *bungaku* as a mode of expression via letters.

Furthermore, I will attempt to take a step back and introduce another perspective by which to examine language reforms in the following section by specifically examining the issue of racialization. I believe race plays a vital role in the formation of "national language" and is significant in understanding the global context in which these language reforms were advocated, debated, and implemented.

PART II

Race and Language Reform

I WISH TO HERE BRIEFLY PROVIDE A HISTORICAL NARRATIVE OF RACE, how it began to denote what it is in the modern world order. As I stated in the introduction, we must be mindful of the fact that race is fabricated. In order to give its imagined existence the appearance of the real, the concept of race needs to be constantly produced and reproduced, along with other indexes of identity, such as national community and national language. While I discuss the uses of racial categories in history, we must constantly examine race via the ideological world order that reproduces and reifies these categories as such.

As many historians of race have remarked, it was only in the eighteenth century that race appeared as a concept to categorize human beings through physical characteristics, primarily skin color.[1] Prior to this, social status by birth and religion provided a far more prevalent form of self-identity. Through their encounters with Africa, Europeans had of course recognized that they had lighter pigmentations, but race did not become the dominant taxonomy of classification. In effect, the idea of "whiteness" as indicative of a pan-European "superior" race was slow to develop before the eighteenth century.

The advent of "enlightenment" and modern science marked the beginning of change. As a means to turn away from religion, race became one of the defining indexes organizing humans as part of the animal kingdom rather than as "children of God." The well-known father of physical anthropology, Johann Friedrich Blumenbach (1752–1840), published *On the Natural Varieties of Mankind* in 1776. There he introduced the authoritative classification of races, which he divided into five: Caucasian, Mongolian, Ethiopian, American, and Malay. He was the first to trace the white race to the Caucasus. "Mongolians" referred to those in

Asia, including China and Japan; "Ethiopians" to the "dark-skinned" inhabitants of Africa; "Americans" to the natives of the New World; and the "Malays" were the Polynesians and the aborigines of Australia. Such classifications were imported to Meiji Japan through the geography of *Yochi shiryaku* (*An Abridged Account of the World*, 1870), compiled by Uchida Masao and used as a school textbook.

Once such a classification took form, the hierachizing of the categories soon followed. In the 1798 work *Outline of the History of Humanity*, the German philosopher Christoph Meiners aestheticized "whiteness" as "beautiful," which he further linked with "intelligence." In the same vein, "darker" people were designated as "ugly" and "semi-civilized."[2] Such categorizations set the stage for the full-blown biologism and racism fueled by nineteenth-century Social Darwinism.

This racial taxonomy was inextricably connected with the emergence of Europe as the "civilized" center through which the world was defined. In the fifteenth to sixteenth centuries, Europe had emerged as a self-conscious unit.[3] Despite many internal differences, it began to identify itself as a "continent," despite the lack of any geographical basis for this determination. There can be seen a gradual shift in the world order as Europeans identify themselves as "the West" vis-à-vis non-Europeans (the Rest, as Stuart Hall famously described them).[4] The privileged site of "whiteness," although in appearance tied to "Europeans," was thus tightly linked with colonial expansion and the ideological world order that it produced. In this regime, the whiteness of "the West" became the standard regulating this world order, while the Rest were viewed as the deviation from the standard. It is important to keep in mind that this notion of the "West" is not at all monolithic. For example, Britain colonized Ireland and the Irish were not considered "white" in the United States until the late nineteeenth century. Similarly, Jews and Italians were not considered white. It is not difficult to see that the category of the West is highly unstable.[5] Precisely because of this, however, many forces have come to reproduce and reify this structure of the West and the Rest.

The West and the Rest are always already in a cofigurative relation, to borrow Naoki Sakai's term.[6] Cofiguration is a mechanism of semantic correlation by which a collective represents itself vis-à-vis the other. It is a relationship of equivalence, but this equivalence can never sustain itself, as there would inevitably be a difference that is identified as "excess" or "lack." The West is the regulative idea by which the Rest is evaluated. In effect, the excess or lack will invariably be attributed to the Rest. It is, furthermore, a structure of desire. The West will always present itself as the goal to which the Rest aspires, but remains ultimately inaccessible, which is a necessary condition for its status as object of desire.

When Japan joined the international community in the late nineteenth century, the world was already racialized. The Tokugawa Shogunate closely followed the fate of Qing China, which had survived two Opium Wars in the mid-nineteenth century and became semi-colonized as a result. Japan thus had to desperately avoid becoming China, and this meant becoming a "first-rate nation" in a world that designated Asia as "semi-civilized." In other words, joining the world order but avoiding the trap of colonialism meant internalizing "the West" as the object of desire and invariably approximating it.

The racial taxonomy produced in eighteenth-century Europe was transmitted to Japan even before the Meiji Restoration (1868).[7] However, the most influential works on racial taxonomy appeared after the Restoration, especially through the writings of Fukuzawa Yukichi. In *Shōchū bankoku ichiran* (*All Countries at a Glance: Pocket Edition*, 1869), he defines the five races in the following manner:

1. White race: They have the fairest skin. . . . They are the most intelligent and capable of attaining the highest level of civilization.
2. Yellow race: Their skin is yellow like oil. . . . They are capable of endurance and diligence but are limited in intelligence and slow in making progress.
3. Red Race: Their skin mixes red and brown and is like copper. . . . They are aggressive and combative in nature, and always vengeful.
4. Black Race: Their skin is black and their hair curly like sheep. . . . They are indolent in habit and have not attained progress.
5. Brown Race: Their skin is brown like rust. . . . They are fierce and strongly vengeful.[8]

Here one can clearly see the racial hierarchy organized by the framework of Social Darwinism. This racial hierarchy was inextricably tied to geography: the "white race" is in Europe, the "yellow race" in Asia, the "black race" in Africa, etc. Fukuzawa himself fully endorsed this view. Such classification also shapes his *Sekai kunizukushi* (*The Countries of the World*, 1869), which was used as a school geography textbook.[9] In effect, the study of geography marked the very internalization of such racial hierarchy. In his *Bunmeiron no gairyaku* (*An Outline of a Theory of Civilization*, 1875), Fukuzawa organizes the stages of civilization into three categories: "uncivilized" (*mikai*), "half-civilized" (*hankai*), and "civilized" (*bunmei*). Given the world order encountered by Meiji Japan, Fukuzawa had no choice but to situate Japan among the half-civilized.

The race war in Meiji Japan was very much a pursuit of "whiteness" in this racial order. Predictably, as the Japanese were designated as "yellow," an affinity was established with those in China and Korea. In the 1880s, Kōakai (The Society of Asianism), a group that promoted the goal of Asian consolidation, was founded. This group fostered integration and a collective sense of solidarity among Asians in an attempt to ward off the threat of Western imperialism. Even within this organization, however, Japan sought to claim the position of leader. The power struggle in East Asia, in other words, reflected Japanese desire to assume the status of the West. As a result, Japan soon strove to become a colonial power itself. As early as 1876, Japan subjected Korea to unequal treaties that imposed harsher conditions than those forced upon Japan by the United States. After its victory in the first Sino-Japanese War (1894–95), Japan invaded Taiwan and then later annexed Korea in 1910.

Force was not the only means Japan used to emulate the West. In fact, Japan presented itself as the object of desire for East Asian countries. It became the East Asian center for gaining "Western knowledge," resulting in a large influx of students from China and Korea. Japan quickly defined itself as the educator of East Asia. As I will show, it was precisely in this context that Ueda Kazutoshi, the founder of *kokugo*, attempted to define Japanese as the common language of Asia. In this way, Japanese could gain recognition as one of the few "imperial" languages, such as English. Learning Japanese, therefore, was seen as a means to acquire access to modern—and so Western—forms of knowledge.

4

Racializing the National Language

Ueda Kazutoshi's Kokugo *Reform*

Having looked extensively at the first two decades of the Meiji period, we now turn to Ueda Kazutoshi and his reforms. I am deeply indebted to the many works on Ueda, but, as I mentioned in the introduction, much previous scholarship has demonized Ueda as the father of linguistic nationalism, and the overemphasis of nationalism and ethnocentrism in such scholarship has swayed many away from the process of racialization that I wish to highlight in this chapter. These works focus on Japan's de-Asianization or de-Sinification project, which are extremely important in thinking about Japanese imperialism in East Asia. But the narrow focus on Japanese ethnocentrism in relation to China, Korea and other colonies has resulted in a concealment of race as a major index of identity by which language was defined. There is, of course, no way to deny that Ueda was a nationalist, as he did define *kokugo* as the "spiritual blood of the Japanese people" (*Nihonjin no seishinteki ketsueki*). But we must remind ourselves that nationalism and racism reinforce one another—not through the relationship of cause and effect, but in the sense that the formation and reification of one in many cases foster the other. Therefore, the premise of this chapter is that racism is critical to the foundation of modernity, and we must be mindful of all its slippages into ethnocentrism and nationalism.

Just as we have seen in the previous chapters, we need to keep in mind that many of the terms that we currently take for granted, such as *jinshu* or *minzoku*, didn't mean then what they mean now. The term *jinshu* (now denoting "race") was in flux, and its use still very unstable, as we shall see in more detail later. The term *minzoku*, which we now often translate as "ethnic nation" or "ethnicity," was not yet in wide use.[1] This does not mean that the terms were not used; it simply signifies the chaotic conditions in which what constitutes a "nation" or "national community" was being probed.

Again, racialization must be understood as a form of social categorization based on physical traits, arbitrarily yet decisively chosen to determine one's place in society. Racial categories are fabricated and hierarchized and "whiteness" is construed as an object of desire. We must also remind ourselves that multiple indexes of identity must be constructed and need to work in tandem for a given index of identity to constitute itself. As such, race cannot be divorced from be ethnicity or nationality. They are all mutually invasive. Hence it is important to define the varying logics that form or shape the forces of identification. Here I want to focus on the logic of equality and "naturalization," two of the defining characteristics of modernity that reify and foster racism. I would like to do so in light of how Ueda posits the "Japanese language" and show how his reform is complicit with the project of racialization.

In his "Kokugo to kokka to" ("National Language and Nation"), an essay based on a series of talks he gave and published soon after Japan's victory in the First Sino-Japanese war in 1895, Ueda defines the relationship between the nation and its national language in the following manner:

> A language, for the people who speak, is the symbol of the spirit of compatriots, just like the blood shared by their bodies. Taking the Japanese national language as an example, the Japanese language is the spiritual blood of the Japanese people. The nation of Japan is maintained by this spiritual blood, and the Japanese race (*Nihon no jinshu*) is unified by this most potent and long-preserved chain. Therefore, when visited by a crisis, as long as this voice resonates, our forty million compatriots will listen to it and come to help one another.... On learning of good news of victory, the celebration song for the emperor echoes from Chishima through Okinawa.[2]

In this infamous passage, Ueda posits a logic of equality among forty million people, a figure which includes those from Chishima (currently the Kuril islands, north of Hokkaidō) to Okinawa. These are boundaries which were still very much contested at that time. On the one hand, as he states elsewhere, this appears "democratic," as he argues against the production of a language that is controlled solely by the upper class or intellectuals. Yet, on the other hand, there is danger in this logic of equality: "equality" provides a grounding for comparing individuals and producing differences. If one speaks a dialect, one is "marked" as a minority. The façade of equality, which can never sustain itself, always produces excess and/or lack. The dominant regulative idea will then be used to explain the excess and/or lack.

Positing *kokugo* as "the spiritual blood of the Japanese people," Ueda also mobilizes the logic of "naturalization." These forty million people "naturally" speak this "Japanese language"—so a given person that belongs to this community necessarily is endowed with certain abilities "naturally." This "Japanese language" binds them together like a chain, and precisely because of this, if a crisis occurs to anyone who belong to this community, the community will offer help to those in need.

As many scholars have remarked, Ueda did not believe in one "race" speaking one language. Despite this, however, he states: "For a nation to be established, we must acknowledge that there must be one race that is the pillar of the nation. In order to realize our movement, we need the *yamato* spirit of loyalty and patriotism and the *yamato minzoku* that possess this nation's language."[3] Ueda's ethnocentrism has often been pointed out, but it is worth noting the very common logic of national community at play here, which is complicit with the logic of equality and naturalization that was posited earlier. "Equality" is inextricably linked to the need for assimilation because of the logic of "naturalization." Equality, which should fundamentally be about "rights," slips into a *need* to be "equal." It is not that we are simply "equal," but that we need to become the "same." Take one's language ability, for example. One is naturally endowed with such an ability. However, ultimately, our language ability is an individual ability—one person is better at Japanese than I am or vice versa. But when one's ability becomes the source of judgment regarding whether one "rightfully" belongs to a given national community, a hierarchy is inevitably instituted among the speakers. The standard by which such judgment is made is by the "imagined majority"—in this case the *yamato minzoku*.

This is also one defining characteristic of a national community: a part of a whole functioning like a synecdoche that defines the nation. In other words, a nation will always have an imagined dominant majority, a part of a whole that sets the standard by which a given nation is defined. This majority is allegedly somewhere—like the *yamato minzoku* in Japan, whites in the United States—but it can only be imagined and thus in need of continuous fabrication. This is precisely why *anyone* can be suddenly marked as a minority in this framework.

Having thus established the powerful majority, Ueda then claims the following in "Kokugo kenkyū ni tsuite" ("On the Study of *Kokugo*"):

> We, the members of this research group, are ones who show great respect and love for the *kokugo* of the Great Japanese Empire. We do not fall behind anyone, especially in investigating [language] in our scholarly endeavors, and in pursuit of [*kokugo*'s] expansion. . . . We are the ones who have made a lifelong commitment to creating a common language of Asia (*Tōyō zentai no futsūgo*): a language that anyone involved in scholarship, politics, and business in Asia—whether this person be Korean, Chinese, European, or American—would need to know.[4]

This *Tōyō zentai no futsūgo* was later renamed *Tōa kyōtsūgo* (language common to all of Asia), the education which Ueda and his disciples later tried to implement in Japan's colonies. Despite his fanatic nationalism, Ueda never conceptualized *kokugo* as a language that belonged only to the Japanese. In fact, he attempted to conceptualize *kokugo* as a language equivalent to French, English, and Spanish, that would be spoken beyond a single nation. In short, he conceptualized Japanese as an imperial language, and thus he conceptualized it as "white." At the onset of modernity in Meiji Japan, the marker of whiteness consisted in possessing a nation-state. Nation formation was thus of the utmost necessity. But the unit of the nation was only one form of whiteness. As the desire to be "white" was inevitably frustrated, it needed to further find ways to reinforce its whiteness. In effect, Japan had to possess an empire in which Japan was the center. The Japanese language that Ueda conceptualized was an imperial language which could be spoken by anyone in the Japanese empire. It was thus not simply a national language (to a degree, of course, it is, as the *yamato minzoku* are the true masters and "authentic" speakers of Japanese language), but it had to be reborn not as a national language but as an imperial language, always already racialized.

Thinking about *kokugo* this way, Ueda's conception of race becomes rather suggestive. He claims:

> Any nation has one or a few races. Therefore, I do not believe that national subjects should be limited to one race. For example, among the Westerners, there are Italians, French, and Germans, just as among the Japanese people, there are people of imperial descent (皇別), descendants of Amatsukami and Kunitsukami (神別), as well as those descendants of the feudal domains (藩別).[5]

One can easily see that the terms "nation" and "race" are in flux here, but perhaps most interestingly, for Ueda, *jinshu* is conflated with class. The imagined "whiteness" is in many ways a matter of class or privilege. Those who belong to the most "civilized," privileged community do so precisely by laying claim to what is imagined as "civilized."

What is involved in such a construction of *kokugo* as whiteness? How can Ueda produce such *kokugo* with any sense of reality? In order to unravel this complex process, I wish to focus on two elements in Ueda's reform: his obsession with the "present" and "speech"—both of which have been primarily attributed to his study of cutting-edge linguistic theories in Germany. But before elaborating on Ueda's reform, I wish to briefly discuss the forms of literary history that his contemporaries were compiling, all in the name of nation formation. That will help show what Ueda's conception of the "nation" was responding to, and it will allow me to highlight how he radically departs from the nation to produce his "white" imperial language.

As mentioned before, *bungaku* was language, and it is thus not a coincidence that language textbooks featured literary histories. The literary histories that Meiji ideologues took as their model arose in late seventeenth- to early eighteenth-century Europe. They embodied a growth of "the historical sense" that accompanied an increasing interest in the individual's place in history.[6] Following this trend, there was an increase in the biographical reading of poetry, which became prominent in the eighteenth century. Literary histories were compiled accordingly by focusing on the process of creation by individual poets and emphasizing the writer's background. With the advent of Social Darwinism in the nineteenth century, moreover, the focus further shifted to social evolution, which placed the individual in a shared sociological space. By logical extension, literary texts were deemed an expression of the social, political, and cultural environment of a given work's production. Perhaps the most far-reaching work in this vein is *History of English Literature* (1863) by Hippolyte Taine, known as the founder of the sociological study of literature. Positing the famous "race-milieu-moment" as a formula that constructs literary history, Taine sought to identify the national *Volk* expressed through texts, capturing the *Volk* as a product of its political, social and natural environment.

It is important to note here that Taine recognized the relationship between language and race in his project of social organization. Any "social organization" requires various indexes of identity. That is to say, when the question is how to create a society that is equal to itself and different from other societies, one requires a principle of organization. Defining "race" in this race-milieu-moment formula, Taine says the following: "What we call the race is the innate and hereditary dispositions which man brings with him to the light, and which, as a rule, are united with the marked differences in the temperament and structures of the body."[7] Race was the primary index in his social organization project. In his framework, racial disposition was then affected by what he called the milieu, which refers to the environment, as well as what he called "moment," which signified the "momentum" of past and present traditions.

Taine's work was widely read by Meiji ideologues, who sought to compile their own works of literary history. Literary historians in Japan started compiling histories closely following Taine's model in 1890.[8] Their works marked a shift in the way literary historians situated texts. The traditional, antiquarian literary studies were a study of "dead" texts, as it were. Instead, new scholars of "national literature" (*kokubungaku*) sought to read texts as a reflection of the time, of social organization, and of the people's inner spirit. We thus see many references to words like "*jinsei no kagami*" (mirror of life), "*jisei no han'ei*" (reflection of the time), and *shakai no hansha kagami* (a reflective mirror of society) in situating works of literature.[9] Such compilation of history was often characterized as a "scientific approach" to literature, referring to the Social Darwinian framework upon which their narratives were written.[10]

In describing texts as a reflection of time, literary historians constantly linked the texts to people's *shin-teki seikatsu* (internal lives) and *kanjō shisō* (emotions and thoughts). Mikami Sanji and Takasu Kuwasaburō's *Nihon bungakushi* (*History of Japanese Letters*, 1890), for example, claims that "literature is a reflection of people's mind" which embodies emotions, customs and taste.[11] Haga Yaichi, in compiling *Kokubungakushi jikkō* (*Ten Lectures on National Literary History*, 1899), says that literary history traces "the thoughts and feelings of our ancestors, expressed through our national language."[12] Takeshima Hagoromo sought to discover the "vicissitudes of our people's spirit" (*kokumin ga seishin no hensen*) and identify their "internal movements" (*naimen teki katsudō*).[13] Mikami and Takasu's *Nihon bungakushi*, which included writings of "history, philosophy, political studies and also science," highlights the mutual relationship between the writings and socio-political phenomena: "literature is affected by politics, influenced by religion, and accompanies the transformation in feelings and customs," but literature also takes on power of its own and "becomes that which affects politics, religion, emotions and manners."[14] In his *Kokubungakushi jikkō*, Haga also claims, "The individual was produced by the historical time and expressed the historical time through literature, but the individual also shaped the spirit of the time."[15] As many critics have noted, among the many objectives that literary historians had was the production of a national collective with a shared history by identifying the "Japaneseness" inscribed in literary works.

The link between literature, history, and nation that these literary histories infallibly create must be examined in the context of the "new modern time" that Japan adopted in the first decade of Meiji period, which significantly altered the sense of time and space. As shown by Narita Ryūichi, and later more extensively by Stephan Tanaka, Japan adopted the Western calendar in 1873, which forced people to reorient their lives.[16] One of the decisive changes here can be seen in the redefinition of nature, with which the lunar calendar had close affinity. Nature was reconfigured as "milieu," a conceptual site that provided the means to permanence and transhistorical spirit. Tanaka discusses how the discovery of "milieu" in the Japanese archipelago—and hence the removal of nature's earlier significance—allowed historians to find a shared space that linked the people of the past to the present as "Japanese." The production of history as narrative, as Tanaka aptly points out, must also be historicized in this context, because it is history that "provides the technology to establish that permanence of place and simultaneously a narrative of change (development)."[17] The result of this narrative was on the one hand a sense of the global (because it shares a narrative structure with its Western counterparts) and on the other a sense of the particular of being "Japanese." The apparently contradictory forces of permanence and change are inscribed in narratives of literary history, which is clearly implicated in this new linear, homogeneous time.

In defining *kokugo*, Ueda retained the internal focus, one that is similar to the literary historians. In his "Kokugo to kokka to," Ueda claims the following:

> The language that a given citizenry (*jinmin*) speak and their characteristics are very intricately connected. What one citizenry feels via a phenomenon or what the citizenry thinks about anything is reflected in its language. Thus I do not hesitate to designate language as a manifestation of the speakers' thoughts and emotions in their spiritual life.[18]

His definition of language is almost identical to how literary historians situated "literature." Yet Ueda departs radically from that perspective by focusing on the "present." In "Nihon gengo kenkyūhō" ("Research Methods on the Japanese Language"), a text based on a lecture Ueda delivered in 1889, he says:

> Language has life and death. Language has its genealogy. In the language we now employ, there are things that have been alive for decades and others that have been assimilated recently. . . . The benefits will be great if we investigate what currently exists as compared to investigating photographs.[19]

By "photographs," he means written scripts, and I will return to his focus on spoken language later in the chapter. But what he is promoting here is a focus on what "currently exists," rather than going back into the past like literary historians. This focus on the present can also be seen from his "Kokubungaku shogen" ("Preface to National Literature"), compiled in 1890. A textbook of national literature, which primarily takes quotes from the Tokugawa and Meiji periods, this text was written prior to his trip to Germany. The plan was to publish a series of volumes, but they never appeared. In planning these volumes, however, Ueda interestingly reversed the conventional order and started with the "present."[20] Literary history of the time typically began in antiquity and proceeded to the present, tracing the "Japaneseness" that had seemingly existed from antiquity. As we saw in the previous chapter, *kokubun* scholars attempted to define what made certain prose or poetry "Japanese," focusing on things like *te ni o ha* particles. This was, of course, an attempt to privilege the *kundoku* style, a local system of grammar that parsed *kanbun*, and hence differentiating (or constructing) "Japanese" prose from *kanbun*. Ueda's insistence on the present went directly against such a method of producing "Japan." The implication of Ueda's rejection is rather radical. In the creation of *kokugo*, when the constructed continuity of a nation is of utmost importance, *kokugo* in Ueda's conceptualization severs itself from the past. It features a revolutionary view, an attempt to "nationalize" by rejecting the past. Perhaps more accurately, the past by which "Japan" was constructed until now is rejected.

I do not mean to posit Ueda as an anti-nationalist or non-nationalist. After all, he posits "Nihongo" as "the spiritual blood of the Japanese people."[21] In many ways, it is precisely because he conceptualized *kokugo* as an imperial language that ought to be spoken by those beyond "Japan" that he had to sever his *kokugo* from the "Japaneseness" that was created by literary histories. This "Japan" was too limited, as literary histories, through the privileging of the "milieu," posited the link between language and the political, the social and natural environment. In such a paradigm, the "shared Japan" is geographically and socially bound. In order to posit *kokugo* as the unifying force of Asia, the embodiment of "imperial whiteness," Ueda needed to sever *kokugo* from the literary history model. Ueda thus negates one form of the "national" and nationalism to re-form it with the more expansive view of conceptualizing an empire. Yet, as we have seen, he retains a part of the Taine model, the "internal focus" that is further evidence of the logic of "naturalization" that we saw earlier. This is inextricably linked to his privileging of the *yamato minzoku*. In this paradigm, *yamato minzoku* will always be the most authentic and "natural" speakers of the Japanese language. In order to sustain this center, everyone else will be "racialized" or marked as "a minority" that can only fall short of linguistic mastery.

It must also be noted that in the literary history model, race does not appear as an index of identity; instead, the subjects are "Japanese people" or "our people." There is here an erasure, suggestive of a disavowal. Given that Japan entered an already heavily racialized world order, it was vital to disavow "yellowness." *Minzoku* (what eventually became ethnicity or ethnic nation) was produced as a focal point by which to differentiate the Japanese from the Chinese and Koreans and hence claim superiority. The Japanese could disavow their "yellowness" if they could act "white" vis-à-vis the rest of East Asia. This is part of the reason why the terms *jinshu* and *minzoku* were still in flux at the time of Ueda's writing. The textual fluctuations show us that these indexes of identity do not have any fixed, concrete existence. Japanese intellectuals were still probing various ways in which they could act "white," whether consciously or otherwise. To ignore such fluctuation and focus exclusively on ethnocentrism, therefore, can only result in complicity with this disavowal.

The link to *kokugo* and Japanese thoughts (*shisō*) and emotions needs further elaboration, especially in light of how such discourse was later used in the colonies to justify Japanese language education. On the one hand, it is something "internal" and hence limited to the so-called "Japanese people." But it is also a *shisō* that Japan attained through its efforts to "modernize" since the Meiji Restoration. And *kokugo* is the ultimate embodiment of this "modernized" Japan. This is precisely why Ueda retains the link between *shisō* and internal life that was employed by literary historians. Language embodies the development of *shisō*—and that is precisely the "Japanese" (modern) *shisō* that ought to be disseminated in the colonies.

Such privileging of *kokugo* is everywhere apparent, especially as a regulative idea by which other languages were studied in the framework of comparative linguistics. Comparative linguistics was a form of "science" not only in Japan but throughout Europe. Take for instance an example I gave earlier in chapter 1 of this book, an ideological view proposed by Friedrich von Schlegel (1772–1829): Indo-European languages were "inflectional languages," which, Schlegal claimed, could express "complex ideas through a single word: the root contains the main idea, the syllables that serve to form derived words express accessory modifications, and the inflections express variable relations." For Schlegel, these languages, as the most advanced form of languages, were the only medium that could bring about "any improvement of the human spirit."[22] Notice here the inextricable link between language and human "progress." In contrast, the "isolating languages," among which he classified "Chinese," showed no inflection, were "made up of monosyllables that we cannot even call roots," and could only be "lifeless," hence the least advanced and an impediment to progress.

Ueda's curriculum in Hakugengaku (then a term for Linguistics) at Tokyo Imperial University, through which he produced a great many linguists who were deployed to the colonies to theorize Japanese language education, was primarily comparative linguistics. Ogura Shinpei (1882–1944) focused on Korean, Iha Fuyū on the Ryūkyū language, Kindaichi Kyōsuke on Ainu, Ogawa Naoki on Taiwanese—in fact, he was later sent to Taiwan to teach Japanese.[23] Kindaichi later recalls that the reason he selected the Ainu language was because Ueda lamented that there were no Ainu language specialists around him. Among the students, there was also Kanazawa Shōsaburō, who studied Korean, Ainu, and Ryūkyū, and would later go on to publish *Nikkan ryōkokugo dōkei ron* (*Common Origins of Japanese and Korean Languages*, 1910) and *Nissen dōso ron* (*Common Ancestry of Japanese and Koreans*, 1929), which I will touch upon later. I certainly cannot do justice to the details of the studies that these scholars offered. Of course, they were extremely sincere in their endeavors, attempting to lay out the varying structures of existing languages. Despite the varying nature of the studies, however, such comparative linguistics presented a structure of "knowledge" that was always already racialized, making *kokugo* the embodiment of "progress" among the "East Asian languages," the medium for human development to attain the desired level of whiteness.

In his *Kokugogaku jikkō* (*Ten Lectures of the Study of* Kokugo, 1916), Ueda delineates *kokugo*'s position vis-à-vis other East Asian languages. The Ryūkyū language, for example, is for him a "dialect" of *kokugo* and, despite its apparent difference, they are in a sibling relationship.[24] The Ryūkyū language, he claims, contains elements that are "extremely similar to quadrigrade conjugation (*yodan katsuyō*)" of *kokugo*, "a characteristic very similar to Japanese before the Nara period," suggesting that the Ryūkyū language is quite behind its time.[25] In his discussion of Korean, Ueda delineates their similarities and says the following:

> Despite the fact that Korean language and literature have such similar characteristics as our *kokugo* and share the history of development, they each differ markedly in the development of national literature (*kokumin bungaku*). In Korea, there is no such thing that can be called 'national literature' written in Korean in a pure sense. This is a result of the ethnic nation's character, but also their obsession with their admiration for the powerful and their devotion to Chinese literature. As a result, they never worked toward improving their own national language.[26]

This is rather ironic, as Ueda is critical of written language or what is considered to be national literature in Japan, but the supposed lack of national literature in Korea (which of course is not true) is used as a sign of backwardness, positing Japanese *kokugo* as more superior and hence more progressive.

How then were such ideological views applied to *kokugo* education in the colonies?

Kokugo education was not systematically carried out in all Japan's colonies. In more ways than one, it appears to have been a process of trial and error. Take Okinawa, for example. Despite what Ueda says about the affinity of the two languages, in practice, it was necessary to first train translators. After that, they created textbooks that would print Japanese with glosses in the Ryūkyū language.[27] In Korea, the Japanese language was taught in public schools even before the annexation of Korea in 1910, but the forceful implementation of Japanese-only education did not begin until the 1930s. The variation of the actual practices of *kokugo* education in the "colonies" is beyond the scope of this chapter. But it is worth noting the issues at stake when *kokugo* education in the colonies was contemplated, and how they engage with the racialization of language that I am discussing. To do so, let me focus on the project of assimilation in Korea.

As Yasuda Toshiaki succinctly discusses, after the annexation of Korea in 1910, the term 国語*kokugo* (or *kugo* in Korean), which until then referred to the Korean language, was changed to signify Japanese, and Korean simply became *Chōsengo* (or Korean).[28] The "Chōsen kyōikurei" ("Edict of Education in Korea"), published August 24, 1911, offers an interesting glimpse into the ideology underlying the educational policies to be implemented in Korea. Articles 2 and 8 are pertinent:

> Article 2: Education will be carried out based on the imperial edict to cultivate good and loyal national subjects (*kokumin*).
>
> Article 8: The common school (*futsū gakkō*) is a space that will offer common education (*futsū kyōiku*) that is the core of national subject education; it will be a place that is mindful of physical development, a place to teach *kokugo* and moral education to cultivate characteristics of national subjects and offer knowledge and techniques that are necessary for the lives of national subjects.[29]

Note the inextricable link established between *kokugo* and the production of loyal and upright national subjects, signifying "imperial subject" in these articles. *Kokugo* was further linked to the "modern," which is evident in *kokugo* textbooks. *Kokugo chōsa iinkai* (the Committee of *Kokugo* Research) was founded in 1902, with members such as Ueda Kazutoshi, Maejima Hisoka (the writer who called for the abolishment of *kanji* as early as 1867), and Ōtsuki Fumihiko, the compiler of the dictionary *Genkai* (*Sea of Words*). It published two textbooks based on members' research into various dialects: *Kōgohō* (*Grammar of Spoken Language*, 1916) and *Kōgohō bekki* (*Additional Grammar of Spoken Language*, 1917). In the preface to the latter work, Ōtsuki writes:

> In Tokyo, there is the imperial palace and the government. As a result, people of the entire country are beginning to emulate the Tokyo dialect. As such, it is clear that the Tokyo dialect needs to be the target for our spoken language of the entire nation. But the Tokyo dialect of the vulgar people has too strong an accent, so we can't take that. So we took as our target the language of those in Tokyo who are educated. In addition, we collected those words widely in use in the entire nation and set our rules. The rules of spoken grammar that we put forth in this book were produced in this manner. Taiwan and Korea have entered our honorable country. In order to make the vulgar natives (*dojin*) like those of us in this honorable country, it is first important to teach our spoken language.[30]

I will return to the issue of the Tokyo dialect later. The clear assumption in this passage is that Taiwanese and Korean natives are less developed and that the only way for them to "enter our honorable country" is through the language of *kokugo*. The Japanese language embodies "civilization." Such discourse was rampant around the time of annexation. Take, for example, Horie Hideo's 1905 essay entitled "Nihongo no sekaiteki chii" ("The Status of Japanese Language in the World"):

> Our *kokugo* is something that our fifty million compatriots are always speaking, communicating with one another and exchanging knowledge. The *shisō* of the Japanese ethnic nation (*minzoku*), the civilization itself, is engrained in our *kokugo*. *Kokugo* is not only our cherished treasure, but for anyone to engage with Japan, trade with us, wish to research our world, and desire to absorb oneself in the advantages of this civilization, it is of the utmost importance that they study this Japanese language.[31]

The more "inauthentic" speakers of *kokugo* (the language of whiteness) they can create, the more "authentic" the imagined dominant majority become. That is to say, by continuing to produce minorities and the less civilized other, the more "white" the "authentic" *yamato minzoku* become. Whiteness, which can never be fully accessed, can only be reaffirmed through the continuous reproduction of the less-white.

It was in this context that the theory of "common origins" of Japanese and Korean (both in terms of language and ethnicity) were introduced. Kanazawa Shōsaburō, who studied with Ueda at Tokyo Imperial University, delineated the commonality between Korean and Japanese in his *Nikkan ryōkokugo dōkeiron*, arguing that Korean was in fact a "branch of Japanese" (the English translation is provided along with the original text). The logical conclusion that one derives from such a theory is that precisely because of this, it is easy for Koreans to learn the "civilized" language of Japanese.[32]

The need for such "inauthentic speakers" is inextricably linked to the fact that *kokugo*, as defined by Ueda, has no fixed, concrete existence. This is clear from the fact that Ueda's rejection of the past is accompanied by his obsession with spoken language. In his "Nihon gengo kenkyūhō," he asserts that the object of linguistics is "language as such" (*gengo sono mono*), which he qualifies as the following:

> The most scientific definition of language is this: it is a spoken sound unit that is uttered by a person's mouth, heard by another person's ear; it is a sign (*fuchō*) that people use to communicate their thoughts. Language is sound, thus written script (*moji*) is not language. If one likens it to a person, [written scripts] are like photographs that capture one moment, one instance, which means that, while the sound can change, the script will remain the same. . . . Until now, it seems that scholars of Japanese language have only studied these photographs. I must say that they have only studied a single period of language.[33]

Here, "language as such" is defined first and foremost by "a spoken sound unit" uttered by someone and heard by another. Despite the fact that it is a "sign" (*fuchō*), it is defined against "written script," which, as Ueda's photograph metaphor tells us, does not manifest the change in sound. For Ueda, *kokugo* was equivalent to the language of "voice," and *bungaku* or *kokubun* was equivalent to the language of *moji* (letters). In other words, for Ueda, *gengo* (*kokugo*) and *moji* (*kokubun*) constituted two separate modes of expression, one via voice, and the other via letters.

Such emphasis on the present and "spoken" language engages well with the forms of linguistics that Ueda studied in Germany. As the study of Western linguistics tried to establish itself as part of the growing body of natural sciences in the nineteenth century, scholars sought to focus on "living" languages as opposed to "dead" languages, which were presumably the object of study of classical philologists from which linguistics sought to differentiate itself.[34] The "living" language referred to the language "currently in use," and precisely because of this, it privileged sound and the pronunciation of words and phrases.

What we find is a desire to sever "*gengo*" from all past writings; it was not only "literary writings," as many critics have pointed out. Such an interpretation derives from an anachronistic positing of the division between language (*gengo*) and literature (*bungaku*) that has yet to be produced.

We see here Ueda's desire to prioritize the present, and yet, significantly, this "present" does not include present writings. For Ueda, written scripts are like photographs that can only be a static representation of language at a given moment. As he acknowledges, language has a genealogy, but what makes something language is its phonetic manifestation in the present. It is only the sound that changes—or rather, it is the changes in sound that make a language, language. In effect, he proposes a radical reinvention of "language" through spoken sound. It must thus be noted that *gengo*, in this case, is far from an equivalent of Saussurean *langue*, as it completely excludes writing. In this dynamic, Ueda is still driven by the need to consolidate spoken language as *kokugo*, and writing with it comes sometime in the future.

But if Ueda were to reject all past writings, where then does he turn to create his *kokugo*? He must find an entirely different source of language that is untapped, or one that has yet to be *registered* as language. The implication is that anything that is already written, already somewhere functioning as a sign, cannot be included. Such production of language is fundamentally impossible. Language will always retain its past trace, whether spoken or written, whether one is conscious of this or not. For a given language to be a sign, it must fundamentally be repeatable, carrying within itself a trace of all previous utterances. A sign is a mark that is necessarily displaced from one utterance to the next, but a sign cannot be a sign without repetition.

What Ueda sought, however, was the production of new language through the collection of dialects that are actually being "currently used somewhere." In more ways than one, *Kōgohō* and *Kōgohō bekki*, the textbooks compiled and published in 1916 and 1917 that I referred to earlier, were clearly in line with his views. Take, for example, Ueda's "Hyōjungo ni tsukite" ("On Standard Language"), published over a decade before the textbooks. Here, he sets forth the need for a standardized language based on an extensive study of currently used language:

> Among the many languages that are spoken in one country, [the standard language] is one that most people everywhere in the country can understand, unlike the local dialects that are only spoken in a certain locale. . . . Although the standard language is an ideal form, if we trace its origin, it is one form of dialect. And that dialect, through a number of artificial polishings, attains transcendental status. . . . The standard language must correctly transcend local dialects. In addition, it must be collected and selected from the actually existing essence, to which we add our research and solidify unification. As such, the standard language must be one that is possible to be spoken in real life. No, it must be spoken by someone somewhere in the present.[35]

As we saw earlier in the preface to *Kōgohō bekki*, ultimately he and his followers selected the "Tokyo dialect of the educated men" to produce such standard language. But most importantly, there is an obvious contradiction in this passage that stems from the impossibility of what Ueda seeks. On the one hand, he claims that "standard language" is an "ideal" form of language that can be understood by people in the country. It is something that is "artificially" produced, one that "transcends" all local languages. Yet it is also something that "has to be spoken by someone somewhere in the present," as it is a language that is "collected." Ueda falls into a bind here: he must acknowledge the non-existence of standard language, as it has to be artificially produced. Yet it must be an existing language.

It is important to recall that the desire underlying Ueda's project is to create a new "national," based on a language that can be equal to English, French, and other colonialist languages, which will eventually become "the common language of Asia." Whether or not Ueda was actually conscious of this is not an issue. But the rejection of "writing" and positing of the "spoken" is not just about implementing the cutting-edge German linguistic theories he had studied. In light of the contemporaneous movement to construct "Japan" and "Japaneseness" through preexisting texts that were linked to the *volk* of the nation, Ueda's obsession with spoken language represents a radical rejection of a certain type of nationalism. At the level of methodology, Ueda was also arguing against the attempt to find a standard of grammar in past writings; the standard for consolidating his *kokugo* had to be found in the present—in the spoken language which had yet to be developed. He thus sought to create *kokugogaku* as a study to establish *kokugo*. His rejection of the past, therefore, was not limited to past writings, but was also the study of them. What he sought, in other words, had yet to exist: both language as *gengo* and the form of study that produces this language.

Yet in "Hyōjungo ni tsukite" such rejection leads him to a paradox, an interesting one that requires unpacking. As Ueda himself admits, the standard language does not exist; it can only be an ideal form. Spoken languages vary infinitely, and it is, as Ueda's definition of sound (language) suggests, constantly changing. Any attempt to halt the changes, which is ultimately what "standardization" signifies, can only fall short. And yet, it must also be said that it is precisely this gap between the "ideal" and the "actual" that allows Ueda to empower *kokugo*. *Kokugo* is an idea that is empty; it is an ideal form to which one aspires and yet one can never actually reach.

Ueda was certainly not alone in conceptualizing a language based on collection of dialects. Although he was the central figure in these projects, there were many similar attempts that endorsed Ueda's views. Take the many *kōgo bunten* (spoken language dictionaries) that began to appear around at the turn of the century. Even when Ueda himself was not involved in their compilation, they specifically excluded the many "literary" works that sought to incorporate *genbun'itchi* prose. Furthermore, many *kōgo bunten* took the form of "collection" of dialects. In effect, a discursive condition in which the idea of collection of dialects leads toward the establishment of *kokugo* began to gain consensus around this time.

There is also a regional specificity in standard language. Ueda claims that it ought to emulate a specific Tokyo dialect: "What I mean by Tokyo language refers to the language that educated people speak in Tokyo."[36] By "educated" he is defining it against "Edo dialect" such as ベランメー. Interestingly, however, while the many *kōgo bunten* often designate Tokyo dialect as the potential standard, most spend more time and space "collecting" not the Tokyo dialect but other local dialects.[37] In effect, here too, we find a gap between the ideal and actual: Tokyo dialect, which is presumably the model of "ideal," remains empty, while the actual "collection" is centered on local dialects. In effect, the ideal form (that is, Tokyo dialect) is being produced precisely through local dialects. It is a formation through the identification of "deviation": once the "deviation" is identified, so is the "standard" form. I must of course add here that "local dialects" are also being produced in this process as "deviation."

Whether Ueda was conscious of this or not, the emptiness of *kokugo* is precisely what allowed him to empower *kokugo* as an object of desire. This is precisely the structure of racialization. It is not present, but it appears to be present. It is an object that can never be possessed, but it is supposed to be somewhere. The many subsequent reforms in the colonies thus featured a production of imperfect/inauthentic "Japanese speakers," the invariably hierarchized "subjects" who "desire" to belong to the Japanese Empire, thereby further enabling *kokugo* to act "white." Such repetition can only empower it even further.

When scholarship focuses almost exclusively on ethnocentrism in Ueda's language reform, it loses sight of racialization and becomes complicit with the project of racialization itself. It is around the time Ueda was writing that the concept of *minzoku* became stablized as ethnicity or ethnic nation, though his own writings still show some instability. Race was always on the minds of Japanese intellectuals, who were forced to negotiate with their violently labeled "yellowness." In order to disavow this "yellowness" and act "white" in East Asia, they began to revolve their entire nation/empire building project around ethnocentrism. The absence of race in previous scholarship is also symptomatic of the archive-centered Japan Studies field. By simply focusing on the object of knowledge, one can completely lose sight of this disavowal.

I cannot overemphasize the importance of reinscribing race in our work to critically engage with our field. The very fact that Japan Studies exists in its current form is already a product of racialization. Just as a racialized worldview entered Japan in the Meiji period as a form of science, we too have inherited the structure of the forms of knowledge which are very much implicated in such a framework. We don't have to look too far. Western philosophy presents itself as the "normative philosophy" while "Japanese philosophy" is merely a yellow version of that. Area Studies, which was produced as the world reorganized itself at the end of World War II with the United States as center, reproduces this framework. If we simply ghettoize ourselves in the "study of Japan" as an object, without calling attention to how such an object becomes constituted in the first place, and without calling attention to the always already structured raciality inscribed in it, we can only become complicit with this structure of racialization.

5

Tropes of Racialization in the Works of Natsume Sōseki

This chapter complements the previous one, analyzing the works of Natsume Sōseki by returning to the tropes of racialization. As I stated in the introduction, I seek to make several interventions by bringing in Sōseki here. First, this will allow me to address one problem in Japan Studies scholarship where Ueda is often attacked as an evil linguistic nationalist while Sōseki is deemed a figure of resistance to nationalism and imperialism. Such a tendency is extremely reductive, as it refuses to consider modernity in a structural sense.

Second, apart from a few essays on rhetoric that Sōseki wrote—like "Shaseibun" ("On Sketching," 1907) and "Sōsakuka no taido" ("On the Attitude of Creators," 1908)—Sōseki's works are rarely taken up in the scholarship on language reform. Of course, Sōseki was a fiction writer, but his theoretical works, such as *Bungakuron* (*Theory of Literature*, 1906) and *Bungaku hyōron* (*Literary Criticism*, 1907), offer a radical view of language, providing a unique alternative to those of Ueda and the other advocates of reform. Furthermore, they responded to a shared historical time. As we shall see below, not only Ueda but Sōseki also engaged with the notion of literary history prevalent in their era.

Finally, introducing race into this dynamic is an important intervention in itself. Race studies have long contemplated the link between race and language, while studies of language reform have continued to efface the inextricable role race played in the formation of "national languages." The concealment of such major indexes of identity—which the proponents themselves often recognized—should by no means be reified through our practices. As I will delineate later in the chapter, Japan Studies in North America has been complicit in the effacing of race as a major index of identity.

In order to free race from biologism, I will continue to construe race not as a fixed category, but as a fluid one. As I have discussed, "civilization," and hence race, embodies a movement toward "whiteness." The telos that is "whiteness" is inextricably linked to "privilege," whether it be the "West" in all its incarnations, social status, "cultivated taste," or the "proper" use of language—such as pronunciation, grammar, and so forth. These are means to racialize and thus produce a hierarchy among people. Without thinking about race in this way, it is impossible to understand how racial categories have transformed throughout the course of history. Such a view of race is vital to analyzing Sōseki's works and, more broadly, to understanding the complexity of race that lies at the core of modernity.

Although the primary focus of this chapter is Sōseki's theoretical works, I will first discuss his other works, particularly *Sanshirō* (1908) and "Mankan tokoro dokoro" ("Travels in Manchuria and Korea," 1909) where tropes of racialization surface compellingly. I do so for two primary reasons. The first is to show how conscious Sōseki was about race, how racial tropes figure ubiquitously in his works. Second, it will also allow me to highlight the problematics of Sōseki scholarship, especially the way scholars treat racial tropes evident in his works. I should add here that my interest is not to determine whether Sōseki was a nationalist or not or even racist or not. Such questioning is itself rather naïve, as it individualizes issues that are by nature structural. By uncovering the tropes of racialization embedded in his works, I will show that the complexity of race and nation eludes such manner of problematization.

THE FLUIDITY OF RACE IN SŌSEKI'S WORKS

As I mentioned, there has been a strong trend in Sōseki scholarship to valorize him as an anti-imperialistic, anti-colonialist figure. Komori Yōichi has, in his various works on Sōseki, been representative of this trend, but he is definitely not alone.[1] In the last decade or so, however, this trend has begun to be questioned. Park Yuha, for example, boldly shows in her *Nashonaru aidentitī to jendā* (*National Identity and Gender*) that such an image is symptomatic of a desire to make Sōseki more admirable than he actually was, and is the mere result of disavowing the many textual manifestations of Sōseki's clear imperialistic tendencies. In addition, Shibata Shōji's *Sōseki no naka no "teikoku"* (*"Empire" Within Sōseki*) also examines the ubiquity of imperialist discourse in Sōseki's oeuvre. As these works show, Sōseki was very much a product of his time.

Valorization of the West, together with anti-Chinese sentiment, defined Japan's modernization process in a variety of ways, and these appear everywhere in Sōseki's fiction, essays, journal, and letters. One obvious example is "Mankan tokoro dokoro," a travelogue that he wrote based on his visit to the colonies upon the invitation by the then president of the South Manchurian Railway Company, Nakamura Zekō (1867–1927). The following is a notorious passage where Sōseki describes the "Chinese coolies" that he sees upon arriving in Manchuria:

> On the pier, there were crowds of people; most of the people there, however, were Chinese coolies. Even one of them appeared filthy, but two together was even more unsightly (*migurushii*). When they were all huddled together, however, it was indecent (*futeisai*). . . . As soon as we had docked, the crowd of coolies started buzzing and swarming like angry wasps.[2]

As many scholars have pointed out, Sōseki here uses the discourse of hygiene, a discourse of modern superiority. Sōseki further animalizes the "coolies" here. In fact, throughout the text, he repeatedly characterizes the "coolies" as having physical prowess that Japanese could never have, endowing the former with a rather primitive animalism. Such an association between coolies and animals is clearly on par with a common racist discourse to which the Japanese were also subjected, as the Russian Tsar Nicholas II famously referred to the Japanese as "monkeys" during the Russo-Japanese War.

Scholars have debated much about this kind of vulgar racism in "Mankan tokoro dokoro," but there are also more subtle forms of racial tropes in this text. Take a look at the following passage, where Sōseki expresses a sense of surprise upon finding beautiful architecture in Fushun when visiting a coal mine:

> When we went up on to the embankment where the water tower had been erected, I was able to take in the whole town at a glance. It had not yet been completed, but all the buildings were brick and the architecture was even worthy of illustration in *Studio*. One would have never imagined that this place was managed by Japanese. . . . The buildings included a church, theater, hospital, school, and, needless to say, the miners' living quarters. It would have been great to take them to the center of Tokyo and gaze at during a walk. When we asked Matsuda, he informed us that they had been built exclusively by Japanese engineers (*SZ* 16:253; tr. 133).

The buildings do not appear to be "managed by Japanese," suggesting that they look "Western" as they are "worthy of illustration" in the English journal *Studio*. Sōseki is then told that they were indeed built by Japanese engineers. The center shifts here—the West is the ultimate center, but the Japanese, who are capable of reproducing such buildings in Fushun, act "white" in the colonies. The desire to make Japan "white" exists strongly in Sōseki, as it did in many of his contemporaries.

We must be cautious about overemphasizing what we may refer to as "vulgar racism," as this might make us lose sight of the complexity that is involved in the issue of race. Take the following passage from Park, where she discusses Sōseki's overtly imperialistic gaze, inscribed in his characterization of the same "Chinese coolies":

> Sōseki's gaze vis-à-vis this 'filth' is clearly in accord with that of the South Manchurian Railway Company (SMR) = imperialism. What brings about this gaze is precisely the self-awareness of an 'enlightened figure' (*bunmeijin*) that, like the SMR, attempts to exclude the unhygienic and unsanitary. Such a gaze, shared by the SMR and Sōseki, goes beyond the simple sense of surprise in seeing "differences" and becomes

> "discriminatory." This was precisely because hygiene had established itself as an ideology for the strong nation-state, which invariably produced discrimination. When such a gaze is projected on to other ethnicities and nations, it produces racism.[3]

To be fair to Park, I must add here that she is arguing against scholars who view Sōseki as an anti-imperialistic and anti-colonialist figure who existed beyond racism. Too many scholars, including such critics as Kawamura Minato, have taken up "Mankan tokoro dokoro" and remarked that Sōseki was being "humorous," and hence "lacked the feeling of racism."[4] Yet Park's desire to establish Sōseki as an imperialist figure leads her, perhaps inadvertently, to simplify racism and categories of ethnic difference. I do not disagree that the gaze here is imperialistic. But racism is not limited to such a gaze being "projected on to other ethnicities and other nations," as Park claims. This gaze is racist even within a single nation or ethnicity. To perceive racism only when such a gaze is applied to other nationalities or ethnicities can only reify and ultimately endorse the biologism of racial or ethnic categories. In effect, despite Park's desire to expose Sōseki's uncritical application of imperialist tropes, her failure to question the fixed binary of self and other makes her own work complicit with this same structure of racism.

We must again remind ourselves that neither race nor ethnicity is a fixed category. In fact, as we shall see later, the same racializing gaze is, in Sōseki's works, projected onto others within the confines of Japan. I should also add that Park is in fact quite conscious of the internal hierarchy that exists within Japan. In her other chapters on Sōseki, for example, she explores how the countryside is discovered as an "inferior" place, against which Tokyo as center can claim its status as enlightened.[5] Significantly, however, race is not introduced in this discussion. That is to say, Park would not characterize this as racial discrimination. Despite her otherwise compelling analysis of imperialist discourse in Sōseki, she either disregards race or only mobilizes it when it is projected onto an ethnic or national other. I cannot stress highly enough the importance of freeing the discussion of race from biologism and reified ethnic categories. If we consider racism to be produced only when national or ethnic boundaries are crossed, we inevitably fix race as that which exists objectively in the world.

Such biologism further makes us lose sight of the complex ways in which Sōseki addressed the issue of race. Take his 1908 *Sanshirō*, for example. At the beginning of this well-known novel, the namesake protagonist travels to Tokyo from his native Kyūshū to begin his illustrious career at Tokyo Imperial University. At the time, one had to be a graduate of one of eight *kōtō gakkō* (or "colleges") around the country to even be eligible to take the entrance examination at Tokyo Imperial University, thus effectively marking Sanshirō as "white" and part of the elite. Yet he is also "black," as he is described as a "black man from Kyūshū" (*Kyūshu no otoko de iro ga kuroi*) who is likened to the African prince Oroonoko.[6] As the train travels to Tokyo, Sanshirō notices women's skin color "gradually becoming whiter" (*shidai ni shiroku naru*) (5). Precisely because of this, Sanshirō notices the woman he ends up spending the night together with at an inn in Nagoya, characterizing her as "*iro ga kuroi*," or "black," which he further describes as a "Kyūshū color" (5). In Meiji Japan, Tokyo was a center marked as white, while Kyūshū was a "backward" site associated with "black" people. Kyūshū continues to be described as a "backward" site, as shown by Sanshirō's dialogue with a fellow student:

> 'Where did you go to college?'
>
> 'Kumamoto.'
>
> 'Oh, really? My cousin went there. I heard it's a terrible place.'
>
> 'Yes, barbaric' (142; tr. 114).

What is important here is that racial hierarchy is mobilized not only with the non-Japanese, but within the confines of Japan itself. In other words, contrary to what Park believes, anyone can be subjected to this racial discourse in Sōseki's works. Moreover, race is not fixed in *Sanshirō*, as mobility is not restrictive, which is evident from the fact that Sanshirō, a "black man" from Kyūshū, can become "white" as a Tokyo Imperial University student. Using the movement of the train from Kyūshū to Tokyo, which aligns with skin color "gradually becoming whiter," Sōseki suggests a teleological movement toward whiteness, a movement toward civilization, here clearly embodied by Sanshirō.

To further this racialization of center-periphery, *Sanshirō* even hierarchizes "Westerners." Take the following scene where Sanshirō and a man whom we later discover is Hirota Sensei encounter "Westerners" at a train station:

> Sanshirō noticed four or five Westerners strolling back and forth past the train window. One pair was probably a married couple; they were holding hands in spite of the hot weather. Dressed entirely in white, the woman was very beautiful. Sanshirō had never seen more than half a dozen foreigners in the course of his lifetime. Two of them were his teachers in college, and unfortunately one of those was a hunchback. He knew one woman, a missionary. She had a pointed face like a smelt or a barracuda. Foreigners as colorful and attractive as these were not only something quite new for Sanshirō, they seemed to be of a higher class (*jōtō*). He stared at them, entranced. Arrogance from people like this was understandable. He went so far as to imagine himself traveling to the West and feeling insignificant among them. When the couple passed his window he tried hard to listen to their conversation, but he could make out none of it. Their pronunciation was nothing like that of his Kumamoto teachers (19; tr. 15).

Just as the Kyūshū Japanese are racially marked as "inferior" to those in Tokyo, so too are the Westerners here. In comparison to the beautiful couple that Sanshirō sees, the Westerners in Kyūshū whom he had met were a "hunchbacked" teacher or a woman with a face like a fish. Moreover, the pronunciation of the language they speak, which is clearly a marker of class, had been entirely different from that of the Westerners in Kumamoto. In other words, in *Sanshirō* even the Westerners become "whiter" as they approach Tokyo, which greatly highlights the fluidity of race. In more ways than one, what Sōseki demonstrates is that there is no essential whiteness, for this category is internally divided. We can only speak of whiteness in the plural, and this difference is profoundly hierarchal.

Hirota's view, on the other hand, appears to reify the common understanding of Westerners. Looking at the same couple, he says the following:

> 'Beautiful,' he murmured, releasing a languorous little yawn. Sanshirō realized what a country boy he must appear; he drew his head in and returned to his seat. The man sat down after him. 'Westerners are very beautiful, aren't they?' he said. . . . 'We Japanese are sad-looking things next to them. We can beat the Russians, we can become a "first-class power," but it doesn't make any difference. We still have the same faces, the same feeble little bodies' (20; tr. 15).

Hirota homogenizes the Westerners as a superior race, while degrading all Japanese as having the "same faces, the same feeble bodies." Later in the novel, Sanshirō asks Yojirō about Hirota: "He talks about how dirty Tokyo is and how ugly the Japanese are, but has he ever been abroad?" Yojirō responds, "Are you kidding? . . . He's like that because his mind is more highly developed than anything in the actual world. One thing he does do is study the West in photographs. He's got tons of them—the Arc de Triomphe in Paris, the Houses of Parliament in London—and he measures Japan against them!" (76; tr. 63). There is an internal contradiction in *Sanshirō*, as the text shows: on the one hand, Sanshiro's musings on the various kinds of "whiteness," on the other Hirota's comments on whiteness as fixed and homogenous. In the secondary scholarship, Hirota has often been equated with Sōseki himself, and precisely because of this, his views have been privileged. However, it is clear that Sanshirō's reflections on the internal hierarchy that exists between Westerners, as well as the various instances in the text that use racial tropes to organize the modern world in which *Sanshirō* takes place, destabilize the view that Hirota posits.

Even among the Tokyo elites, there exists a racialized hierarchy that defines them. The constant reminder that Sanshirō is a Kyūshū "black" man is one such example, but women are of course not exempt from this dynamic. Mineko, the heroine with whom Sanshirō falls in love, is endowed with many markers of whiteness: she is talented in English; Sanshirō is always noticing her "white teeth"; she has a white flower with her when Sanshirō first sees her; Sanshirō is awed by her Western-style living room. Many of the male characters further refer to her as "an Ibsen woman." Interestingly however, her skin is described as follows:

> [Sanshirō] thought about the skin of the young woman he had seen by the University pond. It was a tawny, foxlike shade, the color of a lightly toasted rice cake, its texture incredibly fine. That was the only way for a woman's skin to be (34; tr. 27).

In contrast, Yoshiko, a sister of Nonomiya, the man whom, we presume, Mineko was going to marry, is described as *aojiroi* ("pale" but literally "blue-white"), despite being a Kyūshū woman. Why are these racial markers present? Both Mineko and Yoshiko are "white" to the extent that they are sisters of Tokyo Imperial University graduates, are well-educated, and are expected to marry into the elite circle. Yet the decisive difference is that Nonomiya's wealthy parents, who send money to buy Yoshiko a violin, are alive, while Mineko's are not. This becomes apparent when Mineko's brother Satomi Kyōsuke decides to marry. Mineko must be married off first, as her brother can only take care of one dependent. Mineko and Yoshiko are exchangeable to the degree that they are both sisters of elites. So as to highlight this point, the man Mineko marries at the end of the novel is someone who had initially asked for Yoshiko's hand. Yoshiko had the luxury to refuse to marry, but Mineko did not. It is as if Sōseki is highlighting the fact that race is about class and privilege.

As Shibata Shōji has shown, Tokyo elites in the novel are endowed with a racial duality.[7] Again, Sanshirō is a Kyūshū "black" boy at Tokyo Imperial University—Shibata in fact remarks that *shiro*, the term for white, can be found in Sanshirō's name.[8] Mineko, with all her markers of whiteness, has tawny skin. Hirota Sensei, allegedly the most sophisticated intellectual, who has a nose that is "so very straight it looked Western," is referred to as "great darkness" (*idainaru kurayami*) (14, tr. 11; 128, tr. 103). Shibata attributes such duality predominantly to the tension between the "modern" and "premodern," or more specifically, he claims that it represents "not only [Japan's] inability to rid itself of the premodern, but [that] modernization is being controlled precisely by it." He equates this with Sōseki's understanding of modernity.[9] Although I agree to an extent, it does not fully explain the complexity of this duality.

To further explore this point, let us continue to dwell on the representation of the center and periphery in *Sanshirō*. Interestingly, there is a strange temporal lag established between Tokyo and Kyūshū: in comparison to Tokyo, Kyūshū "was far away and had the fragrance of the past, of which Yojirō called the years before Meiji 15" (80; tr. 65). Yojirō also says to Sanshirō, "You just arrived from the provinces (*inaka*) of Kyūshū. Your brain is still back in Meiji 1" (72; tr. 59). On the one hand, Kyūshū represents the "past" from which Tokyo, as a "white" center, has already grown out of. However, Kyūshū is also valorized as a "nostalgic" site throughout the text. The nostalgic image of the mother constantly appears in the mind of Sanshirō as he tries to acclimate to Tokyo. When Sashirō first meets Yoshiko, another Kyūshū woman, she is described like this: "She smiled at him, moving the spare flesh of her cheeks, and her pallor took on a nostalgic (*natsukashii*) warmth," which evokes "a shadow of his mother at home far away" (59; tr. 49).[10] In addition, Kumamoto may be associated with "blackness" and "backwardness," but it is not without "light." Omitsu is a black-faced woman but her name, *mitsu* (光), also suggests "brightness." If Kyūshū is simply backward and premodern, why is it associated with "lightness" and a profound sense of nostalgia?

In more ways than one, Kyūshū is a site that is arrested in the past, a place that is not contaminated by the hustle and bustle of the city that is overwhelmed by "whiteness." Kumamoto, or the *inaka* in general, is often posited as a site of authenticity for any given nation-state. It is a place that is putatively left behind by the center, the movement toward civilization, but it is also a site that retains the precontaminated self. In this sense, it has a double role in sustaining the modern structure of the nation state. First, it becomes a reference point by which the center constitutes itself as superior and more progressive. Second, it is redefined as an unsullied place where the authentic "natives"—those who have yet to be contaminated by the center—exist. Of course, this space can only be putatively posited, because no place can be fully free of the movement toward modernization, as Sōseki was well aware. This is a structural issue for any nation-state. The countryside retains the remnant of the past while the center becomes increasingly "white," ostensibly destroying the national authenticity it once had. In such a way, the "fictive ethnicity" that binds the national community finds its home.[11] This cannot be characterized simply as a tension between the "premodern" and "modern"—it is the structure of modernity itself.

THE LITERARY HISTORY MODEL AND SŌSEKI'S INTERNAL FOCUS

As we have seen, there is a tension within which Sōseki posits racial tropes. On the one hand, there are, as in "Mankan tokoro dokoro," examples of what we may refer to as "vulgar racism," animalizing the coolies that he saw in Manchuria and describing them as "filthy." Yet, on the other hand, Sōseki also frees race from biologism and ethnic categories, and uses racial tropes to hierarchize those within the same ethnic nation. How does such duality play out in his theories?

Just like Ueda Kazutoshi, Sōseki engages with the literary history model I introduced in the previous chapter with Hippolyte Taine, which posits race as a defining index by which to compile works of literature. As we have seen, literary historians appropriated such models to posit a national collective with a shared history. Inscribed within it was an internal focus, where the texts were constantly linked to people's *shin-teki seikatsu* (internal lives) and *kanjō shisō* (emotions and thoughts). Ueda was no different in this regard. Despite his ultimate departure from it, Ueda retained the internal focus of this model because *kokugo* was defined as a means to solidify the national community. Sōseki's decision to revert to psychological theories in his definition of what he calls "literary substance" is not unrelated to such a focus on internal life. Moreover, literary history also used the historical divisions that corresponded with origin (*kigen*), development (*hattasu*), transformation (*hensen*), and decline (*suitai*). When Sōseki says, "I vowed to determine what psychological necessity there was for literature—for its emergence, its development and its decline," he was very much in the same vein as the history of his day.[12]

This internal focus that Sōseki deployed is inextricably linked to the objective of *Bungakuron*, which he lays out in his famous preface to the work. He ventured to "resolve the most essential question: What is literature?" after becoming aware of the following:

> In reflecting on my own past . . . I realized that, despite lacking a solid scholarly foundation in classical Chinese, I nonetheless believed myself able to appreciate fully the Confucian classics. Of course, my knowledge of English was not particularly deep, but I did not believe it to be inferior to my knowledge of classical Chinese. For my sense of like and dislike between the two to be so widely divergent despite my having roughly equal scholarly abilities must mean that the two were of utterly different natures. In other words, what is called "literature" in the realm of the Chinese classics and what is called "literature" in the realm of English must belong to different categories and cannot be subsumed under a single definition (*SZ* 18:9; tr. 44).

Many scholars have written on this well-known passage. Despite his "equal scholarly abilities" in English and classical Chinese, Sōseki could not understand why his sense of "like and dislike between the two [could] be so widely divergent." Based on the divergence of his "taste," therefore, Sōseki sought a definition of "literature" that could accommodate the works of *kangaku* and English. In other words, he sought a universal definition of "literature" that transcends national, cultural, and linguistic categories.

In order to clarify how Sōseki sets out to do so, let us briefly examine the famous formula (F+f) that he posits as "literary substance" (*bungakuteki naiyō*). For Sōseki, literary substance is represented through this formula, where F refers to "focal impressions or ideas" and f signifies emotive factors that are attached to F. It is important to understand F within the waveform of consciousness model: F is at the summit of the waveform as the focal point (where an idea or impression exists) and it is accompanied by f (emotions) at the lower fringes of consciousness. In other words, at a given moment, a given idea or impression appears to have focal intensity. When another F follows, the former F loses focus and is peripheralized in our consciousness.

This F is by no means easy to grasp. It is clearly in the mind, but Sōseki is silent as to how it gets there. When F constitutes itself as F, it is already an impression or a concept in the mind that is divorced from the specificity of expression. That is to say, he is silent about the process of mediation that invariably exists for F to be itself in the first place. In addition, the quotes he uses throughout *Bungakuron* are primarily derived from English sources, but the "Englishness" of the quotes are never brought to the fore. Moreover, he further refuses to translate them, whether the original be English, Japanese, or *kanbun*. The linguistic hierarchy that invariably exists between these languages are erased even in the act of writing *Bungakuron*. That is to say, all the languages are devoid of relation to one another.

It is probably obvious by now that Sōseki's choice to appropriate the internal focus inscribed in these literary histories critically departs from both Ueda and the literary historians. Following Taine's formula of "race-milieu-moment," literary historians sought specifically to produce a shared sense of "Japanese-ness" in the texts they compiled. Ueda, departing from this project and severing *kokugo* from "Japanese-ness," sought to define *kokugo* as an imperial language, hence a "white" language, whose most authentic speakers were *yamato minzoku*. What may have appeared to be a radical departure on the part of Ueda seems rather tame in comparison to what Sōseki attempted. By seeking to be equal to the West, Ueda reinforced the global racial organization within which Japan found itself, while Sōseki tried to posit (F+f) in a context completely severed from the global hierarchy of nation-states and of racial organization altogether.

Sōseki thus attempts to posit a linguistically-neutral entity in his formula (F+f), but there is an inevitable tension that arises from positing a universal, linguistically-neutral entity in order to define literary substance.[13] He is forced to theorize the manner in which to represent (F+f). It is precisely for this reason that he turns to rhetoric.[14] What was important for Sōseki is that rhetoric not only deals with representation, but traditional rhetoric assumes a universal idea that is unaffected by space and time. Its view of literature was represented by the famous phrase of Aristotle, "Poetry is finer and more philosophical than history; for poetry expresses the universal, and history only the particular." Poetics posits the *idea* through rhetorical tropes and figures, as it lends itself to the universal.

This view was one that was still prevalent among aesthetic theories of the eighteenth century.[15] With the trend toward empiricism, theorists began to privilege sensation and the direct experience of nature over the indirect experience of nature via linguistic representation. Nevertheless, they deemed that the degree of pleasure that these experiences produced was stronger in the latter than the former. Joseph Addison, for example, says the following about comparing nature and art:

> If we consider the works of *nature* and *art*, as they are qualified to entertain the imagination, we shall find the last very defective in comparison of the former; for though they may sometimes appear as beautiful or strange, they can have nothing in them of that vastness and immensity, which afford so great an entertainment to the mind of the beholder.[16]

Yet later he says the following:

> The pleasures of these secondary views of the imagination, are of a wider and more universal nature than those it has when joined with sight; for not only what is great, strange, or beautiful, but anything that is disagreeable when looked upon, pleases us in an apt description.[17]

In effect, "art" may be defective in comparison to "nature," but the pleasures of description are "wider and more universal" than the experience of nature by sight alone. As such, when mediated by language, nature is made more universal than nature itself. Language is not defined as a means for mimesis, but a means to the universal. This view was certainly not limited to Addison, but was a perspective shared by the aesthetic theories of such writers as Lord Kames and Edmund Burke.[18]

Catering to such idea of the universal behind traditional rhetoric, Sōseki thus attempted to retain F as a linguistic-neutral entity. Yet precisely because of this model, he inherited the problematic of direct and indirect experience, which perhaps unwittingly leads him into a bind. Sōseki's discussion on direct and indirect experience appears most concretely in Book II, Chapter 3, where he discusses the quantitative and qualitative changes in the emotive factor f. In his discussion of the illusions that are attached to emotive f, he says:

> It goes without saying that an emotive f that arises from direct experience and one that arises from indirect experience are different in terms of strength and content. This difference is the reason that things that are not acceptable in the natural world under ordinary circumstances become acceptable; things that are unpleasant to the ear or conditions ordinarily unbearable in the natural world can produce pleasure when transformed into indirect experience. In other words, when things that we do not consider beautiful or things that we long to eliminate both mentally and physically appear as f in literature, not only do we reserve our apprehension, but we at times tend to welcome them (*SZ* 18:113).[19]

Sōseki refers to this process as extraction (*chūshutsu*), which is a process of dissociation of self, morality, and intellect from the "real." For example, what one may deem terrifying in real life can take on beauty in literary expression. The "self" consciously or otherwise dissociates him or herself from real terror (and from the real eminent danger) and sees beauty in its representation.

What this discussion betrays is the very fact that (F+f) is a linguistic medium, which goes directly against Sōseki's attempt to neutralize it. If F is always already F, then whether the experience is direct or indirect should not even become a problem.[20] Critics have often noted the importance of universality in *Bungakuron*. However, they have linked it primarily to psychological theories, and as such, have often severed the link between language and F. Too often blindly following Sōseki's argument without questioning his confusion or contradictions, not many scholars have questioned the dilemma Sōseki found himself in.

There is also another glaring contradiction in *Bungakuron*. Despite all these attempts to universalize F and sever it from language, Sōseki uncritically posits a national community. This appears most compellingly in his positing of *shūgōteki* F (aggregate or group F), a discussion of which occurs in Book V of *Bungakuron*. We know that Sōseki was rather invested in this discussion, as he heavily edited his notes on Book V upon publication. Here he moves from the realm of psychology to sociology, from individual consciousness to collective consciousness.[21]

There are three types of group F, though the first, which he calls imitation (*mogiteki ishiki*), is perhaps the most pertinent:

> We call 'imitative' that consciousness easily dominated by outside forces. By dominated we mean to say that as it moves from A to B, it naturally falls into step with others and takes a similar course of action. In other words, it is the type of consciousness that arises from the imitation of taste, "isms," and the experience of others. Imitation is a necessary social glue. A society without imitation would be like a heavenly body ungoverned by the laws of gravity. It would splinter into pieces and before long would collapse altogether. . . . The ability to live in a society of adults without inviting constant mishaps indicates that one's thought, one's actions, and one's language (*gengo*) are adapted to that society (*SZ* 18:320–21; tr. 123–24).

Sōseki then goes on to say that while "normal imitation is done with subjective imitation," there are other forms of imitation that "are commanded by nature." These include "an imitation that is forced upon us by something stronger than individual will. Imitation tends to banish irregularities from society and bring each of its members into an orderly and equal (*byōdō*) array" (*SZ* 18:321–22; tr. 125). "Imitation," in other words, is a "glue" that sustains a community, which is "natural" or "commanded by nature." Moreover, it is quite compelling that this community is, among other things, defined by "thought" and "language." Such positing of a community is on a par with Hippolyte Taine's "race-milieu-moment," in which it is assumed that a given community has, inherent in itself, a natural commonality in "thought" and "language." In addition, it is one that aligns "its members into an orderly and equal array." Equality, as we saw in the previous chapter, is one major ideology of the nation-state which invariably hierarchizes its members, as differences will inevitably be identified. What Sōseki posits here, in other words, is the foundation of a racially-organized world order. Despite his rigorous analysis of the various categories he deploys, Sōseki is curiously silent on how such a "collective" comes into being. It is simply assumed. In effect, the racial hierarchy that he erased by concealing the means of representation is reintroduced in such a positing of group F. Nowhere in *Bungakuron* does he attempt to reconcile this contradiction.

BELLETRISTIC RHETORIC AND SŌSEKI'S "TASTE"

Let us now turn to another branch of rhetoric with which Sōseki engaged. Just as dominant as the psychological-philosophical vein of rhetoric was belletristic rhetoric, which is of particular interest here because of its emphasis on the development of "taste." Taste, it should be recalled, was the very reason why Sōseki began this monumental project in the first place. Let me first provide a brief discussion of the trends in belletristic rhetoric both in England and in Japan to contextualize Sōseki's project. Practitioners of belletristic rhetoric sought to cultivate people's taste through literary appreciation. The most prominent practitioner of belletristic rhetoric was Hugh Blair, whose *Lectures on Rhetoric and Belles Lettres* (1783) was widely read. Belletristic rhetoric thus engaged with the ongoing debate that developed throughout the eighteenth century on taste as a discriminator of aesthetic judgment. Just like the psychological-philosophical vein of rhetoric, it emerged as a movement against classical rhetoric. With economic development and the concomitant creation of a new reading public, needs of course changed. For those who lived in the world of commerce and trade, the power of persuasion in English was more valuable than knowledge of Greek or Latin, which was a reflection of upper-class erudition. Characterizing this shift and the rise of belletristic rhetoric, Wilbur S. Howell noted that it was "a change from the convention of imperial dress to the convention of the business suit."[22] Such a change also coincided with the development of nationalism, which further contributed to the shift toward English.

We must not forget that this shift was racialized. It was not a coincidence that English studies and belletristic rhetoric developed quickly in Scotland, as the need for formal training in English arose "to promote ethnic English culture among the Scottish middle class."[23] The Scottish were, in other words, not "white," and in order to assume "white" status, they had to master "Englishness." Sōseki found himself in the middle of such a racialized setting when he studied in England at the turn of the century. He tells us in the preface to *Bungakuron* that he first went to Cambridge to pursue his studies, but he was quickly disillusioned and considered going "north to Scotland or across the sea to Ireland" (*SZ* 18:6; tr. 41). Ultimately, he decided against it, since he "quickly realized that both places were ill-suited for the purpose of practicing English" (*SZ* 18:6; tr. 41). The meaning here is that "white" English was only spoken at the center. But the very reason that he considered Scotland and Ireland is precisely because "rhetoric" and "literature" were being taught outside of England.[24] In the mid-to-late eighteenth century, the University of Edinburgh developed a teaching curriculum of lectures based on selections taken particularly from English literature in order to produce young men with "cultivated English taste."[25] In describing Blair's work, Robert Crawford says, in his *Devolving English Literature*, that "Blair's works had been geared to a task of cultural conversion, of Anglicizing upwardly mobile Scots to make them acceptable Britons."[26] Racial hierarchy thus existed within one nation despite the seeming non-"biological" difference.

This exemplifies the "fictive ethnicity" around which a nation is produced. Along with pronunciation, "proper grammar," and so forth, the authentic imaginary majority possesses, within themselves, a "cultivated" taste to which all "non-whites" must aspire. This question of aspiration returns us to the question of racial teleology, the movement to become "white." Such an ideal majority does not, of course, exist, and precisely for this reason it is never achievable. What is important, however, is that the reality of achievability is present to foster the desire to become the authentic majority.

Works of belletristic rhetoric in Japan arose around the same time that literary histories began to be compiled, and closely followed their British counterparts in defining their own *raison d'être* in the cultivation of taste. The first work of impact was Takata Sanae's *Bijigaku* (*A Study of Belles Lettres*, 1889), followed by Tsubouchi Shōyō's *Bijironkō* (*Thoughts on Belles Lettres*, 1893) and Shimamura Hōgetsu's *Shin bijigaku* (*A New Study of Belles Lettres*, 1902).[27] Takata elsewhere preached the need to nurture "taste," the ability to distinguish the beautiful and non-beautiful, and explained that this was the primary reason he compiled *Bijigaku*.[28] While the modes of categorization in *Bijigaku*, such as the figure of speech and style of composition, were adopted from works of Western rhetoric, most notably Bain's *English Composition and Rhetoric*, the examples were primarily taken from Japanese and Chinese poetry.[29] *Bijigaku*, while establishing aesthetic criteria of style and expression, was the first to "cultivate the style of composition to express one's thoughts." Takata continues, "Only after studying rhetoric can one find a refined taste in literature; and once enlightened with a refined taste in literature, one's heart or mind will move toward loftiness and elegance, and further develop honor."[30] The study of rhetoric, which according to Takata cultivates refined taste, ultimately leads one to loftiness and elegance, which embodies national character. I must add here that insofar as it is an aspiration and thus a movement, it also threatens the very concept of national character, hence the need for a fictive ethnicity that is anchored in the past.

These works, used as textbooks, produced the ideal form of "national character," but their obsessive catering to Western rhetoric and style betrays their desire to become "white" at two levels: they claim whiteness by showing that Japanese examples adhere seamlessly to Western-style rhetoric, and they promise that the "taste" that is cultivated through the use of such rhetoric is "white." It was not a coincidence that Takata argued that English should become Japan's official language until two years prior to the publication of *Bijigaku*.[31] By virtue of the fact that these works were used as textbooks, they were endowed with an authority by which to judge what was (and what was not) cultivated taste. These texts became a standard by which the presumably "equal" speakers of the Japanese language were hierarchized.

Let us now see how Sōseki responded to this trend. As many critics have noted, the main concern with which Sōseki started out his project was how to theorize taste in universal terms.[32] In this sense, *Bungakuron* should have been more about small f than large F. Sōseki spends most of this long treatise discussing F, but he takes up taste again in *Bungaku hyōron*.[33] While contemporaneous studies of rhetoric sought to cultivate refined "national" taste, we again find Sōseki seeking "universality" in the domain of taste.

Sōseki first acknowledges that most experiences of taste are singular, that they very rarely match with others. But there are cases in which they *do* match, and some are actually a result of necessary correspondence. It is very rare, he says, to identify universal taste in the likes and dislikes of literary materials themselves, but we are very likely to find universality of taste in "order, length, and structure (*keizoku shōchō*) of materials used in literary works."[34] In other words, this universal taste is a reaction not to the material itself but to "the relationship and distribution between the materials." This is what he identified as "form" (as opposed to literary substance) in *Eibungaku keishikiron* (*On the Study of Form in English Literature*, 1924).[35] "Form," Sōseki argues, appeals to taste and can produce universal taste. Form is divided into three, descriptions of which he gives in English: "1) Arrangement of words as conveying the meaning, 2) arrangement of words as conveying combinations of sounds, 3) arrangement of words as conveying combinations of shapes of words."[36] Of course, he does not argue that universal taste can be claimed in all three cases: in fact, *Eibungaku keishikiron* is all about where to identify that universality. For example, he argues that the "arrangement of words as conveying the meaning" is the easiest for which to claim universality because they appeal to the intellect. As long as the arrangement of words follows the "intellectual flow," the demands of the intellect (which is universal) will be met (*SZ* 33:12). On the other hand, he says that the "arrangement of words as conveying combinations of sounds"—including the rhythm, melody and sound of words—is the most difficult for which to claim universality. The focus of his rigorous search for universality in taste is clearly on the formalistic aspect of language.

Let us compare Sōseki's discussion to Hōgetsu's *Shin bijigaku*, which was also greatly influenced by the study of psychological-philosophical rhetoric and in many ways shares much of the rhetorical paradigm. Despite the apparent similarity, we find that Hōgetsu arrives at completely opposite conclusions. In discussing the methods of study in rhetoric, Hōgetsu has the following to say:

> There are two parts to a study that takes a word as a base unit: one that studies the character of words and the other their mutual relationships. To study the character of the words, we identify their parts of speech based on types, and examine their inflection, conjugation, and change based on their usages. . . . The study of relationships between words theorizes concord, government, and order.[37] When two or more words are strung together, concord refers to the agreement of gender, number, tense and person; government refers to case relationship; and order refers to the sequence of nouns, verbs, etc. These rules all come from the customs (*shūkan*) of a given national language. They embody national characteristics. Within the respective national languages, what agrees with these rules ought to be deemed right and those that disagree ought to be considered wrong because of its divergence from custom.[38]

When Hōgetsu attributes such rules to custom, he has in mind, for instance, inverted phrases that are not necessarily in "logical" order. Here is an example he provides: he claims that "*boku wa Ōsaka e ikō*" (I am going to Osaka) is just as grammatically correct as "*ikō Ōsaka e*" (To Osaka, let's go), but he suggests that it may not be so in other languages.[39] According to Hōgetsu, therefore, rules that govern the sequence of words ought to be determined within a given national language because they embody national character.

For Sōseki, the formal aspect of language was a site of universality. Sōseki thus sought universality in the very area that his contemporaries sought national specificity. Sōseki's literary apparatus thus gives us a critical model by which to examine national literature and rhetoric, presenting itself as a foundation for multiple criticisms.

At the same time, however, we must again note Sōseki's duality. Despite these attempts to seek universality, he cannot escape positing the particular. Even *Bungaku hyōron*, a work that attempted to theorize "universal taste," is not exempt from this. Discussing the study of foreign literature, Sōseki claims:

> Japanese people do not have enough practice in English to make out the nuanced shades and tones. Thus there will be times when a foreigner might say that a given expression is obnoxious, whereas we don't find it so. There will be times that we gloss over as a common phrase what is actually lofty and divine. Japanese people are not very perceptive about these things and hence are probably not as acute as those scholars in England. . . . Without a doubt, this problem arises from the difference in languages . . . the common assumption that foreigners possess the standard by which to evaluate foreign literature, whereas we don't, and thus we must abide by their theory. . . . Until now you thought a certain way about a given work, but, listening to the criticism of Mr. X—which is very different from yours and which appears rather forced to you—you conclude that what he feels must be correct since he is a native critic. You then think that what you felt before must have been a mistaken and vulgar feeling, and since it is a mistaken feeling, it must be corrected. . . . You then begin to discard the feelings you had until then and move toward what you *think* is right (*SZ* 19:39–40; tr. 233–34).

As much as Sōseki is arguing against an uncritical valorization of native scholars' literary criticism, the units "we" (the Japanese) and "they" (the foreigners) remain completely fixed. That is to say, while he tries to critique the category of the "native," he remains in fact complicit with it, as the boundary between the self and other remains intact. Although Sōseki takes a critical stance via the creation of "Japanese-ness" in the development of bellestristic rhetoric in Japan, he here replicates the very units he questioned. Such an uncritical positing of the "Japanese" subject is, needless to say, integral to the racialized world order, which assumes a commonality and equality amongst those within the confines of Japan. It is a repetition of his Group F which he posited in *Bungakuron*, a collective that has "naturally" come together that shares language, thought, and action.

• • •

In lieu of a conclusion, I would like to end this chapter with an observation on Sōseki scholarship in North America. In light of the ubiquity of racial tropes in his works, it is rather astonishing that scholarship on Sōseki does not address it. In fact, the silence on racial tropes extends far beyond scholarly remiss, which is evident in the English translations of literary works. Take *Sanshirō*, for example. When Sanshirō notices the "skin color of women becoming progressively 'whiter,'" the translator, Jay Rubin, renders the passage as follows: "he had noticed the complexions of local women getting lighter and lighter."[40] I of course realize that translations of literary works need to read smoothly, and that they should avoid awkwardness in the English to make the work more accessible to the general public. But such racial erasure seems to be significant. I view this as symptomatic of our field, as it is consistent with other translations of modern Japanese fiction. Edwin Mcllelan, who translated Sōseki's *Kokoro*, commits a similar erasure. Here is the passage where the narrator describes the time he first spots Sensei at the beach: "I was in a relaxed frame of mind, and there was such a crowd on the beach that I should never have noticed him had he not been accompanied by a Westerner. The Westerner, with his extremely pale skin, had already attracted my attention when I approached the tea house."[41] What is translated as "extremely pale skin" is in Japanese "*sugurete shiroi hada*," which should perhaps be translated as "supremely white skin." In the novel, this is a decisive moment in which Sensei is marked as "white." For Sensei is, as we later find out, a graduate of Tokyo Imperial University who is wealthy enough to live with his wife without working.

Such a tendency of racial erasure is of course not limited to the works of Sōseki. In the translation of Mori Ōgai's "Maihime," or "Dancing Girl," by Richard Browning, when Toyotarō, the narrator/protagonist of this novella, first meets Elis, a German girl with whom he has an affair, he remarks how she was startled when he approached her "and stared at my yellow face" (*ki naru omote*). Browning translates this as "my sallow face."[42] Elis's face, on the other hand, is described as "*chi no gotoki iro no kao*," literally "a face that is like milk," which Browning ends up rendering as "pallid face."[43] The reference to his "yellow face" is an indication that Toyotarō is rather self-conscious of his "yellow-ness" in front of a "milky" white woman, but such an obvious indication of racialization is completely erased from the translation. I want to emphasize that I do not wish to disparage these translators. In fact, these works are all first-rate translations. However, we cannot simply brush these erasures aside as an attempt to avoid awkwardness in English. Rather, this is a structural problem of translation that reflects the field itself.

What then is the ideological ground upon which such effacement of racial tropes rests? While I can only provide a cursory observation here, it is first of all connected to the Cold War politics to which we owe the establishment of area studies, a structure of study with which we remain complicit even today. The translators I have cited are of the generation that was recruited to reconfigure the image of the "enemy Japanese" into that of the tamed, domesticated ally who were capable of understanding a "beauty" that was translatable to an American readership. This was vital in the Cold War era. At the same time, as Takashi

Fujitani has shown, it was also crucial for the United States to present an antiracist image of itself within the new world order, which had tremendous impact on postwar policies vis-à-vis Japan.[44]

Furthermore, "literature" became a site where the "universality of the human condition" was to be debated and learned.[45] Even the postwar SCAP-led educational reform designated literature as a vehicle for "the development of the human spirit." The Fundamental Law of Education (*Kyōiku kihonhō*, 1947) contains the following passage in its preface: "We shall esteem individual dignity and endeavor to bring up the people who love truth and peace, while education aimed at the creation of culture, general [*fuhen*] and rich in individuality, shall be spread far and wide."[46] In response to such calls for reform, high school textbooks at the time featured literary history, and defined literature as a site where "universal man" was to be discussed. This narrative tells us that "world literature," regardless of "linguistic" or "racial" differences, represents a site of "mutual understanding" given the universality of the realm of literature.[47] I am certainly not trying to claim that translators were conscious of racial erasure, as we cannot establish any facile causal relation between such institutional policies and individual choices. However, it is not too hard to imagine that these external forces somehow worked to conceal the racial tensions so obviously present in the Japanese texts. This type of universalism violently effaces the racialized world order and naively equates all people under the category of "human." At the same time, however, this category retains a telos of "whiteness."

I must emphasize here that the Cold War scheme is but one manifestation of the structural problems governing modernity, in which racial hierarchy is produced and reproduced. As much as we like to believe that we are now beyond such naivete, we become complicit with such erasure if we do not reinscribe race in our study.

NOTES

All translations from the Japanese, unless otherwise noted, are mine.

INTRODUCTION

1. See Lee Yeounsuk, *"Kokugo" to iu shisō* (Tokyo: Iwanami shoten, 1996); Osa Shizue, *Kindai Nihon to kokugo nashonarizumu* (Tokyo: Yoshikawa kōbunkan, 1998); Komori Yōichi, *Nihongo no kindai* (Tokyo: Iwanami shoten, 2000); Yasuda Toshiaki, *Teikoku Nihon no gengo hensei* (Tokyo: Seori shobō, 1997), *Kokugo to hōgen no aida—gengo kōchiku no seijigaku* (Tokyo: Jinbun shoin, 1999), and *"Kokugo" no kindaishi: teikoku Nihon to kokugo gakusha tachi* (Tokyo: Chūkō shinsho, 2006). In English, see also Paul H. Clark, *The Kokugo Revolution: Education, Identity and Language Policy in Imperial Japan* (Berkeley: University of California Press, 2009).

2. Works by Michel Foucault, such as *Discipline and Punish* (New York: Pantheon, 1977); *The History of Sexuality* (New York: Pantheon, 1978); and his numerous lectures on governmentality (see especially *Security, Territory, Population: Lectures at the College de France 1977–1978* [New York: République Française, 2007]), have been appropriated in numerous works.

3. See, for example, Yamamoto Masahide, *Kindai buntai hassei no shiteki kenkyū* (Tokyo: Iwanami shoten, 1965) and *Genbun'itchi no rekishi ronkō* (Tokyo: Ōfūsha, 1971).

4. Harry D. Harootunian, *History's Disquiet: Modernity, Cultural Practice, and the Question of Everyday Life* (New York: Columbia University Press, 2000), 48.

5. Harootunian, *History's Disquiet*, 46.

6. Benedict Anderson, *Imagined Communities: Reflections on the Origin and Spread of Nationalism* (New York: Verso, 1983).

7. Such a master narrative of preceding scholarship inevitably does violence to many brilliant analyses to which I am deeply indebted. There are also notable exceptions.

Nakayama Akihiko, for example, deliberately refuses to succumb to such ideological critiques. See, for example, "'Hon'yaku' suru/sareru 'kokugo-Nihongo,'" *Kan* (January, 2001): 152–62, and "Tonji toshite no kenryoku—Ueda Kazutoshi 'Kōgohō' 'Kōgohō bekki,'" *Bungaku* (March-April, 2006): 127–41. See also Sakai Naoki, *Shizan sareru Nihongo Nihonjin: "Nihon" no rekishi-chiseiteki haichi* (Tokyo: Shin'yōsha, 1996) and Kamei Hideo, *Meiji bungakushi* (Tokyo: Iwanami shoten, 2000).

8. Yasuda Toshiaki, "Kindai Nihon gengoshi no shoronten," *Kan* (January, 2001): 163. There is, of course, much value to works that seek to identify commonalities between nations, especially to counter the idea that the Japanese experience was unique. Yet when the commonality of the process of nationalization is stressed to the extent that the process itself becomes predetermined, it can only result in a teleological narrative.

9. This tendency is, I believe, stronger in Osa's and Yasuda's works than in Lee's and Komori's.

10. It is with hesitation that I include Lee Yeounsuk in such a group of scholars, because of her brilliant analysis of the debate between Baba Tatsui and Mori Arinori. There she claims, "The conceptualization of 'the Japanese language' as a single unified language—an understanding undoubtedly present today—did not exist; this understanding was historically constructed" (*"Kokugo" to iu shisō*, 12). There are, however, several slips here and there. For example, she (alongside others) lumps together the first two decades of the Meiji period as the pre-*kokugo* era. Since the origin of *kokugo* lies with Ueda Kazutoshi, her examination of the pre-Ueda writers can only fall short of Ueda's endeavors.

11. Typically translated as "Chinese characters," "Chinese writing," and "Chinese learning," respectively.

12. See, for example, Kamei, *Meiji bungakushi*; Komori, *Nihongo no kindai*; and Yamada Shunji, "Koe o chōetsu suru genbun'itchi," *Bungaku* (March–April, 2006): 70–83.

13. Komori, *Nihongo no kindai*, 108–9 and 111.

14. See Saitō Mareshi, *Kanbunmyaku no kindai* (Nagoya: Nagoya daigaku shuppankai, 2005); "Rai San'yō no kanshibun," in *Koten Nihongo no sekai: kanji ga tsukuru Nihon* (Tokyo: Tokyo daigaku shuppankai, 2006); *Kanbunmyaku to kindai Nihon* (Tokyo: NHK Books, 2007); "Gen to bun no aida," *Bungaku* (November–December, 2007): 91–98.

15. As I have argued extensively in my *Concealment of Politics, Politics of Concealment* (Stanford, CA: Stanford University Press, 2007) the equation *bungaku* = literature had yet to take form in the early Meiji period. *Bungaku*, though now a standard translation for "literature," was closer to "knowledge," a body of texts endorsed as a form of learning.

16. Lee, *"Kokugo" to iu shisō*, 93–94.

17. The italicized words are originally in English. Quoted in Lee, *"Kokugo" to iu shisō*, 107.

18. It is worth noting here that despite the "newness" of this form of knowledge, the textbooks still adhered to the pre-existing genre: written in 7–5 rhythm prose, they were designed to be read out loud and memorized. They were further structured in a two-layered manner where the upper layer featured printed prose and the lower calligraphy. This system allowed students to practice calligraphy through transcribing prose. Through such practices of repetition, both oral and written, the racialized world order was disseminated and internalized.

19. Sakai Naoki, "Reishizumu sutadīzu e no shiza," in *Reishizumu sutadīzu josetsu*, ed. Ukai Satoshi, Sakai Naoki, Tessa-Morris Suzuki, Ri Takanori (Tokyo: Ibunsha, 2012), 3–68. For other discussions on racialization, see Etienne Balibar and Immanuel Wallerstein, *Race,*

Nation, Class: Ambiguous Identities (New York: Verso Books, 1991) and Rey Chow, *Not Like a Native Speaker: On Languaging as a Postcolonial Experience* (New York: Columbia Univeristy Press, 2014).

20. Sakai, "Reishizumu sutadīzu e no shiza," 16.

21. Balibar and Wallerstein, *Race, Nation, Class*, 37.

22. Frantz Fanon, *Black Skin, White Masks*, trans. Charles Lam Markmann (New York: Grove Press, 1967), 18.

23. Fanon, *Black Skin, White Masks*, 18.

24. Natsume Sōseki, *Nōto*, in *Sōseki zenshū*, vol. 21 (Tokyo: Iwanami shoten, 1997). See also Shibata Shōji, *Sōseki no naka no teikoku: "kokumin sakka" to kindai Nihon* (Tokyo: Kanrin shobō, 2006), 21.

PART I. "PRE-NATION": LINGUISTIC CHAOS

1. The rate of literacy varied considerably based on regions. See Richard Rubinger, *Popular Literacy in Early Modern Japan* (Honolulu: University of Hawai'i Press, 2007).

2. Fukuchi Gen'ichirō, "Bunron," compiled in *Buntai*, ed. Katō Shūichi and Maeda Ai, *Nihon kindai shisō taikei*, vol. 16 (Tokyo: Iwanami shoten, 1989), 78.

3. Toyama Masakazu, "Rōmajikai o okosu no shui," *Tōyō gakkai zasshi*, vol. 39 (December 1884): 228–33.

4. See, for example, Kamei Hideo, *Kansei no henkaku* (Tokyo: Kōdansha, 1983), and Komori Yōichi, *Kōzō to shite no katari* (Tokyo: Shin'yōsha, 1988) and *Buntai to shite no monogatari* (Tokyo: Chikuma shobō, 1988) for insightful analyses of Futabatei's experiment in *Ukigumo* (*Floating Clouds*, 1887). In English, see also Indra A. Levy, *Sirens of the Western Shore: The Westernesque Femme Fatale, Translation and Vernacular Style in Modern Japanese Literature* (New York: Columbia University Press, 2006).

5. Mozume Takami, "Genbun'itchi," in *Kindai buntai keisei shiryō shūsei: hasseihen*, ed. Yamamoto Masahide (Tokyo: Ōfūsha, 1975), 265–289; B.H. Chamberlain, "Gen-bun itchi," in *Kindai buntai keisei shiryō shūsei: hasseihen*, ed. Yamamoto Masahide (Tokyo: Ōfūsha, 1975), 358–360.

CHAPTER 1. COMPETING "LANGUAGES"

1. Maejima Hisoka, "Kanji onhaishi no gi," in *Kokugo kokuji kyōiku shiryō sōran*, ed. Nishio Minoru and Hisamatsu Sen'ichi (Tokyo: Kokugo kyōiku kenkyūkai, 1969), 18.

2. Mori Arinori, "Hoitonī ate shokan," in *Mori Arinori zenshū*, vol. 1 (Tokyo: Senbundō shoten, 1972), 309. As we shall see shortly, the main gist of his idea was to adopt the English language.

3. Nanbu Yoshikazu, "Moji o kaikaku suru gi," in *Kokugo kokuji kyōiku shiryō sōran*, ed. Nishio Minoru and Hisamatsu Sen'ichi (Tokyo: Kokugo kyōiku kenkyūkai, 1969), 21.

4. Nishi Amane, "Yōji o motte kokugo o shosuru no ron," in *Meiroku zasshi*, vol. 1, ed. Yamamuro Shin'ichi and Nakanome Tōru (Tokyo: Iwanami shoten, 1999), 37. I have used William Reynolds Braisted's translation and made minor alterations to clarify my arguments; see "Writing Japanese with the Western Alphabet," in *Meiroku Zasshi: Journal of the Japanese Enlightenment*, trans. William Reynolds Braisted (Cambridge, MA: Harvard University Press, 1976).

5. See Lee, "*Kokugo*" *to iu shisō;* Kamei, *Meiji bungakushi;* Saitō Mareshi, "Gen to bun no aida"; and Naoki Sakai, *Voices of the Past: The Status of Language in Eighteenth-Century Japanese Discourse* (Ithaca, NY: Cornell University Press, 1991). Moreover, it is worth noting here that actual spoken language did not become an object of much inquiry until the 1880s. For example, even as the multitude of dialects divided Japan in early Meiji, *chihō shūshū* (collection of provincial dialects), a group assigned to gather and study the existence of different dialects in order to see how best to standardize them, only began in 1885. Moreover, the surge in *kōgo bunten* (grammar books of spoken language) did not begin until the mid to late 1890s. See Nakayama, "Tonji toshite no kenryoku," and Nakayama Akihiko, "'Bun' to 'koe' no kōsō—Meiji sanjūnendai no kokugo to bungaku," in *Media hyōshō ideorogī*, ed. Komori Yōichi, Takahashi Osamu, and Kōno Kensuke (Tokyo: Ozawa shoten, 1997), 227–55.

6. This should not be taken to mean that I will trace the history of phonocentrism in early Meiji. Such an enterprise could only retrace—and thus fall short of—what Karatani Kōjin's study has shown in his *Nihon kindai bungaku no kigen* (*Origins of Modern Japanese Literature*, 1980). This study significantly altered the study of language in Meiji Japan by arguing that phonocentrism—manifested in the form of the suppression of figurality—was integral to the production of a new *écriture* that led to new epistemic discoveries such as "interiority" and "landscape." Instead, I seek to identify the presence of other "sounds" that are privileged in the arguments for reform, ones that are not necessarily integral to the production of "phonocentric" discourse.

7. See Tsuchiya Michio, *Kokugo mondai ronsōshi* (Tokyo: Tamagawa daigaku shuppanbu, 2005), especially pages 22–33.

8. For a survey of nineteenth-century development in linguistics, see R. H. Robins, *A Short History of Linguistics* (London and New York: Longman, 1997) and Lia Formigari, *History of Language Philosophies* (Philadelphia: John Benjamins Publishing Company, 2004). In Japanese, see Kazama Kiyozō, *Gengogaku no tanjō: hikaku gengogaku shōshi* (Tokyo: Iwanami shoten, 1978). Also, I should add that by "Western linguistic theories" in this chapter, I refer to those that found their way to Japan, shaping the arguments for reform, and certainly not the entire theoretical development of Western linguistics.

9. Mori, "Hoitonī ate shokan," 309–10, emphasis mine. Also, for general reactions to Mori's proposal, see Ivan Parker Hall, *Mori Arinori* (Cambridge, MA: Harvard University Press, 1973), 189–95.

10. Though composed as a letter to Whitney, the letter was published to reach a wider public audience.

11. Quoted in Formigari, *History of Language Philosophies*, 136–37. See Friedrich von Schlegel, "On Indian Language, Literature, and Philosophy," in *The Aesthetic and Miscellaneous Works of Friedrich von Schlegel*, trans. E. J. Millington (London: George Bell and Sons, 1875).

12. Quoted in Formigari, *History of Language Philosophies*, 137.

13. I do not mean to suggest here that the encounter with the West is the sole reason behind Mori's criticism of "Chinese schools," since the criticism of *kangaku*'s lack of utility (a criticism of its textual study, for example) was one that had already appeared internally within *kangaku*. But the idea that "Chinese language"—by which Mori refers not only to *kanji* and *kanbun* but also to *kanbun kundokutai*—was a hindrance to progress clearly aligned with an ideological view inscribed in comparative linguistics.

14. Katō Hiroyuki, "Hakugengaku ni kansuru gian," in *Meiji ikō kokugo mondai ronshū*, ed. Yoshida Sumio and Inoguchi Yūichi (Tokyo: Kazama shobō, 1964), 63. In accordance with comparative linguistics, Katō here emphasizes syntax and inflections (or lack thereof) in order to differentiate "*shinago*" from "our language." "*Shinago*" therefore is the equivalent of "Chinese" in Western linguistic theories.

15. Tanaka Katsuhiko, "Seiyōjin wa shinago o dō mitekitaka: Augusuto Shuraihyā no baai," in *Gengo bunka* (March, 1985): 5–15. See also Osa, *Kindai Nihon to kokugo nashonarizumu*, 29, and Komori, *Nihongo no kindai*, 106.

16. Seth Jacobowitz, *Writing Technology in Meiji Japan: A Media History of Modern Japanese Literature and Visual Culture* (Cambridge, MA: Harvard University Asia Center, 2015), 104.

17. Mori, "Hoitonī ate shokan," 306–7.

18. See Lee, "*Kokugo*" *to iu shisō*, 10–13. She brilliantly argues that Mori's references to "Japanese" and "language in Japan" did not mean the same thing.

19. See Robins, *A Short History of Linguistics*; Formigari, *History of Language Philosophies*.

20. This is important precisely because Mori, as Lee Yeounsuk persuasively argues, did not argue for the abolition of "the language used in Japan," a fact often overlooked by those who cast Mori as a deranged anti-nationalist. It must be added, however, that his criticism of what he refers to as "Japanese" gets harsher in his "Education in Japan" and also in "Remarks of Mr. Mori," a speech he gave at the meeting of the National Educational Association in 1872. See "Education in Japan," in *Shinshū Mori Arinori zenshū*, vol. 5 (Tokyo: Bunsendō shoten, 1999), and "Remarks of Mr. Mori," in *The Address and Journal of Proceedings of the National Educational Association* (1872): 105–10.

21. Mori, "Education in Japan," 185–86.

22. Ivan Parker Hall claims that "[Mori] seems to contradict himself flatly in mid-letter," referring to his statements that say, on the one hand, "the only course to take . . . is to start anew, by first turning the spoken language into a properly written form, based on a pure phonetic principle" and, on the other, "spoken language is too poor to be made, by a phonetic alphabet, useful as a written language." However, if we accept that "phonetic principle" refers to the criterion by which to define a new language and the clause "by a phonetic alphabet" as referring to using the alphabet and simply transcribing the spoken, there is no contradiction. See Hall, *Mori Arinori*, 191.

23. Neither of Mori's proposals was implemented, nor did they garner much support. However, they prompted Baba Tatsui to write *An Elementary Grammar of the Japanese Language* to argue against Mori's claim that "spoken language in Japan" was too poor and unsystematic for the new age. As Lee claims, Baba's work is the first attempt at "descriptive grammar" to show a certain systematicity of "spoken Japanese" as a "living" language. However, it is ironic, as Lee states, that Baba wrote this work of grammar in English. In fact, his endeavor exposed the weakness of the very language he took up in his work and supported Mori's criticisms of it.

24. I am here referring to the "linguistic Orientalism" in which scripts from ancient Egypt to contemporary Japan were lumped together.

25. Maejima, "Kanji onhaishi no gi," 18.

26. Yamamoto Masahide, "Bunken kaisetsu" in *Kindai buntai keisei shiryō shūsei: hasseihen*, ed. Yamamoto Masahide (Tokyo: Ōfūsha, 1975), 23.

27. Kamei, *Meiji bungakushi*, 61–62. According to Fukuchi Gen'ichirō, this language was apparently very similar to the spoken language prevalent among the former samurai class, should the character *sōrō* be taken out.

28. Lee claims that "What underlies Maejima's argument is the utilitarian perception that language is a tool, that language, and the letters that represent the sound of the language, is not the true object of knowledge; it is, rather, a tool that communicates the object of knowledge. From such a perspective, letters ought to correspond faithfully to sound and must also have 'the benefit of everyone uttering the same sound for the same character.' At the core of Maejima's rejection of *kanji* was the ideology of 'practical knowledge' (*jitsugaku*), the idea that true knowledge is in the 'the thing itself' and not the 'language' [that mediates it]. Maejima accordingly thought that *kanji* were inappropriate for the acquisition and communication of modern knowledge" (Lee, "*Kokugo*" *to iu shisō*, 29–30). I do not disagree that Maejima sought an easier medium by which to study "modern knowledge," but I am reluctant to endorse the view that the "core of his argument" is shaped by a utilitarian view of language as "practical knowledge," which is equated with a "Western view," as Lee seems to suggest.

29. Maejima Hisoka, "Kokubun kyōiku no gi ni tsuki kengi," in *Meiji ikō kokugo mondai ronshū*, ed. Yoshida Sumio and Inoguchi Yūichi (Tokyo: Kazama shobō, 1964), 39.

30. On *sodoku* and *kangaku* studies in the late Edo period, I consulted Nakamura Shunsaku, *Edo jukyō to kindai no "chi"* (Tokyo: Perikansha, 2002); Tsujimoto Masashi, *Manabi no fukken* (Tokyo: Kadokawa shoten, 1999); and Takai Hiroshi, *Tenpōki, shōnen shōjo no kyōyō keisei katei no kenkyū* (Tokyo: Kawade shobō shinsha, 1991). I have also learned a great deal from Saitō Mareshi, *Kanbunmyaku no kindai* and *Kanbunmyaku to kindai Nihon*, as well as Maeda Ai, "Kindai dokusha no seiritsu," in *Kindai dokusha no seiritsu*, vol. 2, *Maeda Ai chosakushū* (Tokyo: Chikuma shobō, 1987).

31. This process was further individuated. We ought not imagine a classroom full of students all studying under one teacher and at the same level. In private families, it was either the father or elder brother who taught *sodoku*. Many started *sodoku* between the ages of five and ten, and on average seven or eight. See Tsujimoto, *Manabi no fukken*, 62.

32. Of course, this does not mean that they were not taught any meaning of the texts during the *sodoku* phase, but the main objective of *sodoku* was to recite and memorize the texts. Also, they started right off with the Four Books, without any other training. The typical order was *Great Learning* (大学, Da xue), *Analects of Confucius* (論語, Lun yu), *Mencius* (孟子, Mengzi) and *The Mean* (中庸, Zhong yong). The *sodoku* of the four classics ended around ten years of age for quick learners and no later than thirteen or fourteen for others.

33. Despite the importance of later stages, however, it is essential to note that when they were done with the first stage, the students could read other *kangaku* texts without the help of a teacher. *Sodoku* even taught *kanbun* grammar; those who could not compose well were made to do *sodoku* repeatedly. See Takai, *Tenpōki, shōnen shōjo no kyōyō keisei katei no kenkyū*, 149.

34. See Noguchi Takehiko, *Ogyū Sorai: Edo no Don Kihōte* (Tokyo: Chūō kōronsha, 1993).

35. Wakabayashi Torasaburō and Shirai Kowashi eds., *Kaisei kyōjujutsu*, vol. 1 (Tokyo: Fukyūsha, 1884), 29.

36. Tsujimoto, *Manabi no fukken*, 70–71.

37. See Tsujimoto, *Manabi no fukken*, especially pages 146–56.

38. For a detailed analysis of different *kanbun kundokutai*, see Saitō Fumitoshi, "Kinsei kindai no kanbun kundoku," *Nihongogaku* (June 1998): 56–62; "Kinsei ni okeru kanbun no kundoku to ondoku," in *Nagoya daigaku kyōyōbu kiyō* 37 (1993): 1–24; and "Meiji shoki ni okeru kanbun kundokutai," in *Jōhō bunka kenkyū* 1 (March 1995): 184–76.

39. Saitō Mareshi, "Gen to bun no aida," 95.

40. It is, as Lee seems to suggest, easy to think that Maejima's argument for the use of *kana* derives from his urge to identify with the West. Maejima himself appears to adhere to this idea when he says the following: "When I say that *kanji* ought to be abolished, I do not mean to say that we should also abolish *kango*, i.e., words, diction, and language that we imported from China. What I mean is to employ not their letters but *kana* and write down the words as they are. This is just like countries like England adopting Latin words as they are and making it their national language, spelling them in their own national orthography" ("Kanji onhaishi no gi," 18). In this line of argument, as Lee suggests, Maejima clearly sees a parallel between the relationship between Latin-English and *kanbun-kana* scripted *kokugo* (Lee, *"Kokugo" to iu shisō*, 30–31).

41. Susan L. Burns, *Before the Nation: Kokugaku and the Imagining of Community in Early Modern Japan* (Durham, NC: Duke University Press, 2003), 511, and Nakamura, *Edo jukyō to kindai no "chi,"* 122.

42. Saitō Mareshi, "Rai San'yō no kanshibun: kinsei kōki no tenkanten," 207.

43. Komori, *Nihongo no kindai*, 106.

44. Maejima, "Kokubun kyōiku no gi ni tsuki kengi," 40.

45. Saitō Mareshi, "Gen to bun no aida," 93.

46. Saitō Mareshi, *Kanbunmyaku no kindai*, 218.

47. Nanbu, "Moji o kaikaku suru gi," 21.

48. There are exceptions to this. Watanabe Shūjirō, for example, argues for the use of the "Tokyo kotoba" (Tokyo language) in "Nihonbun o seiteisuru hōhō," published in 1875. It is doubtful, however, that Meiji literati shared the notion of "Tokyo language."

49. See, for example, the following passage by Ōta Zensai, who, in 1828, takes up the controversy over /i/, /u/, /e/ sounds: "The difference in these three pairs of sounds (*i, yi, e, ye, u, yu*) is quite subtle, so it is fine to say that they are the same sounds in our everyday use. But we must use the correct *kana* when we decipher the correct sound (*on'in o tadashi*) and render them in *kana* scripts." Quoted in Furuta Tōsaku, "Ongiha 'gojū-on zu' 'kanazukai' no saiyō to haishi," in *Shōgaku dokuhon binran*, vol. 1, ed. Furuta Tōsaku (Tokyo: Musashino shoin, 1978), 376.

50. Hirata Atsutane, a well-known nativist, referred to the fifty-sound syllabary grid as "itsura no oto," 五十の音 with "*kowe*" glossing the characters for *oto*. See also Sakai, *Voices of the Past*.

51. As one can imagine, there were numerous systems of *kanazukai* prevalent in the Edo period, and a comprehensive survey of these varying systems is beyond the scope of this chapter. For a detailed discussion, see Kuginuki Tōru, *Kinsei kanazukairon no kenkyū: gojū-on zu to kodai Nihongo onsei no hakken* (Nagoya: Nagoya daigaku shuppankai, 2007). Also, for the history of the fifty-sound syllabary grid, see Mabuchi Kazuo, *Gojū-on zu no hanashi* (Tokyo: Taishūkan shoten, 1993). On debates over *kanazukai* in the late Edo to the early Meiji period, I found Furuta's "Ongiha 'gojū-on zu' 'kanazukai' no saiyō to haishi"

most helpful. See also Sakai, *Voices of the Past*, and Burns, *Before the Nation* for a discussion on textual strategies of Edo intellectuals.

52. This scholarly turn toward *kogaku* was on a par with the movement in *kangaku* classics I briefly discussed earlier. One of the pivotal figures in Edo Confucianism, Ogyū Sorai, claimed that *kangaku* classics ought to be read through *kaon* ("original" sounds) and not in *kundoku* to recover the texts' original meaning.

53. In conceptualizing these "voices," I owe a great deal to Naoki Sakai's discussion on the status of language in the eighteenth century, which he lays out in his *Voices of the Past*.

54. See Komori Yōichi's discussion of Ogyū Sorai, Motoori Norinaga, and Ueda Akinari. He discusses how they shared the idea that "sound" can be derived from *kanji* characters (*Nihongo no kindai*, 16).

55. In addition to Sakai, *Voices of the Past*, see also Noguchi Takehiko, "Gojū-on zu to genrei: ongi to gengo nashonarizumu no keisei o megutte," in *Edo shisōshi no chikei* (Tokyo: Perikansha, 1993), 273–302. See also Maruyama Ryūji, "Gojū-on zu: sono gensetsu kūkan" in *Fuji joshi daigaku kokubungaku zasshi* 50 (1993): 136–45 and Kawamura Minato, *Kotodama to takai* (Tokyo: Kōdansha, 1990).

56. See, for example, Furukawa Masao, *Eiri: Chie no wa* (1870–72) and Sakakibara Yoshino, *Shōgaku dokuhon* (1873). See also Furuta, "Ongiha 'gojū-on zu' 'kanazukai' no saiyō to haishi."

57. There are exceptions to this. Fukuzawa Yukichi, for example, promoted the teaching of *iroha* over the fifty-sound syllabary grid, claiming that the former was "knowledge" while the latter was "science." His rationale was that *iroha* was the "easier" medium and more "practical" for everyday use, and hence it ought to be learned first. See "Shōgaku kyōiku no koto II," in *Fukuzawa Yukichishū*, vol. 12 (Tokyo: Iwanami shoten, 1981), 105.

58. Furuta, "Ongiha 'gojū-on zu' 'kanazukai' no saiyō to haishi," 385.

59. As a poetic sequence with its series of words, *iroha* was a model by which to learn calligraphy (*tenarai*), and its importance in calligraphy practices continued even in the Meiji period. On *tenarai juku*, see Tsujimoto, *Manabi no fukken*.

60. That the fifty-sound syllabary grid embodies grammar necessary for conjugation is an awareness that dates back to the end of the eighteenth century.

61. Katayama Junkichi, *Shōgaku tsuzuriji hen*, quoted in Furuta, "Ongiha 'gojū-on zu' 'kanazukai' no saiyō to haishi," 385–86.

62. Historical *kana* system (or *rekishiteki kanazukai*) refers to a system of spelling that presumably reflects how the words were pronounced in the Heian period.

63. Lee, *"Kokugo" to iu shisō*, 33–34.

64. Nishi, "Yōji o motte kokugo o shosuru no ron," 37.

65. See, for example, Yamamoto, *Kindai buntai hassei no shiteki kenkyū*.

66. Nishi, "Yōji o motte kokugo o shosuru no ron," 43–44.

67. Nishi, "Yōji o motte kokugo o shosuru no ron," 50–51.

68. The translator of *Meiroku zasshi* speculates that Nishi is referring to *kanji* pronunciations such as *go-on*, *kan-on*, and *tō-on* and adds *wa-on* ("Japanese-local" sound) as the fourth. However, seeing that Nishi adds the ninth point, "Decide rules for employing sounds of *kanji*," I find it unlikely that Nishi is also referring to *kanji* sounds here. See Braisted, *Meiroku Zasshi*, 20.

69. See Itō Shingo, *Kinsei kokugogakushi* (Osaka: Tachikawa bunmeidō, 1928), 170–79. See also Sakamoto Kiyoe, "Keichū no Teika kanazukai hihan—shiseikan to no kankei kara" in *Kokubungaku kenkyū* 109 (March, 1993), 82–91.

70. His knowledge of Western linguistic theories is evident in his *Kotoba no ishizue* as well as his *Hyakugaku renkan* (*Encyclopedia*, 1870), in which he introduced the basic categories used in the study of linguistics. His speech, entitled "Katō sensei hakugengaku gian no ken" (On Mr. Katō's Proposal to Establish the Linguistics Department, 1880), displays much knowledge of comparative linguistics theory in referring to Schlegel, Bopp, and others. See Nishi Amane, "Katō Hiroyuki sensei hakugengaku gian no gi" in *Meiji ikō kokugo mondai ronshū*, ed. Yoshida Sumio and Inoguchi Yūichi (Tokyo: Kazama shobō, 1964), 66.

71. Nishi Amane, *Kotoba no ishizue* in *Nishi Amane zenshū*, vol. 2 (Tokyo: Munetaka shobō, 1961), 603. See also Nakayama Rokurō, "Nishi Amane no Nihongo bunpōron," *Gakugei kokugo kokubungaku* 33 (2001): 56–64.

72. Nishi co-edited *Great Learning* with Tsuda Shin'ichirō. See Hattori Takashi, "Nishi Amane to Nihongo no hyōkihō—Nihongo bunten no kijutsu o chūshin ni," *Jōchi daigaku kokubunka kiyō* 22 (March 2005): 54.

73. Quoted in Hattori, "Nishi Amane to Nihongo no hyōkihō—Nihongo bunten no kijutsu o chūshin ni," 54.

74. As a translator of a great many works, he saw the necessity of *kango* and produced many new compounds like *tetsugaku* (philosophy), *shukan* (subjective), *kyakkan* (objective), *shinrigaku* (psychology), and so forth, many of which we still use today. See Yamamoto Masahide, "Nishi Amane no kokugo kaikaku katsudō," in *Gengo seikatsu* 196 (1968): 86.

75. Saitō Mareshi, *Kanbunmyaku to kindai Nihon*, 105.

CHAPTER 2. SOUND, SCRIPTS, AND STYLES

1. Let me reiterate here that this is not to say that *kanbun kundokutai* has been undervalued in recent scholarship. Many scholars have emphasized the importance of this style in their discussions of its role in the political arena, as well as in the translingual practice of Western philosophy and materials.

2. Yano Ryūkei, *Nihon buntai moji shinron*, compiled in *Kyōkasho keimōbunshū*, ed. Saitō Toshihiko, Kurata Yoshihiro, and Tanigawa Keiichi (Tokyo: Iwanami shoten, 2006), 383. Hereafter cited as *New Theory*.

3. I owe a great deal to the recent works of Saitō Mareshi in understanding this shift in *kanbun kundokutai*. See especially *Kanbunmyaku no kindai*, "Rai San'yō no kanshibun," and *Kanbunmyaku to kindai Nihon*.

4. Anderson, *Imagined Communities*, 14–15.

5. Saitō Mareshi, "Gen to bun no aida," 92.

6. Saitō Fumitoshi, "Kinsei kindai no kanbun kundoku," 57. For a detailed analysis of different *kanbun kundokutai*, see also his "Kinsei ni okeru kanbun no kundoku to ondoku," and "Meiji shoki ni okeru kanbun kundokutai," *Jōhō bunka kenkyū* 1 (March 1995): 184–76.

7. "*Gorōzeraru bekarazu*" (不可被御覧) or "*oboshimerare sōrō*" (被思食候) are some such examples. Kamei, *Kansei no henkaku*, 33.

8. Kamei, *Kansei no henkaku*, 32–33. Kamei suggests that this "translated" style had become so ubiquitous, even permeating to literate townspeople and peasants, that if developed, it could have become a common language to consolidate such otherwise disparate linguistic conditions.

9. Kamei, *Kansei no henkaku*, 34; Saitō Mareshi, *Kanbunmyaku to kindai Nihon*, 88–89.

10. It is worth noting here that there was a variation of *kanbun kundokutai* known as ōbun chokuyakutai ("direct-translation style of Western language") that introduced, for instance, formulaic expressions like "*shitsutsu aru*" to denote the condition of "developing or continued action" and relative clauses such as "*suru tokoro no*" that were produced through translation of Western languages. Komori, *Nihongo no kindai*, 113.

11. Saitō Mareshi, *Kanbunmyaku to kindai Nihon*, 105.

12. On the role of newspapers and other print media in language reforms, see Komori, *Nihongo no kindai*, especially chapter 2.

13. Saitō Mareshi, *Kanbunmyaku to kindai*, 255.

14. On the role that *Eisai shinshi* played in the early Meiji period, see Saitō Mareshi, *Kanbunmyaku to kindai*, and Maeda Ai, "Meiji risshin shusse shugi no keifu—*Saikoku risshihen* kara *Kisei* made," compiled in *Kindai dokusha no seiritsu, Maeda Ai chosakushū*, vol. 2 (Tokyo: Chikuma shobō, 1987).

15. See Maeda, "Meiji risshin shusse shugi no keifu," 96.

16. *Enzetsu* (speech) and *sokki* (dictation), media that were produced in Meiji and showed much effectiveness especially in the political arena, also played a crucial role in popularizing *kanbun kundokutai*. See Komori, *Nihongo no kindai*, for a brilliant discussion of *enzetsu* and *sokki*. In English see J. Scott Miller, "Japanese Shorthand and *Sokkibon*," in *Monumenta Nipponica* 49, no. 4 (Winter 1994): 471–87, and Jacobowitz, *Writing Technology in Meiji Japan*.

17. Maejima, "Kanji onhaishi no gi," 17. As Lee Yeounsuk states, however, it is important to note that Maejima did not oppose the use of *kanji* compounds (*"Kokugo" to iu shisō*, 30).

18. There were many causes for anxiety about Japan's status in East Asia during the 1880s, resulting from events such as the Imo Mutiny (1882), the Sino-Franco War (1884–85), and the Kapsin Incident (1884).

19. *Tsuki* (moon) and *Yuki* (snow) are the names of groups to which the advocates of *kana* scripts belonged.

20. Toyama Masakazu, "Kanjiha," in *Kokugo kokuji kyōiku shiryō sōran*, ed. Nishio Minoru and Hisamatsu Sen'ichi (Tokyo: Kokugo kyōiku kenkyūkai, 1969), 33.

21. See Lee, *"Kokugo" to iu shisō*, 38, and Komori, *Nihongo no kindai*, 110–11. While Lee simply points out the contradiction inherent in Toyama's criticism of *kanji*, Komori takes it a step further and claims that Toyama's unwillingness to see this contradiction is a manifestation of colonial ambivalence.

22. Taguchi Ukichi, "Nihon kaika no seishitsu shibaraku aratamezaru bekarazu," in *Kindai buntai keisei shiryō shūsei: hasseihen*, ed. Yamamoto Masahide (Tokyo: Ōfūsha, 1975), 208.

23. I do not mean to argue that the Freedom and People's Rights Movement was an anti-elitist movement. It was simply governed by anti-elitist discourse, given that its primary opponents were Meiji government officials.

24. Quoted in Formigari, *History of Language Philosophies*, 136–37.

25. Quoted in Formigari, *History of Language Philosophies*, 137.

26. I do not mean to suggest that the privileging of sound that we see in 1880s Japan all stemmed from the theories of Western linguistics. As I will detail in the following chapter, the idea that *kanji* (as a "foreign" system of signs) interfered with "Japanese" sound(s) occupied a prominent place in the argument for the superiority of spoken language at the time. This privileging of the "Japanese sound," which was inextricably linked to the fifty-sound syllabary grid we saw in the last chapter, played a critical role in further rejecting *kanbun*.

27. Yatabe Ryōkichi, "Rōmaji o mote Nihongo o tsuzuru no setsu," compiled in *Kokugo kokuji kyōiku shiryō sōran*, ed. Nishio Minoru and Hisamatsu Sen'ichi (Tokyo: Kokugo kyōiku kenkyūkai, 1969), 32; Yatabe Ryōkichi, *Rōmaji hayamanabi* (Tokyo: Rōmajikai, 1885), 1.

28. Yatabe, *Rōmaji hayamanabi*, 1. He actually posits three rules, the last of which I omitted, because it is not directly relevant to this discussion. The third rule reads: "In using the Roman alphabet, we should follow English in the use of consonants and Italian (and hence German and Latin sounds) in the use of vowels."

29. It is not possible for me to reproduce what makes this passage very obviously "written" prose, but here is a "semantic" translation: "The summer had passed, and the fall was at its peak. It was even wintry. On one relatively warm day, many ants gathered. It was to dry the food that they had collected during the summer, which they pulled out of the hole" (Yatabe, *Rōmaji hayamanabi*, 37).

30. Taguchi, "Nihon kaika no seishitsu shibaraku aratamezaru bekarazu," 208.

31. See, for example, Mozume Takami's "Genbun'itchi" and Bunpukusai's "Nihon futsū no bun wa kana nite nichijō setsuwa no mama ni kaki kudasu beshi kaku suru toki wa Nihonjin ni kōdai naru eki aru koto o ronzu," both in *Kindai buntai keisei shiryō shūsei: hasseihen*, ed. Yamamoto Masahide (Tokyo: Ōfūsha, 1975).

32. Although I do not have the time to reflect extensively on the movements to adopt *kana* in this chapter, *rekishiteki kanazukai* would have helped to standardize grammar by systematizing the conjugation of words, since conjugation was inscribed in conventional spelling. It is thus not a coincidence that Nanbu, who gave up on the Roman alphabet after the first decade of the Meiji period, advocated the historical *kana* system.

33. Yamamoto Masahide, "'Kana no kai' kikanshijō no genbun'itchi genshō," in *Ibaragi daigaku bunrigakubu kiyō* 11 (December 1960): 53–71. Advocates of *kana* argued that *kana* scripts were much more practical than the Roman alphabet, because more people were familiar with *kana*.

34. This is true not only of scholarly criticisms, but also of the many anthologies of the linguistic reform movements, as they single out chapter 3 to be included in their volumes. See, for example, *Kindai buntai keisei shiryō shūsei: hasseihen*, ed. Yamamoto Masahide and *Kokugo kokuji kyōiku shiryō sōran*, ed. Nishio Minoru and Hisamatsu Sen'ichi.

35. Mori Ōgai, in 1890, develops such awareness in "Genbunron," in *Buntai*, ed. Katō Shūichi and Maeda Ai, *Nihon kindai shisō taikei*, vol. 16 (Tokyo: Iwanami shoten, 1989).

36. Yano, *New Theory*, 383.

37. I say roughly here, because there are *dogo* that do not have equivalents in *shinago* and vice versa (the example Ryūkei gives for *dogo* is *nagamochi*, denoting "wooden box," which does not have a *shinago*-reading; and for *shinago* he provides *tansu*, meaning "drawers," which does not have a *dogo* equivalent). His focus is on those words that have both

shinago and *dogo*, such as *tsurugi* and *ken* (both denoting "sword"); the former is *dogo* and the latter *shinago*.

38. Yano, *New Theory*, 391.

39. It further engages with arguments like the following. Herbert Spencer, in *The Philosophy of Style* (originally published in 1852), says, "We are told that 'brevity is the soul of wit.' We hear styles condemned as verbose or involved. Blair says that every needless part of a sentence 'interrupts the description and clogs the image;' and again that 'long sentences fatigue the reader's attention. . . .' Regarding language as an apparatus of symbols for the conveyance of thought, we may say that, as in a mechanical apparatus, the more simple and the better arranged its parts, the greater will be the effect produced" (*The Philosophy of Style* [Whitefish: Kessinger Publishing, 2004]: 3–4).

40. See, for example, Tanakadate Aikitsu's "Hatsuonkō" ("On Pronunciation," 1885) to see how articulatory phonetics shaped the arguments for the use of the Roman alphabet.

41. Yano, *New Theory*, 467.

42. Komori, *Nihongo no kindai*, 46.

43. Yano, *New Theory*, 427.

44. His argument is often linked to that of Fukuzawa Yukichi who, since the first decade of the Meiji period, had advocated the reduction of *kanji*, especially because Ryūkei studied at Keiō gijuku (present-day Keiō University), a school Fukuzawa founded in 1867.

45. Lee Yeounsuk, "'Hōjū fuhō' kara 'Yōma bunshō' e," *Geppō*, in *Kyōkasho keimō bunshū*, ed. Saitō Toshihiko, Kurata Yoshihiro, and Tanigawa Keiichi (Tokyo: Iwanami shoten, 2006).

46. Yano Ryūkei, *Keikoku bidan*, vol. 2 (Tokyo: Iwanami shoten, 1969), 21–22. Of course, one of the primary differences between the two essays is that in "Buntairon," he is exploring the narrative form for fiction, while in *New Theory*, he focuses on finding a language for the journalistic media, which can partially explain the difference in focus.

47. I do not mean to suggest that Ryūkei's discussion in *New Theory* succeeds in erasing the dialogic relationship with prior literary tradition inscribed in the styles he discusses, which is fundamentally impossible. However, he seeks to actively conceal the literary tradition by focusing his discussion on orthographic comparisons, such as the number of syllables and visual conciseness.

48. Yano, *New Theory*, 450.

49. Yano, *New Theory*, 451–52.

50. See, for example, Kanda Takahiro's "Bunshōron o yomu" and a column of *Meiji nippō*, entitled "Bunshō no kairyō," both of which are included in *Kindai buntai keisei shiryō shūsei: hasseihen*, ed. Yamamoto Masahide (Tokyo: Ōfūsha, 1975).

51. Saitō Mareshi notes that in the early to mid-Meiji period, the notion of contemporary language versus old language did not signify vernacular versus archaic language (*kōgo* vs. *bungo*), as many scholars of *genbun'itchi* have taken for granted; instead, what marked the difference between contemporary language and old language was *kanbun kundokutai* and *kanbun*. See *Kanbunmyaku to kindai Nihon*, 100.

52. Of course, *kanbun kundokutai* has a long history and had developed much beyond classical *kanbun* even before the Meiji period. But it is decidedly different in the Meiji period, as the absolute authority of *kanbun* had begun to wane.

53. See Saitō Mareshi, *Kanbunmyaku to kindai Nihon*, 96.

54. Namekawa Michio, *Nihon sakubun tsuzurikata kyōikushi 1: Meijihen* (Tokyo: Kokudosha, 1977).

55. Saitō Mareshi, *Kanbunmyaku to kindai Nihon*, 106.

56. Such tendencies were also true for many textbooks that were reprinted in the Meiji period. Saitō Mareshi notes that Rai San'yō's *Nihon gaishi* (*Unofficial History of Japan*, 1827) was published without *kana* suffixes in the pre-Meiji version, hence leaving it up to the readers to decide which suffix to employ. In the Meiji version, however, the *kana* suffixes were clearly in place. See *Kanbunmyaku to kindai Nihon*, 87.

57. Such a view is endorsed even by a critic as sophisticated as Lee Yeounsuk, in her *"Kokugo" to iu shisō*, 93.

58. Ochiai Naobumi, "Shōrai no kokubun," in *Kindai buntai keisei shiryō shūsei: hasseihen*, ed. Yamamoto Masahide (Tokyo: Ōfūsha, 1975), 652.

59. See Kamei, *Meiji bungakushi*, 77–78.

60. Sekine Masanao, "Kokugo no hontai narabi ni sono kachi," in *Kindai buntai keisei shiryō shūsei: hasseihen*, ed. Yamamoto Masahide (Tokyo: Ōfūsha, 1975), 405–6.

61. Sekine, "Kokugo no hontai narabi ni sono kachi," 406. Lee discusses the importance of Sekine's effort to sever the link between *kokubun* and *kobun/gabun* (*"Kokugo" to iu shisō*, 90).

62. On par with such a rhetorical operation, other scholars such as Ōwada Tateki retrospectively applied the dominance of *kokubun* to pre-Meiji schools of *kundoku*. By comparing, for example, the different schools such as *dōshunten, gotōten*, and *issaiten*, he criticized the manner in which *issaiten* destroys Japanese grammar, making it a "slave to *kanbun*." Whether or not *kanbun kundokutai* follows Japanese grammar "correctly" should not matter as long as *kanbun* maintains its status as the original text. It is only when *kanbun kundokutai* is relegated secondary to Japanese grammar—as it is here—that this argument stands. See Ōwada Tateki, "Buntai no itchi o ronzu," in *Kindai buntai keisei shiryō shūsei: hasseihen*, ed. Yamamoto Masahide (Tokyo: Ōfūsha, 1975), 675.

63. *Kokubungaku tokuhon*, ed. Haga Yaichi and Tachibana Senzaburō (Tokyo: Fuzanbō, 1890). See also Haruo Shirane, "Curriculum and Competing Canons," in *Inventing the Classics*, ed. Haruo Shirane and Tomi Suzuki (Stanford, CA: Stanford University Press, 2000), 238–39. The article further discusses the reasons behind the national literature scholars' desire to include Edo-period essays in "national literature."

64. It does appear later, specifically with Ueda Kazutoshi, as he discusses how the Japanese language is still invaded by Chinese characters despite Japan's victory in the Sino-Japanese War (1894–95).

65. Sekine, "Kokugo no hontai narabi ni sono kachi," 408.

66. Komori Yōichi notes that this features an ideological move on the part of the national language reformers, because they sought to conceal the very absence of such *kokugo* (*Nihongo no kindai*, 137). Komori ultimately suggests that the national literature scholars' will to conceal its absence reinforces the colonial unconscious.

CHAPTER 3. ZOKU AS AESTHETIC CRITERION

1. The word "*zoku*," in such compounds as *zokugo* (*zoku* words) and *zokubun* (*zoku* writing), is typically translated as the "vernacular" or "vulgar," posited in opposition to *ga* (elegance). As we shall see below, the meaning of *zoku* is extremely fluid in the early Meiji

period. I will therefore refrain from translating the term and retain the Japanese rendering throughout this chapter.

2. This is a typical perspective not only of *genbun'itchi* scholars of modernization theory (e.g., Yamamoto Masahide and Nanette Twine), but also of literary scholars such as Yamada Yūsaku. See Yamada Yūsaku, *Gensō no kindai: Shōyō, Bimyō, Ryūrō* (Tokyo: Ōfū, 2001). This derives from what Komori Yōichi calls one of the myths of *genbun'itchi*, a manifestation of the literary scholars' desire to claim that literature indeed played a large role in the production of "beautiful" *kokugo* based on *genbun'itchi*. See Komori, *Nihongo no kindai*, 124–25.

3. Kamei, *Meiji bungakushi*, 80.

4. "Gengo torishirabejo hōhōsho," compiled in *Kindai buntai keisei shiryō shūsei: hasseihen*, ed. Yamamoto Masahide (Tokyo: Ōfūsha, 1975), 453. The *Gengo torishirabejo* (Office of Language Inspection) was founded by Kuroda Takuma in 1888, and its primary members were *kokubungaku* scholars Ochiai Naobumi, Sekine Masanao, Konakamura Gishō, Hagino Yoshiyuki, Ochiai Naozumi, and Maruyama Masahiko. Although there were many *kokubungaku* scholars in the group, Kuroda Takuma was a scholar of the French language, hence the group was not entirely limited to *kokubungaku* scholars.

5. Mozume Takami, "Genbun'itchi," in *Mozume Takami zenshū*, vol. 3 (Tokyo: Mozume Takami zenshū hensankai, 1935), 6.

6. Meirokusha was an intellectual society founded in 1874 to promote "civilization and enlightenment."

7. "Nihon bunshōkai kiyaku no shogen," compiled in *Kindai buntai keisei shiryō shūsei: hasseihen*, ed. Yamamoto Masahide (Tokyo: Ōfūsha, 1975), 435.

8. See also Ochiai, "Shōrai no kokubun."

9. Sekine, "Kokugo no hontai narabi ni sono kachi," 409–10. For a close reading of Sekine's piece, see Lee, *"Kokugo" to iu shisō*, 86–94.

10. "Gengo torishirabejo hōhōsho," 454.

11. Such a view is clearly derivative of their *kokugaku* lineage, the ideology of the fifty-sound syllabary grid we saw in the first chapter. For brilliant discussions on *kokugaku* ideology, see Sakai, *Voices of the Past*, and Burns, *Before the Nation*.

12. The Meiji *kokubungaku* scholars did not simply seek to revive the past. As Tomiko Yoda has insightfully shown, the sense of temporality between Edo *kokugaku* nativists and Meiji *kokubungaku* scholars differed considerably. While *kokugaku* "preclude[d] radical differentiation among the past, present, and future," *kokubungaku* harbored the "evolutionary temporality." See Tomiko Yoda, *Gender and National Literature: Heian Texts in the Constructions of Japanese Modernity* (Durham, NC: Duke University Press, 2004), 46. Moreover, as we saw last chapter, Meiji *kokubungaku* was much more accommodating of *kanji/kanbun* influences than were the *kokugaku* nativists, not only because of such evolutionary temporality but because, as Yoda claims, they were "less concerned with primordial purity of native voice" than "the expression of the national" (50).

13. Such a narrative was behind the characterization of the language reforms by *kokubungaku* scholars as a "setback" given their reluctance to embrace *zokubun*. See the works of Yamamoto Masahide.

14. I owe a great deal to the work of Shinada Yoshikazu, who details this process in his *Man'yōshū no hatsumei* (Tokyo: Shin'yōsha, 2001). I am also indebted to works by Sakaki Yūichi, who argues that a surge of *shintaishi* criticism that appeared in the late 1880s and

early 1890s, the very time that *waka* poetry debates began, redefined the course of poetic reform, retrospectively discovering *Shintaishishō* as the origin of modern Japanese poetry. See "Bungaku no 'ba'—'juyō' to 'kenkyū' no hazama—Meiji jūnendai makki ni okeru 'shōka /gunka/shintaishi' no shosō," *Nihon kindai bungaku* 61 (October 1999): 1–13; "'Kindaishi' shi no shutsugen/ aruiwa Shintashishō shohen no kigenka—Meiji nijūnendai zenhan no 'shintaishi' hihan o megutte," *Kokugo kokubun kenkyū* 120 (March 2002): 13–30; "Hitei sareru beki mono to shite no 'zoku'—Meiji nijūnen zenhan no 'shintaishi' hihan o megutte," *Nihon kindai bungakukai Hokkaidō shibu kaihō* 10 (May 2007): 1–18.

15. Hagino Yoshiyuki, "Kogoto," in *Tōyō gakkai zasshi* 4 (March 1887): 38.

16. Such efforts at reform should be read vis-à-vis the conflict between *wabun* scholars and *kokubungaku* scholars in the Meiji period. *Kokubungaku* scholars shunned the gendered ephemerality that was attached to *wabun* and *waka* and sought to expand the discursive horizons of *kokugo* and *kokushi*. For an extensive discussion, see Tomi Suzuki, "Gender and Genre: Modern Literary Histories and Women's Diary Literature," in *Inventing the Classics: Modernity, National Identity, and Japanese Literature*, ed. Haruo Shirane and Tomi Suzuki (Stanford, CA: Stanford University Press, 2000), 71–95.

17. Hattori Motohiko, "Waka kairyōron o yomu," in *Meiji karon shiryō shūsei*, ed. Koizumi Tōzō, *Meiji Taishō tanka shiryō taisei*, vol. 1 (Kyoto: Ritsumeikan shuppanbu, 1940), 94. See also Taketsu Yachiho, "Kokugaku waka kairyō fukaron" (1887).

18. Mikami Sanji, "Uta no ron," *Tōyō gakkai zasshi* 5 (March 20, 1888): 24.

19. As we saw in the previous chapter, Toyama and Yatabe were active in their calls for orthographic reform, as Toyama sought to reject *kanji* and Yatabe sought to adopt the Roman alphabet. Neither, however, sought to implement their orthographic experiments with *Shintaishishō*.

20. Yatabe Ryōkichi, "Shintaishishō jo," compiled in *Nihon gendaishi taikei*, vol. 1 (Tokyo: Kawaide shobō, 1974), 30.

21. Inoue Tetsujirō, "Shintaishishō jo," in *Nihon gendaishi taikei*, vol. 1 (Tokyo: Kawaide shobō, 1974), 30.

22. Toyama Masakazu, "Shintaishishō jo," in *Nihon gendaishi taikei*, vol. 1 (Tokyo: Kawaide shobō, 1974), 31.

23. Toyama Masakazu, "Shakaigaku no genri ni daisu," in *Shintaishishō*, vol. 1, ed. Toyama Masakazu, Yatabe Ryōkichi, and Inoue Tetsujirō (Tokyo: Maruya Zenshichi, 1882).

24. Ochiai Naobumi, *Shinsenkaten* (Tokyo: Hakubunkan, 1891), 7.

25. See Shinada, *Man'yōshū no hatsumei*, 116–19. The main purpose of his argument is to show that such emphasis on *chōka* led to the rediscovery of the *Man'yōshū* as a "national" anthology.

26. See for example, Ochiai, *Shinsenkaten*, and Sasaki Hirotsuna, "Chōka kairyōron" (1881), in *Meiji karon shiryō shūsei*, ed. Koizumi Tōzō, *Meiji Taishō tanka shiryō taisei*, vol. 1 (Kyoto: Ritsumeikan shuppanbu, 1940).

27. On their urge to develop national poetry, see Ochiai Naobumi, "Kokubun kokushi o ronjite yo no bungakusha ni nozomu," in *Ochiai Naobumi, Ueda Kazutoshi, Haga Yaichi, Fujioka Sakutarō shū, Meiji bungaku zenshū*, vol. 44 (Tokyo: Chikuma shobō, 1968).

28. What I have translated as "stiff Chinese expressions" here is "*tōkoku no shikaku shimen no ji*," 唐国の四角四面の字.

29. Toyama, "Shintaishishō jo," 32.

30. Sakaki Yūichi makes this point in his "Hitei sareru beki mono to shite no 'zoku,'" 2–3.

31. Hagino Yoshiyuki, "Waka oyobi shintaishi o ronzu," in *Tōyō gakkai zasshi* 3, no. 12 (December 1889): 605–8.

32. For the link between the works of Bakin and the political sphere, see Maeda Ai, "Bakin to Tōkoku—kyō o megutte" and "Meiji rekishi bungaku no genzō—seiji shōsetsu no baai," both in *Genkei no Meiji, Maeda Ai chosakushū*, vol. 4 (Tokyo: Chikuma shobō, 1989).

33. Sugaya Kikuo, *Shiteki rizumu: onsūritsu ni kansuru nōto* (Tokyo: Yamato shobō, 1975).

34. Yano Ryūkei, "Buntairon," in *Keikoku bidan*, vol. 2 (Tokyo: Iwanami shoten, 1969).

35. For a brilliant analysis of *Shintaishishō*, see Kamei Hideo, "Kindaishi sōsōki ni okeru kōsei no mondai—kindaishishi no kokoromi 1," *Bungaku* 52 (January 1984): 1–12, and "Yamada Bimyō no ichi—kindaishishi no kokoromi 2," *Bungaku* 52 (August 1984): 64–74.

36. See for example, Hagino, "Waka oyobi shintaishi o ronzu," 606.

37. Kamei Hideo, "*Omokage* no inritsu," *Bungaku* 52 (November 1984): 13.

38. Takatsu Kuwasaburō, "Shiika o ronzu," *Tōyō gakkai zasshi* 6 (April 1888): 33.

39. Ochiai says the following in his preface to *Shinsenkaten*: "*Tanka* and *chōka* are composed in 5–7 metric rhythm. We acknowledge that the 7–5 metric rhythm is necessary for contemporary tenor (*kinseijin no kuchō*). That is why we have included it in this volume" (7). Ochiai would clearly like us to believe that it was a simple matter of metrical rhythm and that changing from 5–7 to 7–5 was a transition made to cater to contemporary trends and not much more.

40. Tsubouchi Shōyō, *Shōsetsu shinzui*, in *Tsubouchi Shōyōshū, Nihon kindai bungaku taikei*, vol. 3 (Tokyo: Kadokawa shoten, 1974), 112. In translating this text, I consulted Nanette Twine's translation, *The Essence of the Novel: Occasional Papers II* (Queensland: Department of Japanese, University of Queensland, 1981).

41. On the specific link between emotions and *zokugo*, see *Shōsetsu shinzui*, especially "Shōsetsu sōron," 43–51. See also Kamei Hideo, "*Shōsetsu*" *ron: Shōsetsu shinzui to kindai* (Tokyo: Iwanami shoten, 1999), in particular chapter 5, which traces Shōyō's notion of *jō* to the works of Ogyū Sorai. Kamei, in his *Meiji bungakushi*, further emphasizes the point that Shōyō posited *zokugo* in opposition to writing instead of *kanbun*. See Kamei, *Meiji bungakushi*, 68–69.

42. See, for example, his criticism in *Shōsetsu shinzui* that *zokubun* was "verbose" and "long-winded," as well as "unruly" and "ungrammatical" (109). As he makes it clear in "Bunshō shinron" ("New Theory on Style," 1886), however, verbosity includes honorifics, the use of which, according to Shōyō, takes away the "spirit of *zokugo*." Tsubouchi Shōyō, "Bunshō shinron," in *Buntai*, ed. Katō Shūichi and Maeda Ai, *Nihon kindai shisō taikei*, vol. 16 (Tokyo: Iwanami shoten, 1989), 112.

43. Tsubouchi, "Bunshō shinron," 115.

44. As I have argued in my *Concealment of Politics, Politics of Concealment*, Shōyō sought to define the modern *shōsetsu* away from the political sphere in which 7–5 rhythm prose held dominant status.

45. Yamada Bimyō, "Genbun'itchiron gairyaku," in *Yamada Bimyō*, ed. Tsubouchi Yūzō, *Meiji no bungaku*, vol. 10 (Tokyo: Chikuma shobō, 2001), 291–92.

46. Maeda, "Kindai dokusha no seiritsu."

47. Yamada Bimyō, "Genbun'itchiron gairyaku," 293.

48. Bimyō also develops such a view in his "Bun to gochō no kankei 1," *Iratsume* 4, no. 36 (December 1889): 5.

49. See Sakaki, "Bungaku no 'ba'—'juyō' to 'kenkyū' no hazama" and "'Kindaishi' shi no shutsugen/ aruiwa Shintashishō shohen no kigenka." Also see Kaminuma Hachirō, *Jinbutsu sōsho: Izawa Shūji* (Tokyo: Yoshikawa kōbunkan, 1964).

50. Kamei Hideo makes this important alteration to Maeda's essay in his "*Shōsetsu*" *ron*, 148.

51. Tsubouchi, *Shōsetsu shinzui*, 102; Yamada Bimyō, "Ware ware no genbun'itchitai," in *Kindai buntai keisei shiryō shūsei: hasseihen*, ed. Yamamoto Masahide (Tokyo: Ōfūsha, 1975), 627.

52. Much work has been done on the production of new narrative voice in Bimyō's works. See Yamada Yūsaku, *Gensō no kindai*, as well as his "Ichininshō e no kattō: Yamada Bimyō o megutte," *Bungaku* 53 (November 1985): 90–101. In English, see Jim Reichert, *In the Company of Men: Representations of Male-Male Sexuality in Meiji Literature* (Stanford, CA: Stanford University Press, 2006) and Levy, *Sirens of the Western Shore.*

53. He had long shown interest in *shintaishi*, starting with his own *Shintaishisen* (*Selection of New Style Poetry*), 1886.

54. Yamada Bimyō, "Ware ware no genbun'itchitai," 628–29.

55. Maeda, "Kindai dokusha no seiritsu," 138–39. As Yamada Yūsaku points out, moreover, this, like many of the concepts Bimyō sought to develop, is very similar to what Shōyō conceptualized as "elocutionary method" in "Bunshō shinron" and "Doppō o okosan to suru shui." We will soon turn to Shōyō's "elocutionary method." See Yamada Yūsaku, *Gensō no kindai*, 328.

56. Yamada Bimyō, "Ware ware no genbun'itchitai," 629.

57. Yamada Bimyō, "Bun to gochō no kankei 1," 5.

58. In his "Kindai dokusha no seiritsu," Maeda sounds critical of Bimyō for "being unable to escape the curse of *ondoku*," and says that, in spite of the fact that "Bimyō's reading" went against "reciting," it did not signify solitary reading. In a sense, he was right. Bimyō was not advocating solitary reading as Maeda conceptualized it. He sought a new orality. See Maeda, "Kindai dokusha no seiritsu," 139.

59. In "Fuchian taijin no onhihyō o haikenshite gohentō made ni tsukutta zangebun," he claims, "The *onchō* of *da* was quite disagreeable to the ear and it was with great suspicion that I followed such a style. . . . The middle-class style [*desu*/*masu*] has the advantage of being less vulgar, while the low-class style [*da*/*datta*] has the corresponding disadvantage. I employed the low-class style based on the understanding that it is less verbose. But it wasn't the case" (Yamada Bimyō, "Fuchian taijin no onhihyō o haikenshite gohentō made ni tsukutta zangebun," in *Kindai buntai keisei shiryō shūsei: hasseihen*, ed. Yamamoto Masahide [Tokyo: Ōfūsha, 1975], 496–97). For Bimyō's explanation of his decision to switch from *da* to *desu*/*masu*, see also "*Natsukodachi* maeoki" and "Genbun'itchi o manabu kokoroe," both of which are also compiled in *Kindai buntai keisei shiryō shūsei.*

60. Yamada Bimyō, "Genbun'itchiron gairyaku," 293.

61. Yamada Bimyō, "Fuchian taijin no onhihyō o haikenshite gohentō made ni tsukutta zangebun," 496.

62. Many critics have pointed out how this choice was detrimental to the development of the *shōsetsu*, whose theme was interiority, which required the erasure of the voice inscribed in a given language. (See for example Yamada Yūsaku, *Gensō no kindai*, and Karatani, *Nihon*

kindai bungaku no kigen). Perhaps it is true that Shōyō (and more so Futabatei) knew what was more appropriate for the medium of *shōsetsu*. But such a narrative mobilizes the retrospective privilege we have of knowing what *shōsetsu* ought to do. Criticizing Bimyō's choice of *desu/masu* from this perspective, critics often lose sight of the fact that one of the main reasons that Bimyō switched to *desu/masu* was *onchō*, which constituted an important aesthetic criterion for writers of the time.

63. Yamada Shunji, *Taishū shinbun ga tsukuru Meiji no 'Nihon'* (Tokyo: NHK Books, 2002). See also Yamada Shunji, "Koe o chōetsu suru genbun'itchi," *Bungaku* 7, no. 2 (April 2006): 70–83. Yamada suggests that *desu/masu* prose produced a second-person relationship between the writer and reader. As writers narrated events to the readers, readers in turn submitted their responses in the same style of writing, forming, as it were, a dialogue. It is not a coincidence that many speeches were textualized using *desu/masu*.

64. Yamada Yūsaku, *Gensō no kindai*, 331.

65. In *Shōsetsu shinzui*, for example, Shōyō criticized *zokugo* for being "verbose" and "long-winded," as well as "unruly" and "ungrammatical"; in addition to such shortcomings, *zokugo* were at times "incomprehensible" given their regional specificity.

66. Yamada Bimyō, *Nihon inbunron*, part 2, sections 1–3, compiled in *Buntai*, ed. Katō Shūichi and Maeda Ai, *Nihon kindai shisō taikei*, vol. 16 (Tokyo: Iwanami shoten, 1989), 219.

67. Yamada Bimyō, "Tanoshikaretote (aruhito e)," in *Nihon gendaishi taikei*, vol. 1 (Tokyo: Kawaide shobō, 1974), 275. This is the first verse.

68. Kamei, "Yamada Bimyō no ichi," 71. Bimyō sought to destabilize the reading practice through other means as well. One of his most notable efforts can be seen in his attempts to establish new punctuation rules. In "Bunshō fugō no kaishaku," he takes credit for many punctuation marks, such as *kurogoma* (the equivalent of a comma, lit. "black sesame") and *shirogoma* (the equivalent of a semicolon, lit. "white sesame"). See Yamada Bimyō, "Bunshō fugō no kaishaku," in *Kindai buntai keisei shiryō shūsei: hasseihen*, ed. Yamamoto Masahide (Tokyo: Ōfūsha, 1975), 590. Such efforts were on a par with those that tried to eradicate the 7–5 metrical rhythm, which, in more ways than one, functioned to punctuate the syllabically structured verse, phrase, and sentence breaks. Therefore, not only do these commas and semicolon equivalents defamiliarize texts visibly, they also introduce breaks in sentences where they otherwise might not be cut, altering the rhythm by which the sentences are read.

69. See, for example, Yamada Bimyō, "Chōka kairyōron on yonde," in *Yomiuri shinbun* (November 6, 1888), and Yamada Bimyō, "Shōka tsukurikata shogaku" in *Iratsume* 4, no. 28 (October 1889): 9–10.

70. Yamada Bimyō, *Nihon inbunron*, part 1, sections 1–3, is compiled in *Kindai shiika ronshū, Nihon kindai bungaku taikei*, vol. 59 (Tokyo: Kadokawa shoten, 1973), 44.

71. Yamada Bimyō, *Nihon inbunron*, in *Buntai*, 223.

72. Yamada Bimyō, *Nihon inbunron*, in *Buntai*, 224.

73. Ochiai, "Kokubun kokushi o ronjite yo no bungakusha ni nozomu," 11.

74. Tsubouchi, "Bunshō shinron," 109.

75. See Maeda, "Kindai dokusha no seiritsu."

76. Tsubouchi Shōyō, "Doppō o okosan to suru shui," in *Buntai*, ed. Katō Shūichi and Maeda Ai, *Nihon kindai shisō taikei*, vol. 16 (Tokyo: Iwanami shoten, 1989), 192.

77. Tsubouchi, "Bunshō shinron," 112.

78. *Shōsetsu shinzui*, 107. Shōyō was here engaging with principles of Western rhetoric that shunned verbosity, advocating efficiency.

79. The English translations are provided by Shōyō himself.

80. Tsubouchi, "Doppō o okosan to suru shui," 187.

81. Tsubouchi, "Doppō o okosan to suru shui," 188.

82. Tsubouchi, "Doppō o okosan to suru shui," 189.

83. Sekine Masanao, "Kokubun rōdokuhō," *Waseda bungaku* (November 30, 1891): 9–10.

84. Sekine, "Kokubun rōdokuhō," 11.

85. Sekine, "Kokubun rōdokuhō," 12–13.

86. Even though he does not specify the texts of elocution, the textbook he compiled for *kokubun*, entitled *Kintai kokubun kyōkasho* (*Textbook of Contemporary* Kokubun, 1888) should give us a clue. It included passages of *zuihitsu* by Edo writers, which did not differ much from traditional *wabun* textbooks. Lee, *"Kokugo" to iu shisō*, 93.

87. Shōyō is here referring to Richard Whately, who wrote *The Elements of Elocution*.

88. Tsubouchi, "Doppō o okosan to suru shui," 192–93.

89. Tsubouchi, "Doppō o okosan to suru shui," 195.

90. Tsubouchi, "Doppō o okosan to suru shui," 200.

91. Such description is clearly on a par with the ideal form of the modern *shōsetsu*, which he defined in *Shōsetsu shinzui*. As a medium that portrays emotions, it teaches its readers to be lofty and become a means to what he calls "criticism of life" (*jinsei no hihyō*).

92. Lee, *"Kokugo" to iu shisō*, 93–94.

PART II. RACE AND LANGUAGE REFORM

1. See, for example, George M. Frederickson, *Racism: A Short History* (Princeton, NJ: Princeton University Press, 2002) and Michael Yudell, *Race Unmasked: Biology and Race in the 20th Century* (New York: Columbia University Press, 2014). I owe a great deal to Frederickson's work for the ensuing historical discussion.

2. Frederickson, *Racism*, 59.

3. Sakai, "Reishizumu sutadīzu e no shiza," 19.

4. Stuart Hall, "The West and the Rest: Discourse and Power," in *Modernity: An Introduction to Modern Societies*, ed. Stuart Hall, David Held, Don Hubert, and Kenneth Thompson (Cambridge, UK: Blackwell, 1996), 197. For more discussion on the development of Europe as itself, see David Held, "The Development of the Modern State" in *Modernity*, 55–89.

5. Sakai, "Reishizumu sutadīzu e no shiza," 22.

6. Naoki Sakai, *Translation and Subjectivity: On "Japan" and Cultural Nationalism* (Minneapolis: University of Minnesota Press, 1997).

7. See, for example, Watanabe Kazan's *Shinkiron*, where he designates the Japanese as "Tartar" that is equal to "Caucasoid" (*Kazan zenshū*, vol. 1 [Aichi: Kazankai, 1911], 7–8). For an informative discussion on race in early modern and modern Japan, see Yamamuro Shin'ichi, *Shisō kadai to shite no Ajia: kijiku, rensa, tōyo* (Tokyo: Iwanami shoten, 2001).

8. Fukuzawa Yukichi, *Shōchū bankoku ichiran*, in *Fukuzawa zenshū*, vol. 2 (Tokyo: Jijishinpōsha, 1898), 5–6. The base text was S. Augustus Mitchell's *System of Modern Geography*. See also Akiko Uchiyama, "Translation as Representation: Fukuzawa Yukichi's

Representation of 'Others,'" in *Agents of Translation*, ed. Paul Bandia and John Milton (Philadelphia: John Benjamins Publishing Company, 2009), 63–83.

9. Fukuzawa Yukichi, *Sekai kunizukushi*, 6 vols. (Tokyo: Keiō gijuku, 1869).

CHAPTER 4. RACIALIZING THE NATIONAL LANGUAGE

1. See Yasuda Hiroshi, "Kindai Nihon ni okeru 'minzoku' kannen no keisei: kokumin shinmin minzoku," *Shisō to gendai* (September 1992): 61–72.

2. Ueda Kazutoshi, "Kokugo to kokka to," from *Kokugo no tame*, in *Ochiai Naobumi, Ueda Kazutoshi, Haga Yaichi, Fujioka Sakutarō shū, Meiji bungaku zenshū*, vol. 41 (Tokyo: Chikuma shobō, 1968), 110.

3. Ueda, "Kokugo to kokka to," 110.

4. Ueda Kazutoshi, "Kokugo kenkyū ni tsuite," in *Ochiai Naobumi, Ueda Kazutoshi, Haga Yaichi, Fujioka Sakutarō shū, Meiji bungaku zenshū*, vol. 41 (Tokyo: Chikuma shobō, 1968), 114.

5. Ueda, "Kokugo to kokka to," 110.

6. Rene Wellek, *The Rise of English Literary History* (New York: McGraw-Hill, 1983), 48.

7. Hippolyte Taine, *History of English Literature*, vol. 1 (New York: Holt & Williams, 1871) 10.

8. There were, of course, narratives that we can now call "literary history" written prior to this time, but works with the specific title of *bungakushi* (literary history) began in 1890.

9. See Nakayama Akihiko, "Bungakushi to nashonaritii—waisetsu, Nihonjin, bunka bōeiron," in *Kindai chi no seiritsu 1890–1910 nendai*, ed. Sakai Naoki, Narita Ryūichi, Shimazono Susumu and Yoshimi Shunya, *Kindai Nihon no bunkashi*, vol. 3 (Tokyo: Iwanami shoten, 2002), 83–119.

10. On studies of literary history in the Meiji period, see Shinada, *Man'yōshū no hatsumei*; Michael C. Brownstein, "From *Kokugaku* to *Kokubungaku*: Canon-Formation in the Meiji Period," *Harvard Journal of Asiatic Studies* 47, no. 2: 435–60; Suzuki, "Gender and Genre"; Shirane, "Curriculum and Competing Canons"; and Yoda, *Gender and National Literature.*

11. Mikami Sanji and Takasu Kuwasaburō, *Nihon bungakushi* (Tokyo: Kinkōdō, 1890), 5.

12. Haga Yaichi, *Kokubungakushi jikkō* (Tokyo: Fuzanbō, 1899), 6.

13. Takeshima Hagoromo, *Nihon bungakushi* (Tokyo: Jinbunsha, 1906), 2.

14. Mikami and Takasu, *Nihon bungakushi*, 2.

15. Haga, *Kokubungakushi jikkō*, 12.

16. See Narita Ryūichi, "Sōsetsu: Jikan no kindai—kokumin = kokka no jikan," in *Kindai chi no seiritsu 1890–1910 nendai*, ed. Komori Yōichi, et al., *Kindai Nihon no bunkashi*, vol. 3 (Tokyo: Iwanami shoten, 2002); Stephan Tanaka, *New Times in Modern Japan* (Princeton, NJ: Princeton University Press, 2004).

17. Tanaka, *New Times in Modern Japan*, 87.

18. Ueda, "Kokugo to kokka to," 110.

19. Ueda Kazutoshi, "Nihon gengo kenkyūhō," in *Ochiai Naobumi, Ueda Kazutoshi, Haga Yaichi, Fujioka Sakutarō shū, Meiji bungaku zenshū*, vol. 41 (Tokyo: Chikuma shobō, 1968), 182.

20. Lee, *"Kokugo" to iu shisō*, 103.

21. Ueda, "Kokugo to kokka to," 110, and elsewhere.

22. Quoted in Formigari, *History of Language Philosophies*, 136–37. See Schlegel, "On Indian Language, Literature, and Philosophy."

23. Yasuda, *"Kokugo" no kindaishi*, 78.

24. Ueda Kazutoshi, *Kokugogaku jikkō* (Tokyo: Tsūzoku daigakukai, 1916), 74.

25. Ueda, *Kokugogaku jikkō*, 76

26. Ueda, *Kokugogaku jikkō*, 74.

27. Yoshimura Sayaka, "Gaikokugo kara kokugo e: Okinawa ni okeru kokugo kyōikushi 1" *Japanisch als Fremdsprache* 3 (2013): 76–83.

28. Yasuda Toshiaki, *Teikoku Nihon no gengo hensei* (Tokyo: Seori shobō, 1997), 123–25.

29. "Kanpō" (August 24, 1911), 474.

30. Ōtsuki Fumihiko, "Hashigaki," in *Kōgohō bekki*, ed. Kokugo chōsa iinkai (Tokyo: Kokutei kyōkasho kyōdō hanbaijo, 1917), 3.

31. Quoted in Yasuda, *Teikoku Nihon no gengo hensei*, 132–33.

32. For more extensive discussion on Kanazawa, see Yasuda, *Teikoku Nihon no gengo hensei* and *"Kokugo" no kindaishi*.

33. Ueda, "Nihon gengo kenkyūhō," 181.

34. The focus on phonetics had, of course, long been present, ever since the emergence of comparative linguistics at the end of the eighteenth century. However, the urge to establish it as a scientific discipline led linguists to increasingly adopt an "empirical" approach, hence leading them to emphasize "current" and "living" language, as opposed to "dead" languages, as their object of inquiry.

35. Ueda Kazutoshi, "Hyōjungo ni tsukite," in *Kokugo no tame* (Tokyo: Fuzanbō, 1897), 51, 56.

36. Ueda, "Hyōjungo ni tsukite," 62–63.

37. See, for example, *Kōgohō* (Tokyo: Kokutei kyōkasho kyōdō hanbaijo, 1916) and *Kōgohō bekki* (Tokyo: Kokutei kyōkasho kyōdō hanbaijo, 1917). Nakayama Akihiko discusses this point extensively in "Tonji toshite no kenryoku—Ueda Kazutoshi 'Kōgohō' 'Kōgohō bekki.'" See also Nakayama, "'Hon'yaku' suru/sareru 'kokugo-Nihongo.'"

CHAPTER 5. TROPES OF RACIALIZATION IN THE WORKS OF NATSUME SŌSEKI

1. See Komori Yōichi, *Sōseki o yominaosu* (Tokyo: Chikuma shobō, 1995) and *Seikimatsu no yogensha Natsume Sōseki* (Tokyo: Kōdansha, 1999), among others.

2. Natsume Sōseki, "Mankan tokoro dokoro," in *Sōseki zenshū*, vol. 16 (Tokyo: Iwanami shoten, 1957), 80. Hereafter, all citations will be made parenthetically with the designation *SZ*. English translation (slightly modified) is from Natsume Sōseki, *Rediscovering Natsume Sōseki, With the First English Translation of Travels in Manchuria and Korea*, trans. Inger Sigrun Brodey and Sammy I. Tsunematsu (Kent: Global Oriental, 2000), 38–39. Further citations of the translation will also be provided parenthetically.

3. Park Yuha, *Nashonaru aidentiī to jendā: Sōseki, bungaku, kindai* (Tokyo: Kurein, 2007), 140.

4. Kawamura Minato, "'Teikoku' no Sōseki," *Sōseki kenkyū* (1995): 5.

5. Park, *Nashonaru aidentiī to jendā*, 97–128.

6. Natsume Sōseki, *Sanshirō* (Tokyo: Shinchō bunko, 1989), 98. The translation is from Natsume Sōseki, *Sanshirō*, trans. Jay Rubin (New York: Penguin Books, 2009), 79. Hereafter, all citations to this text will be provided parenthetically in the text. When used, citations to translations from Rubin (some slightly modified) will also be provided parenthetically.

7. Shibata convincingly explores the motifs of "light" and "dark" in his chapter on *Sanshirō*. Despite the fact that he aligns these motifs with "modern" and "premodern," Shibata never refers to them in racial terms. He however comes the closest to approaching the question of race. As one can imagine, there are a great many works on *Sanshirō* in both North America and Japan. Despite the ubiquity of racial tropes in this work, I have yet to come across any discussion of them.

8. Shibata, *Sōseki no naka no "teikoku,"* 97.

9. Shibata, *Sōseki no naka no "teikoku,"* 77.

10. See also Iida Yūko, "Onna no kao to Mineko no fuku," *Sōseki kenkyū* 2 (1994): 134.

11. As Balibar reminds us in *Race, Nation, Class*, "No nation, that is, no national state, has an ethnic basis" and "No nation possesses an ethic base naturally" (49, 97).

12. Natsume Sōseki, *Bungakuron*, in *Sōseki zenshū*, vol. 18 (Tokyo: Iwanami shoten, 1957), 10. Translation from *Theory of Literature and Other Critical Writings*, ed. Michael K. Bourdaghs, Atsuko Ueda, and Joseph A. Murphy (New York: Columbia University Press, 2009), 44. Hereafter, all citations to this text will be provided parenthetically in the text. Translations (some slightly modified) will also be cited parenthetically.

13. See Saitō Mareshi, "*Bungakuron* no shatei: disukūru to shite no kagaku," *Bungaku* 13, no. 3 (May-June 2012): 44–55.

14. Many critics have discussed the manner in which Sōseki was deeply invested in rhetoric and style, but very few scholars have noted the importance of rhetoric in *Bungakuron*. The notable exception is Tsukamoto Toshiaki, who has explored the visible traces of rhetoric, especially the psychological-philosophical vein of rhetoric that was prevalent in England at the time of Sōseki's study. See Tsukamoto Toshiaki, "*Bungakuron* no hikaku bungakuteki kenkyū—sono hassōhō ni tsuite," *Nihon bungaku* 16 (1967): 10–33, and "Natsume Sōseki" in *Nihon kindai shōsetsu*, ed. Nakajima Kenzō, Ōta Saburō, and Fukuda Rikutarō, vol. 3, *Hikaku bungaku kōza* (Tokyo: Shimizu kōbundō, 1971), 61–79. The rise of the psychological-philosophical rhetoric was one of the major responses to classical rhetoric that shaped the study of rhetoric. The study of psychological-philosophical rhetoric, as it evolved in the eighteenth century, perceived rhetoric as a means to study man's "mental nature." In effect, unraveling rhetoric became a crucial part of unraveling the mystery of the human mind.

15. My discussion of eighteenth-century aesthetic theories owes a great deal to Ōkouchi Shō, "Sūkō to pikucharesuku," in *Tsukurareta shizen*, ed. Komori Yōichi, et al., *Iwanami kōza bungaku*, vol. 7 (Tokyo: Iwanami shoten, 2003), 173–94.

16. Joseph Addison, "Pleasures of Imagination," in *Selections from The Tatler and The Spectator*, ed. Angus Ross (New York: Penguin, 1982), 377.

17. Addison, "Pleasures of Imagination," 392.

18. Ōkouchi, "Sūkō to pikucharesuku," 178.

19. My translation.

20. For more extensive discussion, see Nakayama Akihiko, "Chinmoku no rikigakuken: riron = han riron toshite no *Bungakuron*," *Hihyō kūkan* 9 (1993): 154–69.

21. On Sōseki's engagement with social theory, see "Introduction" to Natsume, *Theory of Literature and Other Critical Writings*, especially 13–25.

22. Wilbur S. Howell, *Poetics, Rhetoric, and Logic: Studies in the Basic Disciplines of Criticism*, (Ithaca, NY: Cornell University Press, 1975), 158.

23. Franklin E. Court, *Institutionalizing English Literature: The Culture and Politics of Literary Study 1750–1900* (Stanford, CA: Stanford University Press, 1992), 18.

24. See Komori Yōichi and Tomiyama Takao, "Taidan: Rondon ni tatsu Sōseki," *Bungaku* 4, no. 3 (1993): 103–17, and Tomiyama Takao, *Popai no kageni: Sōseki/Faulkner/bunkashi* (Tokyo: Misuzu shobō, 1996).

25. Court, *Institutionalizing English Literature*, 18.

26. Robert Crawford, *Devolving English Literature* (Edinburgh: Edinburgh University Press, 2000), 42.

27. There were, of course, many other works of rhetoric published during these years and many were more concerned with practical rules of grammar and style, elocutionary principles, etc. These three works are representative of a branch of rhetoric that focused on the aesthetic aspects of composition, which is evident from their choice to use *bijigaku* (study of belles lettres) as opposed to *shūjigaku* (a more generic term for the study of rhetoric). For extensive discussions of study of rhetoric in Japan, see Massimiliano Tomasi, *Rhetoric in Modern Japan* (Honolulu: University of Hawai'i Press, 2004); Hayami Hiroshi, *Kindai Nihon shūjigakushi: Seiyō shūjigaku no dōnyū kara zasetsu made* (Tokyo: Yūhōdō, 1988); Hara Shirō, *Shūjigaku no shiteki kenkyū* (Tokyo: Waseda daigaku shuppanbu, 1994).

28. Takata Sanae, "Shūji no gaku o sakan ni sezaru bekarazu," *Yomiuri shinbun*, December 6, 1887.

29. Sugaya Hiromi, *Shūji oyobi kabun no kenkyū*, (Tokyo: Kyōiku shuppan sentā, 1978), 361.

30. Takata Sanae, *Bijigaku* (Tokyo: Kinkōdō, 1889), 4.

31. Hara, *Shūjigaku no shiteki kenkyū*, 5.

32. See Komori, *Sōseki o yominaosu*, 83. See also Ishihara Chiaki, *Tekusuto wa machigawanai* (Tokyo: Chikuma shobō, 2004), 64.

33. *Bungaku hyōron* was originally a series of lectures Sōseki gave under the title "Eighteenth-Century English Literature" at Tokyo Imperial University, which ran from September 1905 to March 1907.

34. Natsume Sōseki, *Bungaku hyōron*, in *Sōseki zenshū*, vol. 19 (Tokyo: Iwanami shoten, 1957), 35. Translations of *Bungaku hyōron* are taken from Natsume, *Theory of Literature and Other Critical Writings*, 230. Hereafter, all references, including the translations, will be provided parenthetically.

35. *Eibungaku keishikiron* was the first of the lectures Sōseki gave at Tokyo Imperial University, though it was the last to be published. It is based on notes taken by four students, but without Sōseki's corrections.

36. Natsume Sōseki, *Eibungaku keishikiron*, in *Sōseki zenshū*, vol. 33 (Tokyo: Iwanami shoten, 1957), 11–12. Most of *Eibungaku keishikiron* is spent on 1 and 2, and it does not touch on 3.

37. Hōgetsu gives these categories in English.

38. Shimamura Hōgetsu, *Shin bijigaku* (Tokyo: Waseda daigaku shuppanbu, 1902), 81.

39. Shimamura, *Shin bijigaku*, 78.

40. Natsume, trans. Rubin, *Sanshirō*, 3.

41. Natsume Sōseki, *Kokoro*, in *Kokoro and Selected Essays*, trans. Edwin Mcllelan (New York: Madison Books, 1992), 3.

42. Mori Ōgai, "Dancing Girl," trans. Richard Browning, *Monumenta Nipponica* 30, no. 2 (Summer, 1975), 155.

43. Mori, "Dancing Girl," 156.

44. Takashi Fujitani, *Race for Empire: Koreans as Japanese and Japanese as Americans During World War II* (Berkeley: University of California Press, 2011).

45. Brian Hurley has written about Edwin Mcllelan's connection to Friedrich Hayek and his neoliberal thought, which, Hurley argues, was one of the defining factors that shaped Mcllelan's translation of Sōseki's *Kokoro*. See Brian Hurley, "*Kokoro* Confidential: Friedrich Hayek, and the Neoliberal Reading of Natsume Sōseki," *Representations* 134, (Spring 2016): 93–115.

46. This excerpt is from the "official" translation of the law, done under the supervision of the Occupation forces. I must note here that such reforms were also severely criticized by Japanese intellectuals at the time, especially those on the left. They claimed that the educational policies that promoted "individualism" were a "remnant of eighteenth-century Western thought." See Oguma Eiji, *"Minshū" to "aikoku": sengo Nihon no nashonarizumu to kōkyōsei* (Tokyo: Shin'yōsha, 2002), 354–68.

47. For an extensive discussion of such policies and how school textbooks reappropriated literary history to such a cause, see Satō Izumi, *Sengo hihyō no metahisutorī: kindai o kiokusuru ba* (Tokyo: Iwanami shoten, 2005).

BIBLIOGRAPHY

Addison, Joseph. "Pleasures of Imagination." In *Selections from The Tatler and The Spectator*, edited by Angus Ross. New York: Penguin, 1982.

Anderson, Benedict. *Imagined Communities: Reflections on the Origin and Spread of Nationalism*. New York: Verso, 1983.

Asukai Masamichi. *Nihon kindai seishinshi no kenkyū*. Kyoto: Kyoto daigaku shuppankai, 2002.

Baba Tatsui. *An Elementary Grammar of the Japanese Language, with Easy Progressive Exercises*. In *Baba Tatsui zenshū*, vol. 1, 3–109. Tokyo: Iwanami shoten, 1987.

Balibar, Étienne. "Racism Revisited: Sources, Relevance, and Aporias of a Modern Concept." *PMLA* 123, no. 5 (2008): 1630–39.

———, and Immanuel Maurice Wallerstein. *Race, Nation, Class: Ambiguous Identities*. New York: Verso, 1991.

Braisted, William Reynolds, ed. *Meiroku Zasshi: Journal of the Japanese Enlightenment*. Cambridge, MA: Harvard University Press, 1976.

Brownstein, Michael C. "From *Kokugaku* to *Kokubungaku*: Canon-Formation in the Meiji Period." *Harvard Journal of Asiatic Studies* 47, no. 2 (1987): 435–60.

Bunpukusai. "Nihon futsū no bun wa kana nite nichijō setsuwa no mama ni kaki kudasu beshi kaku suru toki wa Nihonjin ni kōdai naru eki aru koto o ronzu." In *Kindai buntai keisei shiryō shūsei: hasseihen*, edited by Yamamoto Masahide, 178–81. Tokyo: Ōfūsha, 1975.

Burns, Susan L. *Before the Nation: Kokugaku and the Imagining of Community in Early Modern Japan*. Durham, NC: Duke University Press, 2003.

Chamberlain, B. H. "Gem-bun itchi." In *Kindai buntai keisei shiryō shūsei: hasseihen*, edited by Yamamoto Masahide, 358–60. Tokyo: Ōfūsha, 1975.

"Chōsen kyōikurei." *Kanpō*, August 24, 1911.

Chow, Rey. *Not Like a Native Speaker: On Languaging as a Postcolonial Experience*. New York: Columbia University Press, 2014.

Clark, Paul H. *The Kokugo Revolution: Education, Identity and Language Policy in Imperial Japan*. Berkeley: University of California Press, 2009.

Court, Franklin E. *Institutionalizing English Literature: The Culture and Politics of Literary Study 1750–1900*. Stanford, CA: Stanford University Press, 1992.

Crawford, Robert. *Devolving English Literature*. Edinburgh: Edinburgh University Press, 2000.

Dower, John W. *War Without Mercy: Race and Power in the Pacific War*. New York: Pantheon Books, 1986.

Fanon, Frantz. *Black Skin, White Masks*. Translated by Charles Lam Markmann. New York: Grove Press, 1967.

———. *The Wretched of the Earth*. Translated by Constance Farrington. New York: Grove Press, 1963.

Formigari, Lia. *A History of Language Philosophies*. Philadelphia: John Benjamins Publishing Company, 2004.

Foucault, Michel. *Discipline and Punish*. Translated by Alan Sheridan. New York: Pantheon Books, 1977.

———. *Security, Territory, Population: Lectures at the College de France 1977–1978*. Edited by Michel Senellart. Translated by Graham Burchell. New York: République Française, 2007.

———. *The History of Sexuality*. Translated by Robert Hurley. New York: Pantheon Books, 1978.

———. *The Order of Things: An Archaeology of Human Sciences*. New York: Vintage Books, 1970.

Frederickson, George M. *Racism: A Short History*. Princeton, NJ: Princeton University Press, 2002.

Fukuchi Gen'ichirō. "Bunron." In *Buntai*, edited by Katō Shūichi and Maeda Ai, 77–80. Vol. 16 of *Nihon kindai shisō taikei*. Tokyo: Iwanami shoten, 1989.

Fukuzawa Yukichi. *Bunmeiron no gairyaku*. Edited by Matsuzawa Hiroaki. Tokyo: Iwanami shoten, 1995.

———. *Sekai kunizukushi*. 6 vols. Tokyo: Keiō gijuku, 1869.

———. *Seiyō jijō*. 3 vols. Tokyo: Keiō gijuku, 1872.

———. "Shōchū bankoku ichiran." In *Fukuzawa zenshū*, vol. 2. Tokyo: Jijishinpōsha, 1898.

———. "Shōgaku kyōiku no koto II." In *Fukuzawa Yukichishū*, vol. 12. Tokyo: Iwanami shoten, 1981.

Furuta Tōsaku. "Ongiha 'gojū-on zu' 'kanazukai' no saiyō to haishi." In *Shōgaku dokuhon binran*, vol. 1, edited by Furuta Tōsaku. Tokyo: Musashino shoin, 1978.

Futabatei Shimei. "Yo ga genbun'itchi no yurai." In *Kokugo kokuji kyōiku shiryō sōran*, edited by Nishio Minoru and Hisamatsu Sen'ichi, 133–134. Tokyo: Kokugo kyōiku kenkyūkai, 1969.

Gengo torishirabejo. "Gengo torishirabejo hōhōsho." In *Kindai buntai keisei shiryō shūsei: hasseihen*, edited by Yamamoto Masahide, 450–59. Tokyo: Ōfūsha, 1975.

Haga Yaichi. *Kokubungakushi jikkō*. Tokyo: Fuzanbō, 1899.

———, and Tachibana Senzaburō, eds. *Kokubungaku tokuhon*. Tokyo: Fuzanbō, 1890.

Hagino Yoshiyuki. "Kogoto." *Tōyō gakkai zasshi* 4 (March 1887): 33–46.

———. "Wabun o ronzu." In *Kindai buntai keisei shiryō shūsei: hasseihen*, edited by Yamamoto Masahide, 394–99. Tokyo: Ōfūsha, 1975.

———. "Waka oyobi shintaishi o ronzu." *Tōyō gakkai zasshi* 3, no. 12 (December 1889): 605–8.

Hall, Ivan Parker. *Mori Arinori*. Cambridge, MA: Harvard University Press, 1973.

Hall, Stuart. *The Fateful Triangle: Race, Ethnicity, Nation*. Cambridge, MA: Harvard University Press, 2017.

———. "The West and the Rest: Discourse and Power." In *Modernity: An Introduction to Modern Societies*, edited by Stuart Hall, David Held, Don Hubert, and Kenneth Thompson, 184–227. Cambridge, UK: Blackwell, 1996.

Hara Shirō. *Shūjigaku no shiteki kenkyū*. Tokyo: Waseda daigaku shuppanbu, 1994.

Harootunian, Harry D. *History's Disquiet: Modernity, Cultural Practice, and the Question of Everyday Life*. New York: Columbia University Press, 2000.

Hattori Motohiko. "Waka kairyōron o yomu." In *Meiji karon shiryō shūsei*, edited by Koizumi Tōzō. Vol. 1 of *Meiji Taishō tanka shiryō taisei*. Kyoto: Ritsumeikan shuppanbu, 1940.

Hattori Takashi. "Nishi Amane to Nihongo no hyōki—Nihongo bunten no kijutsu o chūshin ni." *Jōchi daigaku kokubunka kiyō* 22 (March 2005): 45–66.

Hayami Hiroshi. *Kindai Nihon shūjigakushi: Seiyō shūjigaku no dōnyū kara zasetsu made*. Tokyo: Yūhōdō, 1988.

Held, David. "The Development of the Modern State." In *Modernity: An Introduction to Modern Societies*, edited by Stuart Hall, David Held, Don Hubert, and Kenneth Thompson, 55–89. Cambridge, UK: Blackwell Publishers, 1996.

Howell, Wilbur S. *Poetics, Rhetoric, and Logic: Studies in the Basic Disciplines of Criticism*. Ithaca, NY: Cornell University Press, 1975.

Hurley, Brian. "*Kokoro* Confidential: Friedrich Hayek, and the Neoliberal Reading of Natsume Sōseki." *Representations* 134 (Spring 2016): 93–115.

Iida Yūko. "Onna no kao to Mineko no fuku." *Sōseki kenkyū* 2 (May 1994): 130–41.

Inoue Tetsujirō. "Shintaishishō jo." In *Nihon gendaishi taikei*, vol. 1. Tokyo: Kawaide shobō, 1974.

Ishihara Chiaki. *Tekusuto wa machigawanai*. Tokyo: Chikuma shobō, 2004.

Itō Shingo. *Kinsei kokugogakushi*. Osaka: Tachikawa shoten, 1928.

Jacobowitz, Seth. *Writing Technology in Meiji Japan: A Media History of Modern Japanese Literature and Visual Culture*. Cambridge, MA: Harvard University Asia Center, 2015.

Kamei Hideo. *Kansei no henkaku*. Tokyo: Kōdansha, 1983.

———. "Kindaishi sōsōki ni okeru kōsei no mondai—kindaishishi no kokoromi 1." *Bungaku* 52 (January 1984): 1–12.

———. *Meiji bungakushi*. Tokyo: Iwanami shoten, 2000.

———. "*Omokage* no inritsu." *Bungaku* 52 (November 1984): 13–24.

———. *"Shōsetsu" ron: Shōsetsu shinzui to kindai*. Tokyo: Iwanami shoten, 1999.

———. "Yamada Bimyō no ichi—kindaishishi no kokoromi 2." *Bungaku* 52 (August 1984): 64–74.

Kaminuma Hachirō. *Jinbutsu sōsho: Izawa Shūji*. Tokyo: Yoshikawa kōbunkan, 1964.

Kanda Takahiro. "Bunshōron o yomu." In *Kindai buntai keisei shiryō shūsei: hasseihen*, edited by Yamamoto Masahide, 212–17. Tokyo: Ōfūsha, 1975.

Karatani Kōjin. *Nihon kindai bungaku no kigen*. Tokyo: Kōdansha, 1980.

Katō Hiroyuki. "Hakugengaku ni kansuru gian." In *Meiji ikō kokugo mondai ronshū*, edited by Inoguchi Yūichi and Yoshida Sumio. Tokyo: Kazama shobō, 1964.

Kawamura Minato. *Kotodama to takai*. Tokyo: Kōdansha, 1990.

———. "'Teikoku' no Sōseki." *Sōseki kenkyū* 5 (November 1995): 28–38.

Kazama Kiyozō. *Gengogaku no tanjō: hikaku gengogaku shōshi*. Tokyo: Iwanami shoten, 1978.

Kokugo chōsa iinkai, ed. *Kōgohō*. Tokyo: Kokutei kyōkasho kyōdō hanbaijo, 1916.

———. *Kōgohō bekki*. Tokyo: Kokutei kyōkasho kyōdō hanbaijo, 1917.

Komori Yōichi. *Buntai to shite no monogatari*. Tokyo: Chikuma shobō, 1988.

———. *Kōzō to shite no katari*. Tokyo: Shin'yōsha, 1988.

———. *Nihongo no kindai*. Tokyo: Iwanami shoten, 2000.

———. *Seikimatsu no yogensha Natsume Sōseki*. Tokyo: Kōdansha, 1999.

———. *Sōseki o yominaosu*. Tokyo: Chikuma shobō, 1995.

——— and Tomiyama Takao. "Taidan: Rondon ni tatsu Sōseki." *Bungaku* 4, no. 3 (1993): 103–17.

Kuginuki Tōru. *Kinsei kanazukairon no kenkyū: gojū-on zu to kodai Nihongo onsei no hakken*. Nagoya: Nagoya daigaku shuppankai, 2007.

Lee Yeounsuk. "'Hōjū fuhō' kara 'Yōma bunshō' e." In *Kyōkasho keimōbunshū*, edited by Kurata Yoshihiro, Saitō Toshihiko, and Tanigawa Keiichi. Tokyo: Iwanami shoten, 2006.

———. *Ihō no kioku: kokyō, kokka, jiyū*. Tokyo: Shōbunsha, 2007.

———. *"Kokugo" to iu shisō*. Tokyo: Iwanami shoten, 1996.

———. *"Kotoba" to iu gen'ei: kindai Nihon no gengo ideorogī*. Tokyo: Akashi shoten, 2009.

Levy, Indra A. *Sirens of the Western Shore: The Westernesque Femme Fatale, Translation and Vernacular Style in Modern Japanese Literature*. New York: Columbia University Press, 2006.

Mabuchi Kazuo. *Gojūonzu no hanashi*. Tōkyō: Taishūkan shoten, 1993.

Maeda Ai. "Bakin to Tōkoku—kyō o megutte." In *Genkei no Meiji*. Vol. 4 of *Maeda Ai chosakushū*. Tokyo: Chikuma shobō, 1989.

———. "Kindai dokusha no seiritsu." In *Kindai dokusha no seiritsu*. Vol. 2 of *Maeda Ai chosakushū*. Tokyo: Chikuma shobō, 1987.

———. "Meiji rekishi bungaku no genzō—seiji shōsetsu no baai." In *Genkei no Meiji*. Vol 4. of *Maeda Ai chosakushū*. Tokyo: Chikuma shobō, 1989.

———. "Meiji risshin shusse shugi no keifu—*Saikoku risshihen* kara *Kisei* made." In *Kindai dokusha no seiritsu*. Vol. 2 of *Maeda Ai chosakushū*. Tokyo: Chikuma shobō, 1987.

Maejima Hisoka. "Kanji onhaishi no gi." In *Kokugo kokuji kyōiku shiryō sōran*, edited by Nishio Minoru and Hisamatsu Sen'ichi, 17–20. Tokyo: Kokugo kyōiku kenkyūkai, 1969.

———. "Kokubun kyōiku no gi ni tsuki kengi." In *Meiji ikō kokugo mondai ronshū*, edited by Inoguchi Yūichi and Sumio Yoshida. Tokyo: Kazama shobō, 1964.

Maruyama Ryūji. "Gojū-on zu: sono gensetsu kūkan." *Fuji joshi daigaku kokubungaku zasshi* 50 (1993): 136–45.

Meiji nippō. "Bunshō no kairyō." In *Kindai buntai keisei shiryō shūsei: hasseihen*, edited by Yamamoto Masahide, 240–45. Tokyo: Ōfūsha, 1975.

Mikami Sanji. "Uta no ron." *Tōyō gakkai zasshi* 5 (March 20, 1888): 23–28.

———, and Takasu Kuwasaburō. *Nihon bungakushi*. Tokyo: Kinkōdō, 1890.

Miller, J. Scott. "Japanese Shorthand and *Sokkibon*." *Monumenta Nipponica* 49, no. 4 (Winter 1994): 471–87.

Miyake Yonekichi. "Bun no kakikata ni tsukite." In *Kindai buntai keisei shiryō shūsei: hasseihen*, edited by Yamamoto Masahide, 194–95. Tokyo: Ōfūsha, 1975.

Mori Arinori. "Education in Japan." In *Shinshū Mori Arinori zenshū*, vol. 5. Tokyo: Bunsendō shoten, 1999.

———. "Hoitonī ate shokan." In *Mori Arinori zenshū*, vol. 1, 305–10. Tokyo: Senbundō shoten, 1972.

———. "Remarks of Mr. Mori." In *The Addresses and Journal of Proceedings of the National Educational Association, Session of the Year 1872, at Boston, Massachusetts*, 105–10. Peoria, IL: N.C. Nason, 1872.

Mori Ōgai. "Dancing Girl." Translated by Richard Browning. *Monumenta Nipponica* 30, no. 2 (Summer 1975): 151–76.

———. "Genbunron." In *Buntai*, edited by Katō Shūichi and Maeda Ai, 89–101. Vol. 16 of *Nihon kindai shisō taikei*. Tokyo: Iwanami shoten, 1989.

———. "Maihime." In *Gendai Nihon bungaku taikei*, vol. 7. Tokyo: Chikuma shobō, 1969.

Mozume Takami. "Genbun'itchi." In *Mozume Takami zenshū*, vol. 3. Tokyo: Mozume Takami zenshū hensankai, 1935.

———. "Genbun'itchi." In *Kindai buntai keisei shiryō shūsei: hasseihen*, edited by Yamamoto Masahide, 265–89. Tokyo: Ōfūsha, 1975.

Nakamura Shunsaku. *Edo Jukyō to kindai no "chi."* Tokyo: Perikansha, 2002.

Nakayama Akihiko. "'Bun' to 'koe' no kōsō—Meiji sanjūnendai no kokugo to bungaku." In *Media hyōshō ideorogī*, edited by Komori Yōichi, Takahashi Osamu, and Kōno Kensuke, 227–55. Tokyo: Ozawa shoten, 1997.

———. "Bungakushi to nashonaritii—waisetsu, Nihonjin, bunka bōeiron." In *Kindai chi no seiritsu 1890–1910 nendai*, edited by Narita Ryūichi, Sakai Naoki, Shimazono Susumu, and Yoshimi Shunya, 83–119. Vol. 3 of *Kindai Nihon no bunkashi*. Tokyo: Iwanami shoten, 2002.

———. "Chinmoku no rikigakuken: riron = han riron toshite no *Bungakuron*." *Hihyō kūkan* 9 (1993): 154–69.

———. "'Hon'yaku' suru/sareru 'kokugo-Nihongo.'" *Kan* 4 (January 2001): 152–62.

———. "Tonji toshite no kenryoku—Ueda Kazutoshi 'Kōgohō' 'Kōgohō bekki.'" *Bungaku* 7, no. 2 (April 2006): 127–41.

Nakayama Rokurō. "Nishi Amane no Nihongo bunpōron." *Gakugei kokugo kokubungaku* 33 (2001): 56–64.

Namekawa Michio. *Nihon sakubun tsuzurikata kyōikushi 1: Meijihen*. Tokyo: Kokudosha, 1977.

Nanbu Yoshikazu. "Moji o kaikaku suru gi." In *Kokugo kokuji kyōiku shiryō sōran*, edited by Nishio Minoru and Hisamatsu Sen'ichi, 20–21. Tokyo: Kokugo kyōiku kenkyūkai, 1969.

Narita Ryūichi. "Sōsetsu: Jikan no kindai—kokumin = kokka no jikan." In *Kindai chi no seiritsu 1890–1910 nendai*. Vol. 3 of *Kindai Nihon no bunkashi*, edited by Komori Yōichi, et al. Tokyo: Iwanami shoten, 2002.

Natsume Sōseki. *Bungaku hyōron*. Vol. 19 of *Sōseki zenshū*. Tokyo: Iwanami shoten, 1957.

———. *Bungakuron*. Vol. 18 of *Sōseki zenshū*. Tokyo: Iwanami shoten, 1957.

———. *Eibungaku keishikiron*. In *Sōseki zenshū*, vol. 33, 5–66. Tokyo: Iwanami shoten, 1957.

———. *Kokoro*. In *Kokoro and Selected Essays*, translated by Edwin McClellan, 1–236. New York: Madison Books, 1992.

———. *Kokoro*. Tokyo: Shinchō bunko, 2004.

———. "Mankan tokoro dokoro." In *Sōseki zenshū*, vol. 16, 128–227. Tokyo: Iwanami shoten, 1957.

———. *Nōto*. Vol. 21 of *Sōseki zenshū*. Tokyo: Iwanami shoten, 1997.

———. *Rediscovering Natsume Sōseki, With the First English Translation of Travels in Manchuria and Korea*. Translated by Inger Sigrun Brodey and Sammy I. Tsunematsu. Kent: Global Oriental, 2000.

———. *Sanshirō*. Tokyo: Shinchō bunko, 1989.

———. *Sanshirō*. Translated by Jay Rubin. New York: Penguin Books, 2009.

———. "Shaseibun." In *Sōseki zenshū*, vol. 20, 16–23. Tokyo: Iwanami shoten, 1957.

———. "Sōsakuka no daido." In *Sōseki zenshū*, vol. 20, 83–159. Tokyo: Iwanami shoten, 1957.

———. *Theory of Literature and Other Critical Writings*. Edited by Michael K. Bourdaghs, Atsuko Ueda, and Joseph A. Murphy. New York: Columbia University Press, 2009.

Nihon bunshōkai. "Nihon bunshōkai kiyaku no shogen." In *Kindai buntai keisei shiryō shūsei: hasseihen*, edited by Yamamoto Masahide, 435–36. Tokyo: Ōfūsha, 1975.

Nishi Amane. "Hyakugaku renkan." In *Nishi Amane zenshū*, vol. 1. Tokyo: Nihon hyōronsha, 1945.

———. "Katō Hiroyuki sensei hakugengaku gian no gi." In *Meiji ikō kokugo mondai ronshū*, edited by Inoguchi Yūichi and Yoshida Sumio. Tokyo: Kazama shobō, 1964.

———. "Kotoba no ishizue." In *Nishi Amane zenshū*, vol. 2, 599–680. Tokyo: Munetaka shobō, 1961.

———. "Writing Japanese with the Western Alphabet." In *Meiroku Zasshi: Journal of the Japanese Enlightenment*, translated by William Reynolds Braisted, 3–20. Cambridge, MA: Harvard University Press, 1976.

———. "Yōji o motte kokugo o shosuru no ron." In *Meiroku zasshi*, edited by Nakanome Tōru and Yamamuro Shin'ichi, vol. 1, 27–51. Tokyo: Iwanami shoten, 1999.

Noguchi Takehiko. "Gojū-on zu to genrei: ongi to gengo nashonarizumu no keisei o megutte." In *Edo shisōshi no chikei*, 273–302. Tokyo: Perikansha, 1993.

———. *Ogyū Sorai: Edo no Don Kihōte*. Tokyo: Chūō kōronsha, 1993.

Ochiai Naobumi. "Kokubun kokushi o ronjite yo no bungakusha ni nozomu." In *Ochiai Naobumi, Ueda Kazutoshi, Haga Yaichi, Fujioka Sakutarō shū*, 11–13. Vol. 44 of *Meiji bungaku zenshū*. Tokyo: Chikuma shobō, 1968.

———. *Shinsenkaten*. Tokyo: Hakubunkan, 1891.

———. "Shōrai no kokubun." In *Kindai buntai keisei shiryō shūsei: hasseihen*, edited by Yamamoto Masahide, 652–62. Tokyo: Ōfūsha, 1975.

Oda Jun'ichirō. *Karyū shunwa*. In *Meiji hon'yaku bungakushū*, 3–109. Vol. 7 of *Meiji bungaku zenshū*. Tokyo: Chikuma shobō, 1972.

Oguma Eiji. *"Minshū" to "aikoku": sengo Nihon no nashonarizumu to kōkyōsei*. Tokyo: Shin'yōsha, 2002.

Ōkouchi Shō. "Sūkō to pikucharesuku." In *Tsukurareta shizen*, edited by Hyōdō Hiromi, Komori Yōichi, Matsuura Hisaki, Numano Mitsuyoshi, and Tomiyama Takao, 173–94. Vol. 7 of *Iwanami kōza bungaku*. Tokyo: Iwanami shoten, 2003.

Osa Shizue. *Kindai Nihon to kokugo nashonarizumu*. Tokyo: Yoshikawa kōbunkan, 1998.

Ōtsuki Fumihiko. "Hashigaki." In *Kōgohō bekki*, edited by Kokugo chōsa iinkai. Tokyo: Kokutei kyōkasho kyōdō hanbaijo, 1917.

Ōwada Tateki. "Buntai no itchi o ronzu." In *Kindai buntai keisei shiryō shūsei: hasseihen*, edited by Yamamoto Masahide, 672–82. Tokyo: Ōfūsha, 1975.

Park Yuha. *Nashonaru aidentiī to jendā: Sōseki, bungaku, kindai*. Tokyo: Kurein, 2007.

Reichert, Jim. *In the Company of Men: Representations of Male-Male Sexuality in Meiji Literature*. Stanford, CA: Stanford University Press, 2006.

Robins, R. H. *A Short History of Linguistics*. 4th ed. London: Longman, 1997.

Rubinger, Richard. *Popular Literacy in Early Modern Japan*. Honolulu: University of Hawai'i Press, 2007.

Said, Edward W. *Orientalism*. New York: Vintage Books, 1978.

Saitō Fumitoshi. "Kinsei kindai no kanbun kundoku." *Nihongogaku* (June 1998): 56–62.

———. "Kinsei ni okeru kanbun no kundoku to ondoku." *Nagoya daigaku kyōyōbu kiyō* 37 (1993): 1–24.

———. "Meiji shoki ni okeru kanbun kundokutai." *Jōhō bunka kenkyū* 1 (March 1995): 184–76.

Saitō Mareshi. "*Bungakuron* no shatei: disukūru to shite no kagaku." *Bungaku* 13, no. 3 (2012): 44–55.

———. "Gen to bun no aida." *Bungaku* 8, no. 6 (December 2007): 91–98.

———. *Kanbunmyaku no kindai*. Nagoya: Nagoya daigaku shuppankai, 2005.

———. *Kanbunmyaku to kindai Nihon*. Tokyo: NHK Books, 2007.

———. "Rai San'yō no kanshibun." In *Koten Nihongo no sekai: kanji ga tsukuru Nihon*, edited by Tokyo daigaku kyōyō gakubu kokubun/kanbugaku bukai, 189–215. Tokyo: Tokyo daigaku shuppankai, 2006.

Sakai Naoki. *Nihon shisō to iu mondai: hon'yaku to shutai*. Tokyo: Iwanami shoten, 1997.

———. "Reishizumu sutadīzu e no shiza." In *Reishizumu sutadīzu josetsu*, edited by Sakai Naoki, Tessa-Morris Suzuki, Ri Takanori, and Ukai Satoshi, 3–68. Tokyo: Ibunsha, 2012.

———. *Shizan sareru Nihongo Nihonjin: "Nihon" no rekishi-chiseiteki haichi*. Tokyo: Shin'yōsha, 1996.

Sakai, Naoki. *Translation and Subjectivity: On "Japan" and Cultural Nationalism*. Minneapolis: University of Minnesota Press, 1997.

———. *Voices of the Past: The Status of Language in Eighteenth-Century Japanese Discourse*. Ithaca, NY: Cornell University Press, 1991.

Sakaki Yūichi. "Bungaku no 'ba'—'juyō' to 'kenkyū' no hazama—Meiji jūnendai makki ni okeru 'shōka/gunka/shintaishi' no shosō." *Nihon kindai bungaku* 61 (October 1999): 1–13.

———. "Hitei sareru beki mono to shite no 'zoku'—Meiji nijūnen zenhan no 'shintaishi' hihan o megutte." *Nihon kindai bungakukai Hokkaidō shibu kaihō* 10 (May 2007): 1–18.

———. "'Kindaishi' shi no shutsugen/aruiwa Shintashishō shohen no kigenka—Meiji nijūnendai zenhan no 'shintaishi' hihan o megutte." *Kokugo kokubun kenkyū* 120 (March 2002): 13–30.

Sakamoto Kiyoe. "Keichū no Teika kanazukai hihan—shiseikan to no kankei kara." *Kokubungaku kenkyū*, no. 109 (March 1993): 82–91.

Sasaki Hirotsuna. "Chōka kairyōron." In *Meiji karon shiryō shūsei*, edited by Koizumi Tōzō. Vol. 1 of *Meiji Taishō tanka shiryō taisei*. Kyoto: Ritsumeikan shuppanbu, 1940.

Satō Izumi. *Sengo hihyō no metahisutorī: kindai o kiokusuru ba*. Tokyo: Iwanami shoten, 2005.

von Schlegel, Friedrich. "On Indian Language, Literature, and Philosophy." In *The Aesthetic and Miscellaneous Works of Friedrich von Schlegel*, translated by E. J. Millington. London: George Bell and Sons, 1875.

Sekine Masanao. "Kokubun rōdokuhō." *Waseda bungaku* (November 30, 1891): 9–10.

———. "Kokugo no hontai narabi ni sono kachi." In *Kindai buntai keisei shiryō shūsei: hasseihen*, edited by Yamamoto Masahide, 405–13. Tokyo: Ōfūsha, 1975.

Shibata Shōji. *Sōseki no naka no "teikoku": "kokumin sakka" to kindai Nihon*. Tokyo: Kanrin shobō, 2006.

Shimamura Hōgetsu. *Shin bijigaku*. Tokyo: Waseda daigaku shuppanbu, 1902.

Shimizu Usaburō. "Hiragana no setsu." In *Kindai buntai keisei shiryō shūsei: hasseihen*, edited by Yamamoto Masahide, 148–50. Tokyo: Ōfūsha, 1975.

Shinada Yoshikazu. *Man'yōshū no hatsumei*. Tokyo: Shin'yōsha, 2001.

Shirane, Haruo. "Curriculum and Competing Canons." In *Inventing the Classics: Modernity, National Identity, and Japanese Literature*, edited by Haruo Shirane and Tomi Suzuki, 220–49. Stanford, CA: Stanford University Press, 2000.

Spencer, Herbert. *The Philosophy of Style*. Whitefish, MT: Kessinger Publishing, 2004 [1852].

Sugaya Hiromi. *Shūji oyobi kabun no kenkyu*. Tokyo: Kyōiku shuppan sentā, 1978.

Sugaya Kikuo. *Shiteki rizumu: onsūritsu ni kansuru nōto*. Tokyo: Yamato shobō, 1975.

Suzuki, Tomi. "Gender and Genre: Modern Literary Histories and Women's Diary Literature." In *Inventing the Classics: Modernity, National Identity, and Japanese Literature*, edited by Haruo Shirane and Tomi Suzuki, 71–95. Stanford, CA: Stanford University Press, 2000.

Taguchi Ukichi. "Nihon kaika no seishitsu shibaraku aratamezaru bekarazu." In *Kindai buntai keisei shiryō shūsei: hasseihen*, edited by Yamamoto Masahide, 205–8. Tokyo: Ōfūsha, 1975.

Taine, Hippolyte. *History of English Literature*, vol. 1. New York: Holt & Williams, 1871.

Takai Hiroshi. *Tenpōki, shōnen shōjo no kyōyō keisei katei no kenkyū*. Tokyo: Kawade shobō shinsha, 1991.

Takashi Fujitani. *Race for Empire: Koreans as Japanese and Japanese as Americans During World War II*. Berkeley: University of California Press, 2011.

Takata Sanae. *Bijigaku*. Tokyo: Kinkōdō, 1889.

———. "Shūji no gaku o sakan ni sezaru bekarazu." *Yomiuri shinbun*, December 6, 1887.

Takatsu Kuwasaburō. "Shiika o ronzu." *Tōyō gakkai zasshi* 6 (April 1888): 33–39.

Takeshima Hagoromo. *Nihon bungakushi*. Tokyo: Jinbunsha, 1906.

Tanaka Katsuhiko. "Seiyōjin wa Shinago o dō mitekitaka: Augusuto Shuraihyā no baai." *Gengo bunka* (March 1985): 5–15.

Tanaka, Stephan. *New Times in Modern Japan*. Princeton, NJ: Princeton University Press, 2004.

Tōkai Sanshi. *Kajin no kigū*. In *Meiji seiji shōsetsushū* 2, 3–110. Vol. 6 of *Meiji bungaku zenshū*. Tokyo: Chikuma shobō, 1967.

Tomasi, Massimiliano. *Rhetoric in Modern Japan*. Honolulu: University of Hawai'i Press, 2004.

Tomiyama Takao. *Osaru no keifugaku: rekishi to jinshu*. Tokyo: Misuzu shobō, 2009.

———. *Popai no kageni: Sōseki/Faulkner/ bunkashi*. Tokyo: Misuzu shobō, 1996.

———. *Shārokku Hōmuzu no seikimatsu*. Tokyo: Seidosha, 1993.

Toyama Masakazu. "Kanjiha." In *Kokugo kokuji kyōiku shiryō sōran*, edited by Nishio Minoru and Hisamatsu Sen'ichi, 33–36. Tokyo: Kokugo kyōiku kenkyūkai, 1969.

———. "Rōmajikai o okosu no shui." *Tōyō gakkai zasshi* 39 (December 1884): 228–33.

———. "Shakaigaku no genri ni daisu." In *Shintaishishō*, vol.1, edited by Toyama Masakazu, Yatabe Ryōkichi, and Inoue Tetsujirō. Tokyo: Maruya Zenshichi, 1882.

———. "Shintaishishō jo." In *Nihon gendaishi taikei*, vol. 1. Tokyo: Kawaide shobō, 1974.

Tsubouchi Shōyō. "Bunshō shinron." In *Buntai*, edited by Katō Shūichi and Maeda Ai, 103–16. Vol. 16 of *Nihon kindai shisō taikei*. Tokyo: Iwanami shoten, 1989.

———. "Doppō o okosan to suru shui." In *Buntai*, edited by Katō Shūichi and Maeda Ai, 181–204. Vol. 16 of *Nihon kindai shisō taikei*. Tokyo: Iwanami shoten, 1989.

———. "Shōsetsu shinzui." In *Tsubouchi Shōyōshū*, 39–165. Vol. 3 of *Nihon kindai bungaku taikei*. Tokyo: Kadokawa shoten, 1974.

Tsuchiya Michio. *Kokugo mondai ronsōshi*. Tokyo: Tamagawa daigaku shuppanbu, 2005.

Tsujimoto Masashi. *Manabi no fukken*. Tokyo: Kadokawa shoten, 1999.

Tsukamoto Toshiaki. "*Bungakuron* no hikaku bungakuteki kenkyu—sono hassōhō ni tsuite." *Nihon bungaku* 16 (1967): 10–33.

———. "Natsume Sōseki." In *Nihon kindai shōsetsu*, edited by Fukuda Rikutarō, Nakajima Kenzō, and Ōta Saburō, 61–79. Vol. 3 of *Hikaku bungaku kōza*. Tokyo: Shimizu kōbundō, 1971.

Twine, Nanette. *Language and the Modern State: The Reform of Written Japanese*. New York: Routledge, 1991.

———. *The Essence of the Novel: Occasional Papers II*. Queensland, Australia: Department of Japanese, University of Queensland, 1981.

Uchida Masao. *Yochi shiryaku*. Osaka: Meizendō, 1882.

Uchiyama, Akiko. "Translation as Representation: Fukuzawa Yukichi's Representation of 'Others.'" In *Agents of Translation*, edited by Paul Bandia and John Milton, 63–83. Philadelphia: John Benjamins Publishing Company, 2009.

Ueda, Atsuko. *Concealment of Politics, Politics of Concealment*. Stanford, CA: Stanford University Press, 2007.

Ueda Kazutoshi. "Hyōjungo ni tsukite." In *Kokugo no tame*, 51–66. Tokyo: Fuzanbō, 1897.

———. "Kokugo kenkyū ni tsuite." In *Ochiai Naobumi, Ueda Kazutoshi, Haga Yaichi, Fujioka Sakutarō shū*, 114–18. Vol. 41 of *Meiji bungaku zenshū*. Tokyo: Chikuma shobō, 1968.

———. "Kokugo to kokka to." In *Ochiai Naobumi, Ueda Kazutoshi, Haga Yaichi, Fujioka Sakutarō shū*, 108–13. Vol. 41 of *Meiji bungaku zenshū*. Tokyo: Chikuma shobō, 1968.

———. *Kokugogaku jikkō*. Tokyo: Tsūzoku daigakukai, 1916.

———. "Nihon gengo kenkyūhō." In *Ochiai Naobumi, Ueda Kazutoshi, Haga Yaichi, Fujioka Sakutarō shū*, 180–84. Vol. 41 of *Meiji bungaku zenshū*. Tokyo: Chikuma shobō, 1968.

Wakabayashi Torasaburō and Shirai Kowashi, eds. *Kaisei kyōjujutsu*, vol. 1. Tokyo: Fukyūsha, 1884.

Watanabe Kazan. "Shinkiron." In *Kazan zenshū*, vol. 1. Aichi: Kazankai, 1911.

Watanabe Shūjirō. "Nihonbun o seiteisuru hōhō." In *Kindai buntai keisei shiryō shūsei: hasseihen*, edited by Yamamoto Masahide, 154–56. Tokyo: Ōfūsha, 1975.

Wellek, Rene. *The Rise of English Literary History*. New York: McGraw-Hill, 1983.

Yamada Bimyō. "Bun to gochō no kankei 1." *Iratsume* 4, no. 36 (December 1889).

———. "Bunshō fugō no kaishaku." In *Kindai buntai keisei shiryō shūsei: hasseihen*, edited by Yamamoto Masahide, 590–92. Tokyo: Ōfūsha, 1975.

———. "Chōka kairyōron on yonde." *Yomiuri shinbun*, November 6, 1888.

———. "Fuchian taijin no onhihyō o haikenshite gohentō made ni tsukutta zangebun." In *Kindai buntai keisei shiryō shūsei: hasseihen*, edited by Yamamoto Masahide, 495–97. Tokyo: Ōfūsha, 1975.

———. "Genbun'itchi o manabu kokoroe 1." In *Kindai buntai keisei shiryō shūsei: hasseihen*, edited by Yamamoto Masahide, 631–33. Tokyo: Ōfūsha, 1975.

———. "Genbun'itchiron gairyaku." In *Yamada Bimyō*, edited by Tsubouchi Yūzō, 281–96. Vol. 10 of *Meiji no bungaku*. Tokyo: Chikuma shobō, 2001.

———. "Natsukodachi maeoki." In *Kindai buntai keisei shiryō shūsei: hasseihen*, edited by Yamamoto Masahide, 480–84. Tokyo: Ōfūsha, 1975.

———. "Nihon inbunron." In *Kindai shiika ronshū*. Vol. 59 of *Nihon kindai bungaku taikei*. Tokyo: Kadokawa shoten, 1973.

———. "Nihon inbunron." In *Buntai*, edited by Katō Shūichi and Maeda Ai, 215–60. Vol. 16 of *Nihon kindai shisō taikei*. Tokyo: Iwanami shoten, 1989.

———. "Shōka tsukurikata shogaku." *Iratsume* 4, no. 28 (October 1889).

———. "Tanoshikaretote (aruhito e)." In *Nihon gendaishi taikei*, vol. 1. Tokyo: Kawaide shobō, 1974.

———. "Ware ware no genbun'itchitai." In *Kindai buntai keisei shiryō shūsei: hasseihen*, edited by Yamamoto Masahide, 627–33. Tokyo: Ōfūsha, 1975.

Yamada Shunji. "Koe o chōetsu suru genbun'itchi." *Bungaku* 7, no. 2 (April 2006): 70–83.

———. *Taishū shinbun ga tsukuru Meiji no "Nihon."* Tokyo: NHK Books, 2002.

Yamada Yūsaku. *Gensō no kindai: Shōyō, Bimyō, Ryūrō*. Tokyo: Ōfū, 2001.

———. "Ichininshō e no kattō: Yamada Bimyō o megutte." *Bungaku* 53 (November 1985): 90–101.

Yamamoto Masahide. "Bunken kaisetsu." In *Kindai buntai keisei shiryō shūsei: hasseihen*, edited by Yamamoto Masahide, 23–122. Tokyo: Ōfūsha, 1975.

———. *Genbun'itchi no rekishi ronkō*. Tokyo: Ōfūsha, 1971.

———. "'Kana no kai' kikanshijō no genbun'itchi genshō." *Ibaragi daigaku bunrigakubu kiyō* 11 (December 1960): 53–71.

———. *Kindai buntai hassei no shiteki kenkyū*. Tokyo: Iwanami shoten, 1965.

———. "Nishi Amane no kokugo kaikaku katsudō." *Gengo seikatsu* 196 (1968): 86–94.

Yamamuro Shin'ichi. *Shisō kadai to shite no Ajia: kijiku, rensa, tōyo*. Tokyo: Iwanami shoten, 2001.

Yano Ryūkei. "Buntairon." In *Keikoku bidan*, vol. 2. Tokyo: Iwanami shoten, 1969.

———. *Keikoku bidan*, vol. 2. Tokyo: Iwanami shoten, 1969.

———. "Nihon buntai moji shinron." In *Kyōkasho keimōbunshū*, edited by Kurata Yoshihiro, Saitō Toshihiko, and Tanigawa Keiichi. Tokyo: Iwanami shoten, 2006.

Yasuda Hiroshi. "Kindai Nihon ni okeru 'minzoku' kannen no keisei: kokumin shinmin minzoku." *Shisō to gendai* (September 1992): 61–72.

Yasuda Toshiaki. "Kindai Nihon gengoshi no shoronten." *Kan* 4 (January 2001): 163–72.

———. *"Kokugo" no kindaishi: teikoku Nihon to kokugo gakusha tachi*. Tokyo: Chūkō shinsho, 2006.

———. *Kokugo to hōgen no aida—gengo kōchiku no seijigaku*. Tokyo: Jinbun shoin, 1999.

———. *Teikoku Nihon no gengo hensei*. Tokyo: Seori shobō, 1997.

Yatabe Ryōkichi. *Rōmaji hayamanabi*. Tokyo: Rōmajikai, 1885.

———. "Rōmaji o mote Nihongo o tsuzuru no setsu." In *Kokugo kokuji kyōiku shiryō sōran*, edited by Nishio Minoru and Hisamatsu Sen'ichi, 30–32. Tokyo: Kokugo kyōiku kenkyūkai, 1969.

———. "Shintaishishō jo." In *Nihon gendaishi taikei*, vol. 1. Tokyo: Kawaide shobō, 1974.

Yi, Christina. *Colonizing Language: Cultural Production and Language Politics in Modern Japan and Korea*. New York: Columbia University Press, 2018.

Yoda, Tomiko. *Gender and National Literature: Heian Texts in the Constructions of Japanese Modernity*. Durham, NC: Duke University Press, 2004.

Yoshimura Sayaka. "Gaikokugo kara kokugo e: Okinawa ni okeru kokugo kyōikushi 1." *Japanisch als Fremdsprache* 3 (2013): 76–83.

Yudell, Michael. *Race Unmasked: Biology and Race in the 20th Century*. New York: Columbia University Press, 2014.

INDEX

Founded in 1893,
UNIVERSITY OF CALIFORNIA PRESS
publishes bold, progressive books and journals on topics in the arts, humanities, social sciences, and natural sciences—with a focus on social justice issues—that inspire thought and action among readers worldwide.

The UC PRESS FOUNDATION
raises funds to uphold the press's vital role as an independent, nonprofit publisher, and receives philanthropic support from a wide range of individuals and institutions—and from committed readers like you. To learn more, visit ucpress.edu/supportus.